Abstracts of

Frederick County, Maryland Land Records

1773-1778

Libers V, W, BD1, BD2, and RP1

compiled by:

Patricia Abelard Andersen

Damascus, MD

ISBN 978-1-68034-024-2

Cover photo courtesy of Wikimedia Commons.

Now known as Schifferstadt Architectural Museum, this farmhouse was originally built circa 1758 on land Joseph Bruner purchased from Daniel Dulany in 1746. Joseph Bruner sold the land, known as *Schifferstadt*, to his son, Elias Bruner, in 1753. The farmhouse stands today as one of the oldest and most historic buildings in the city of Frederick.

CONTENTS

INTRODUCTION TO FREDERICK COUNTY LAND RECORD ABSTRACTS

This volume includes Libers V, W, BD1, BD2, and RP1 which continues a series of abstracts begun in 1995 with Liber B, the first volume of deeds recorded in Frederick County, and also includes Abstract Indexes for Libers S, T and U. There were no Libers Q or R in Frederick County Deeds.

The type of indexing available in abstracts cannot be replaced with the indexes available, that were prepared by the Circuit Clerks to identify property owners, and to assist the clerks in land property records. Users of these volumes understand much more is involved. The courts indexes do not always identify estate sales, bills of sale, Negro sales or manumissions, or depositions and information within deeds, such as deed boundaries with neighbors, and other documents brought to the court to be recorded. Also, many researchers have difficulty reading the old hand written books, so this also provides a guide and finding aid for the beginning genealogist. The page numbers of the deeds in the original volume are given in the abstracts. Since deeds have been put online at the Maryland State Archives Web Site, the serious researcher is encouraged to obtain copies of deeds of interest.

Abstracts are best used as brief guides and indexes to original records, and at the same time to find people mentioned in deeds who would otherwise be lost in the records (witnesses, adjoining landowners, etc.). This series of abstracts focuses on the names of parties in the deeds; the name of witnesses, when recognized as the usual Justices of the Peace are frequently omitted in these abstracts, nor was the paid alienation fine (always collected) noted in all cases. In most cases the metes and bounds were not detailed, although a few of these abstracts do contain more information; in all cases where it is desired to draw the tract out, the researcher is encouraged to print out an original deed to use.

In addition to the county court land records, some deeds were recorded in the Provincial Court land office. If someone had business at the Provincial Court, e.g. recording the certificate or obtaining their patent or a warrant to survey or resurvey land, it may have been more convenient for them to record their deeds at the state level, instead of in the counties. They cover the colonial period and should always be checked when a transaction cannot be found recorded at the local level.

Any contract (indenture) may be recorded for real or personal property, or for services, if the contracting parties presented the indenture for recording. Most deeds were presented to the clerk for recording during Court Days, when the justices were in town. At this time all deeds were acknowledged before two justices of the peace, or other court officials, and in most instances these justices were also the witnesses. An annotated list of Justices of the Peace active during this period in included in the Appendix. Bills of sale did not require witnesses to be justices, so they were more likely to be neighbors or family members. It appears that when deeds were made on other than court days, the parties went to the homes of the nearest Justices of the Peace, and in those instances you may find that the Justice enlisted other members of his family to serve as witnesses.

At the time of acknowledgment of the deed, the wife generally released her right to a 1/3 life interest in her husband's real property, referred to as her dower rights. Occasionally, she would come in later and record a separate release of dower. Widows, and mothers of sons inheriting property, also had dower rights to release. Deeds made and recorded during court days, were probably agreed upon much earlier. These were more or less, universal "settlement" dates, convenient since most people came to court on court dates. Colonials were knowledgeable about the function of law, and the actions of the courts as they witnessed trials first hand. In colonial days, everyone who was able attended the live dramas offered by the quarterly sessions. Court days in Frederick County were the third Tuesdays of the months of March, June, August and November. The court would meet for several days, and could schedule meetings for several days as required. It is probable that the clerks, or their assistants, then took the "recorded" deeds home with them to write up as time allowed. After recording, the deeds could be picked up and the court record annotated as to who received the deed and what date, sometimes years later.

The signature may differ from the names as recorded in the deed. It was not uncommon for a name to be spelled in a different way three or more times within one document. In the abstracts, the name is spelled consistent with the clerk's spelling. If the family is known to the abstractor, the name may appear in the index only under the most common spelling. The index records only one entry per page, even when there may be several deeds for the party. The clerks were able to read and write a German Script, and when the original deeds' grantor, or witnesses signed the deed in German Script, the clerk copied the signature in German Script. He also apparently tried to copy marks as they appeared. However, all signatures in the deed book were written in the handwriting of the clerk, therefore comparing these signatures from a deed book: one John Smith to another John Smith and saying the signatures were the same; does not imply that it was really the same John Smith or the same signatures on the original deed. Occupations will sometimes help distinguish a man. These are included in the abstracts and the more unusual occupations are indexed in this volume, except for the common "status indicators," of gentleman, planter, yeoman, and farmer. Also be aware that because of spelling inconsistencies, read the index to the volume carefully, looking for possible misreading and/or misspellings in the original, and variant spellings. Be especially vigilant for surnames beginning with "B" or "P". Abbreviations were frequently used in the Record Books. Some of them are also used in these abstracts. Names commonly abbreviated include: Abra'm (Abraham), Alex. (Alexander), Arch'd (Archibald), Benj. (Benjamin), Chas. (Charles), Dan'l (Daniel), Ign's (Ignatius), Jas (James), Jos. (Joseph), Jno. (John), Marg't (Margaret), Morda. (Mordecai), Nath'l (Nathaniel), Nin. (Ninian), Pris'a (Priscilla), Rich'd (Richard), Rob't (Robert), Sam'l (Samuel)., Thos. (Thomas), and Wm. (William).

List of Terms and Abbreviations Used in the Abstracts

AAC	Anne Arundel County
ack	Acknowledgment of the deed by the grantor.
afd/afs'd	aforesaid
AF	Alienation fine. A transfer fee.
BC	Baltimore County
Certificate of Survey:	After a warrant was obtained for land, a settler would contact a surveyor to have an official description of his real estate made. This was presented to the court to obtain a patent.
Commission:	A court order to individuals, as recorded in the deed books, these were generally to resurvey or remark to perpetuate the boundaries of a tract of land where parties may have been in disagreement, or the original bounded trees fallen or in dispute.
Consideration	A required element of a contract, it is what the seller receives to induce him to make a bargain.
dower rights:	A wife or a widow's right to 1/3 of all her husband's real property. This right had to be released whenever he sold property. If not done at the time the deed was made, the widow could come back later and exercise a claim against the property, and sometimes later dower releases were recorded.
draught/draft:	One of the upper branches of a river or creek.
Fieri facias (Fi. Fa.)	Judicial writ directing sheriff to satisfy a judgment from debtors' property.
FC	Frederick County
GS	German Script, in reference to a signature.
Hundred	as in Antietam Hundred, a unit for taxation purposes.
Indenture:	Any written contract. "Indentured servants" comes from this document.
lbs. tob.	Pounds of tobacco. (Legal money in Maryland)
M&B	Metes and bounds - description of real estate boundaries.
Manor of Monocacy	[or Calverton] - A unit of government similar to the Hundred, referred to In deeds, as to be held of the "Manor of Conecocheague" for example. It Does not mean that the land was physically located within the manor survey. The land was in that taxing district for collection or quit rents.
patent	The original land grant from the Lord Proprietary, issued after a certificate of survey was made and returned.
PGC	Prince George's County
pistole	a gold coin used in various European countries.
rsy/rsy'd	resurvey/resurveyed
SMC	St. Mary's County
supersedeas	In some instances use is synonymous with a "stay of proceedings." Here it is most similar to a bond required of one who petitions to set aside a judgment or execution and from which the other party may be made whole if the action is unsuccessful.

[this page intentionally blank]

ABSTRACTS 1773-1778
FREDERICK COUNTY LAND RECORDS
Liber V through Liber RP1

V:1-2 Henry Lazarus recorded 17 Dec. 1773 made 8 Nov. 1773. Whereas Susanna Apple, widow, deceased, died seized in fee of a certain lot #285, in Frederick town, by her will and testament devised her real estate to be divided between her two daughters, Catharine, who married a certain Christian Shull and Margaret who married a certain John Shullman; they in consideration of £24..10 convey said lot. Signed by all four ladies by their marks, before Upton Sheridine and Wm Beatty.

V:2-3. John Stoner recorded agreement 17 Dec. 1773. Whereas there is controversy and dispute arising from the engagement of a mill race & water course, on tract of land called *Mortality*, originally being part of a tract called *Parshers Change* in the possession of Stephen Ramsburg, the said water coming form Tuscarora Creek, for the benefit and advantage of John Stoner. Signed Stephen Ramsburg, John Stoner.

V:3-4. Jacob Miller recorded deed 17 Dec. 1773 made 5 Nov. between Philip Pindle for £157..6, *Resurvey on Mills Folly,* 220 acres. Rachel O. Pindle released dower.

V:5-6. George Creager recorded deed 7 Dec. 1773 from George Baer for £140..2, assigns 61 acres of *Good Luck,* also 78 acres of tract called *The Widow's Chance.*

V:6-8. Edward Thomas recorded deed 17 Dec. 1773 from Ashman Jenkins and Valentine Jenkins his wife, for £105, 114 acre tract seized in fee tail called *Hobson's Choice.* Signed by all three parties.

V:8-10. William Porter of York Co., Pennsylvania, recorded deed 17 Dec. 1773, from James Patterson, seized of two tracts, *Vulkins Lot,* patented 12 March 1761 and *Carolina,* conveyed to him by Benedict Calvert and others, recorded in Liber K:1430, sells for £225, tracts containing 50 and 100 acres. Signed before Wm Blair, Jos Wood. Margaret, wife of James Patterson, released dower.

V:10-11. Peter Waddle recorded deed 17 Dec. 1773 from Stephen Ramsburgh for £225, tract *Resurvey on Nutt Spring,* on side of a hill by the plantation of Alexander Johnson. 114 acres.

V:11-12. Philip Henry Thomas recorded deed 17 Dec 1773 from Thomas Johnson for £100, *Resurvey on Lashmutt's Folly,* 60 acres. Mary wife of said Johnson released dower.

V:13-14. John Chrisman recorded deed 17 Dec. 1773, from Samuel Cookson, for £300, *Timber Ridge,* 60 ½ acres, except for parts previously conveyed by a certain John White or Samuel Cookson, in town called Westminster. Mary, wife of Samuel Cookson released dower.

V:14-16. Mathias Hart, Jr., recorded deed 17 Dec. 1773, from William Pidgeon for £375, land on Great Pipe Creek, called *Bedford,* 167 acres. Rachel Pidgeon released dower.

V:16-17. Jacob Zimmerman recorded deed 17 Dec. 1773 from Thomas Gilbert for £15, tract called *Mountain Frolick,* on west side of Kitoctin Creek. Elizabeth Gilbert released dower.

V:17-18. Francis Deakins recorded deed 17 Dec. 1773 from Jonathan Nixon for £7, tract called *Resurvey on the Farm,* 47 acres. Mary Nixon released dower.

V:18-19. Wm Douglas recorded deed 17 Dec. 1773 from Frederick Nicodemas, Jacob Walker for £252, part of *Coaler's Amendment,* 138 acres. Catharine and Elizabeth wives of Frederick and Jacob released dower.

V:19-21. Joshua Hobbs recorded deed 17 Dec. 1773 from Nicholas Hobbs for £70 , *Here I Begin,* for 50 acres. Elizabeth Hobbs, wife of Nicholas released dower.

V:21-22. Adam Deeds recorded deed 17 Dec. 1773 from Abraham Baker for £45, lot #145 in Sharpsburgh. Elizabeth Baker released dower.

V:22-24. James Sear recorded deed 17 Dec. 1773, from Daniel Dulaney, executor of his father, Daniel Dulaney. On or about 13 Feb. 1752, James Sear and Ninian Veatch paid Daniel Dulaney for tract called *Progress,* and they divided the land on the bank of the Potomac. This is a deed for his moiety of said tract.

V:24-25. Thomas Gassaway recorded bill of sale 24 Dec. 1773 from Nathan Barnes, son of Robert, for £28..8 and £23..2, lot #33 of Chew Farm, plus one bay horse, seven hogs, two feather beds and furniture, unless sums paid by 1 Sept. Next for redemption of bargain. Signed Nathan Barnes, son of Robert.

V:25-26. Andrew Warman recorded deed 24 Dec. 1773 from James Fraser for 5 shillings sterling, part of *Partnership,* containing 7 acres. Signed before Upton Sheridine, John Jacob. Alienation fine paid Wm M. Beall

V:26-28. Solomon Stimpson recorded 24 Dec 1773, made 20 Oct. From Nathaniel Dowden of Frederick Co., for £175 part of *Johnny and Molly's Conclusion,* on east side of Broad Run, containing 100 acres. Susannah Dowden, released dower rights.

V:28-29. Robert Allison of Charles Town, Cecil County, from James Pedan for £1055, part of *Addition to Brooke's Discovery on the Rich Lands,* adjacent to part that Andrew Park and Abraham Hayter made over to Benjamin Peden, for 64 acres. Signed before Wm Blair, Betsy Blair. Kesiah Peden released dower rights.

V:29-31. John Kelly recorded deed 24 Dec. 1773, from Mary Kelly for natural love and affection for him, and for his better maintenance, grants and assigns land where she lives, a part of tract *Dry Fountain,* 100 acres. Signed by mark.

V:31-32. William Yates recorded deed 24 Dec. 1773 from Cornelius Thompson of Frederick County, Virginia, tract called *Dutch Folly,* on bank of Israel Bear Creek, about 3 perches from the bank of the Potomac, 105 acres.

V:32-34. Adam Good recorded deed 24 Dec. 1773, from Mark Alexander for £70 lot #8 in Taneytown. Signed before J.P.'s of Baltimore County, attested to by A. Lawson, clerk.

V:34-36. James Smith of Frederick Town, Innholder, recorded deed 24 Dec. 1773, from Eleanor Charlton of Frederick Town, executor of Arthur Charlton, assigns lots 159, 160 and 161.

V:36-37. Walter Beall recorded bill of sale 24 Dec. 1773 from Erasmus Gill, to cover sundry debts, including Colin Dunlop & sons, £73..15..7, and Barnes and Ridgate, £42... Sells crops of tobacco and corn, at his dwelling plantation, and Negro man Sambo and Negro woman Rachel; one desk, buffet, three tables, four chairs, two beds, iron pot, fire tongs and shovel, washing tub, other household utensils, six geese. Nevertheless if sum paid, sale is void. Signed by Erasmus Gill and Walter Beall before Thomas Price, Jacob Schley.

V:37-39. Jacob Shuh recorded lease 1 January 1774 from John Ransbergh for rents and covenants, leases for term of nine years, one grist mill, one saw mill and dwelling, and ground for a garden on the spring Branch. Yearly rents of £100, and shall grind his grain, and shall clear the head and tail race.

V:39-40. John Creager recorded deed from 3 Jany 1774 Reverdy Ghisclin for £710 part of *Third Addition to Resurvey on Fountain Low,* 710 acres. Mary Ghiselin released dower rights.

V:40-41. Sarah Beatty recorded deed 7 Jan. 1774 from James Beatty for £125 part of *Beatty's Delight* on Linganore one mile from Monocacy River. 100 acres. Elizabeth, wife of James Beatty released dower.

V:41-43. George Brown recorded sale 7 Jan 1774 from Legh Master for £20, bargain made 14 July 1773, for tract called *Jack's Purchase,* on south side of Cobb's Branch, for 5 plus acres; plus part of *Bond's Meadow Enlarged,* on line of tract called *Brown's Plague,* containing 3 1/4 acres. Signed before Ben Nicholson, Thos Sam Pole. Acknowledged before Justices of Baltimore County.

V:43-44. Thomas Burgee recorded deed 7 Jan. 1774, from James Marshall for £90 part of tract *Flag Patch,* near Cat Tail Marsh.

V:44-45. John Hutzle recorded deed 7 Jan. 1774, from Peter Hose for £45, lot #128 in Elizabethtown. Selena, wife of Peter Hose released dower.

V:46-47. John Carter of Baltimore County, recorded deed 7 Jan. 1774 from George Ziegler Senr. For £200 part of *Brother's Agreement,* 100 acres. Margaret, wife of George Sigler released dower.

V:47-49. James Beatty recorded deed 27 Jan. 1774. Whereas Thomas Beatty by his will made in 1768, bequeaths to Thomas Beatty, Charles Beatty, Susanna Maynard, wife of Nathan Maynard, James Beatty and Sarah Beatty all his estate to be equally divided, this deed for £1400, the said Thomas, Charles and Sarah Beatty and Susanna and Nathan Maynard, sells all their rights to said land to James Beatty. Catharine Beatty wife of Thomas and Martha Beatty wife of Charles released dower rights.

V:49-50. James McLaughlin recorded deed 7 Jan. 1774 from Lawrence Shock, late of Frederick County, but now of the colony of Virginia, blacksmith, for £100 assigns tract called *Maiden's Choice,* 100 acres.

V:50-52. Susanna Maynard, wife of Nathan Maynard, recorded deed 27 Jan. 1774 from James Beatty for £220, tract called *Watered Bottom,* standing on Linganore Creek, containing 76 acres. Elizabeth, wife of James Beatty released dower.

V:52-54. Ninian Veatch recorded deed 8 Jany 1774, from Daniel Dulaney Jr. Whereas Daniel Dulaney his father, by writing obligatory dated 13 Feb. 1752, agreed to convey to the same Ninian Veatch and James Sear, for £100 tract called *Progress,* 264 acres, his share of 132 acres, this indenture records details of payments and bond agreements, and makes good the deed to Ninian Veatch.

V:54-55. Benjamin Gassaway recorded deed 28 Jan. 1774 from Robert Gassaway for £113, tract called *Nothing Venture, Nothing Gett,* on Monocacy Creek, near the *Resurvey on Joseph's Kindness,* containing 100 acres. Sarah Gassaway wife of Robert released dower rights.

V:56-57. James McLaughlin recorded deed 31 Jan. 1774 from Stephen Ullerick for £50, part of *Good Neighbor,* 25 acres. Acknowledged before John Stull, Thomas Prather.

V:57-58. Brig. General Haldemond of New York City, devisee and executor of Brig. Gen. Henry Bouquet, deceased, recorded release 14 Jan. 1774 from Hugh Roberts of Philadelphia, Pennsylvania. Whereas, in his lifetime, on or about 20 June 1765, by indenture conveyed to Hugh Roberts *Long Meadow Enlarged,* containing by estimation 4100 acres, and Gen. Haldemond has paid sum owing. Signed Hugh Roberts before Whitehd Humphreys, Joseph Drinker, John Mease.

V:58-60. Peter Hoover recorded deed 24 Jan 1774 from George Bond Sr. for £320, tracts *The Forrest,* on south side of Antietam Creek, 100 acres. Wife's name omitted from dower release.

V:60-61. Jacob Sharrer recorded deed 7 Jany 1774 from Charles Carroll of Annapolis, for £643, three tracts, *McCoy's Delight,* about a mile above Charles Chaney's, containing 100 acres; *Walnut Level,* containing 50 acres, and part of *Kelley's Delight,* containing 607 acres.

V:61-62. Elizabeth Rhinehart recorded divorcement from George Fisher 10 January 1774. I George Fisher of York County, Pennsylvania, married 12 Feb. 1770 to Elizabeth Rinehart, daughter of Valentine Rinehart, but lived together for four months in contention and strife, and after two years, have decided to make separation permanent. Signed by George Fisher before Valentine Flegall, by mark; Frederick Ducker by mark.

V:62-64. Joseph Sprigg recorded deed 14 Jany 1774, from Frederick Haldemond, presently at the City of New York, Major General with his Majesty's Army, for £5,250 sterling, *Long Meadow Enlarged,* 4163 acres, and *Pleasant Spring,* granted John Wrench for 100 acres, and *Small Spring,* 50 acres. Signed by Daniel Dulaney and John Rideout, his attorneys.

V:64-65. Henry Snyder recorded deed 12 January 1774 from Andrew Groob for 1 shillings, lot in Jerusalemtown. Catharine, wife of Andrew Groob released dower.

V:65. John Waggoner recorded bill of sale from Francis Motts 14 January 1774, for £14..18 sell one black mare, one sorrel mare, 10 ½ acres of wheat in the ground, and 4 acres of rye. Nevertheless if sum paid, sale is void.

V:66. Valentine Rhinehart recorded Lie bill from Herman Werker. "Whereas a certain Herman Werker, blacksmith, raised a bad report March, was a year, on Valentine Rinehart, that he the said Valentine Rhinehart would have behaved himself in an unseemly manner having to do in a carnal way with his own daughter, and that he the said Herman Werkin was told so by George Fisher who was married to the said Valentine Rhinehart's daughter which report has been very detrimental to said Valentine Rhinehart, both with regard to the scandal arising from such a report as also cost of law on the case. Now the intention of these lines is that I the above named George Fisher do absolutely deny that ever I said any such thing as is above reported either to Herman Werkin or to any other person whatsoever. I do hereby before these witnesses clear my self of such a charge & do therefore in confirmation of the same subscribe my name and seal this 18th day of December 1773. Signed, Sealed & Delivered Herman Werken, In presence of. [names not recorded].

V:66-67. Nathaniel Pigman recorded mortgage 19 Jany 1774 from Henry Thomas of Charles County for £60, Negro woman Sall and her increase, Negro boys Dick and Jerry. Nevertheless if sum paid before 20 August next, sale is void.

V:67. Doctor John Stephenson of Baltimore Town, recorded bill of sale 29 Jany 1774, for £41..16..1 from Benjamin Griffith, sells one feather bed and furniture, one bay horse, my crop of tobacco.

V:68. Joseph Stallings recorded release 28 Jan. 1774, from Colin Dunlop & Son, merchants of Glasgow, Scotland. Whereas 16 Nov. 1770, he made over six Negroes and their increase to secure loan, he has bargained with John Hawkins, near the Falls of Potomac, for one of the said Negroes, a mulatto girl named Avarilla, for £75, to be paid Adam Stewart on behalf of the said Colin Dunlap, and he releases the said girl from the mortgage. Signed by Adam Stewart.

V:68. Thomas Stone and others [John Rogers, Philip Richard Fendell, trustees for John Barnes and Thos Howe Ridgate] recorded mortgage 2 Feb 1774 from Thomas Brawner, assigns one mulatto boy, Joseph Lizer, one black cow, and two feather beds, provided that if said Thomas Brawner pay amounts, sale is void.

V:69 John Walling recorded marks of cattle 9 February 1774.

V:69-70. Thomas Schley and others recorded agreement February 1774, made 3 January 1772, to dig a well on Market Street in Frederick, and to pay equal shares of the cost, "and likewise to keep said well forever in good repair." Bond signed 20 December 1773. Thomas Schley, George Hoffman, Thomas Polhous, Peter Bucke, Philip Smith, Nicholas Schappart, Nicholas Conradt, Phillip Bultmann, Henrich Lienbough, Jacob Adam, Jacob Zimmerman, Philip Schabboudt, Johannes Wittmer, Valentine Bentz, Johan Simon Fey, ? Gilbert – most of the signatures written in a German Script. Signed before Thos Price, Jacob Miller. Each bound himself in penal sum of £5.

V:70-71. John Goff recorded bill of sale 12 Feb. 1774 from George Collings for £50 one Negro girl, Sarah and her increase.

V:71-72. Thomas Neill recorded deed 19 Feb. 1774 from John (George) Kerr for £350, *Hines Choice,* north east of Stoney Branch of Monocacy Creek, 150 acres. Signed John Kerr. Lettice wife of John released dower.

V:72-74. David Ross recorded deed 22 Feb. 1774, from Frederick William Hawker, for £78, part of *Abstone Forest,* 65 acres. Eve wife of Frederick William Hawker released dower right.

V:74-75. David Ross of Prince George's County, for £54..1.. recorded deed 22 Feb 1774 from Ignatius Thompson, assigns part of tract called *Sideling Hill.*

V:75-76. Peter Shaman recorded bill of sale from William Bowden, taylor for £6, sells one red cow, furniture and housewares. Signed before Jacob Young, Abraham Haff.

V:76-77. Daniel Dulaney of Annapolis, recorded deed 25 Feb 1774 from Stephen Ramsburg for £68..8..9, for tract called *Mortality,* a part of *Tasker's Chance,* 15 3/8 acres.

V:78-79. Charles Warfield recorded deed 1 March 1774 from Nicholas Maccubbin of City of Annapolis, merchant, for £2044..5 sterling, *Resurvey on Justice's Delight,* granted George Becraft 18 April 1768 for 1012 acres; less 85 acres to Phillip Greenwell, 100 acres to William Dickensheets, 200 acres to Allen Farquhar, 20 3/4 acres to Simon Meredith. Signed before Jos Dawson, James Maccubbin.

V:79-80. William Mollison recorded bill of sale 2 March 1774, from William Atchison, for £41..19..2, sells livestock. Signed by mark.

V:80-81. Lawrence Creager recorded deed 19 Jany 1774, from William Diggs Jr. of St. Mary's County, for £30, 50 acres, *Resurvey on Diggs Lot.* Catherine Diggs released dower.

V:82-83. Lawrence Creager recorded release 19 Jany 1774, from Charles Carroll Esq. of Annapolis, part of *Diggs Lot,* 108 acres, mortgaged 17 August 1773.

V:83-84. Lawrence Creager recorded deed 19 Jany 1774 from John Diggs late of Conewago, for 5 shillings, part of *Diggs Lot,* 108 acres.

V:84. William Molleson recorded bill of sale 2 March 1774, from John Atchison for £62..17..5 sells livestock and furniture.

V:85. Jacob Zeller recorded bill of sale 7 March 1774 from Jacob Grove for £20 for being security in a bond due to Michael Myer, assigns two horses to save him from expenses.

V:86. Jacob Hoffman with William Stebens recorded agreement 9 March 1774. Whereas they purchased jointly lots #156, 157 and 158 in Frederick Town, and have agreed to divide them. They agree to allow 4 ft. on either side of their parts to be used for a gate way and path between their lots.

V:87-88. Peter Erb recorded deed 12 March 1774 from Henry Unger for £100, assigns part of tract called *Valleys and Hills, Tims & Wills,* containing 29 acres; also 2nd parcel, *Cool Spring,* contiguous to 1st part, containing 50 acres. Signed by mark. Catharine wife of Henry Unger released dower.

V:88-89. Thomas Beatty recorded deed 12 March 1774 from Thomas Walter for £10, *Barrony Point,* on north side of Linganore, 20 acres. Signed by mark.

V:89-91. Peter Shover recorded deed 12 March 1774 from Charles Beatty for £5 sterling, *Peter's Delight,* containing 41 acres. Martha Beatty released dower right.

V:91-95. Michael Myers recorded deed 12 March 1774 from James Sprigg for £900 part of *Addition to Pile's Delight Enlarged,* land to be sold according to the will of Col. Edward Sprigg deceased in 1752, but was not sold at that time. Richard Sprigg, eldest son and heir at law conveyed land to James Sprigg in 1772, who is now selling land. Metes and bounds given for 1st part containing 921 acres, adjacent to part conveyed by James Sprigg to Joseph Chapline, and a 2nd part, part of *Piles Delight Enlarged,* for 64 acres. Elizabeth Sprigg released dower.

V:95-97. Basil Lucas recorded deed 12 March 1774 from Robert Owen and Mary, his wife, for £66..15 tract called *Hard Struggle,* on Northwest Branch, at the beginning of *Elizabeth's Delight,* 178 acres.

V:97 Benjamin Thrasher recorded cattle marks 15 March 1774.

V:97 Christiana Hann recorded release 15 March 1774 from Devalt Coonce

V:97-98. Colin Dunlop & sons recorded bill of sale 15 March 1774 from Zachariah Barlow for £27..17..7, crop of tobacco and corn, bay horse, all household furniture. Signed by mark.

V:98-99. Colin Dunlop & Sons recorded bill of sale 15 March 1774 from James Shelhorn for £21..4..5, all my crop of tobacco and wheat, one bay horse, seven shoats. Signed by mark.

V:99-101. Joshua Ellis recorded deed 16 March 1774 from Solomon Ellis for £5 sterling, assigns tract *Addition,* beginning at *Resurvey on Choice,* 19 acres. Margaret wife of Solomon released dower.

101. John Dickerson recorded bill of sale 16 March 1774 from Surrat Dickerson for £100, Negro man Charles, feather bed and furniture; two horses, 17 sheep, 27 hogs, 12 head of cattle, housewares enumerated, to pay same b 13 March 1775 with interest, then sale is void.

V:102-103. Henry Griffith Dorsey recorded deed 16 March 1774 from John England for £300, *England's Chance Resurveyed,* 171 acres.

V:103-104. Greenberry Griffith of Charles recorded bill of sale 16 March 1774 from Orlando Griffith for £88..6. If sum paid, sale is void.

V:104-105. Richard Davis Jr. recorded deed 16 March 1774, from Sam'l Buzzard, George Henrich Howard and William Brandenburg for £15, lot #10 in town of Middletown. The three wives came, were examined apart, and released dower, without recording their names.

V:105-106. Joseph Magruder recorded bill of sale 16 March 1774 from Moses Dezelem, one dark bay gelding, one pyed heifer. Signed by mark before John Flemming, John Murphy.

V:106. Thomas Beatty recorded sale 16 March 1774 from John Buffington, for £6, five hogs, household furniture. Signed before George Wolper, Wm Richey.

V:107 Richard Donaldson recorded lie bill from James Norris, 16 March 1774. I have falsely accused and belied Richard Donaldson in regard of stealing a hog. Signed by mark before Richard Williams, Walter Bond, Jay Chaney.

V:107-108. Ephraim Howard recorded deed 16 March 1774 from John Young for one shilling sterling, assigns tract *Duck's Wood,* part formerly sold to Cornelius Carmack by Arnold Livers, 92 acres.

V:108 Suffiah White recorded deed of gift 16 March 1774, from Catherine White, for love and affection for her daughter, all my goods and chattels, debts due. Signed before Benedict Bowman, Adam Haver.

V:109. Mary Chaney, wife of Charles Chaney, recorded deposition 16 March 1774, aged 67 years, sayeth that about 27 years ago she was with Ann Ricketts, who is now wife of Joseph Chaney, son of Richard Chaney, but who was formerly the wife of her son, Ezekiel Chaney, who was with her and delivered a son called Richard Chaney, and was appointed administrator with her of her son Ezekiel Chaney's estate. Signed before John Stull.

V:109-111. Walter White of Prince George's County recorded deed 16 March 1774, from James Ellis for £300, *Good Luck,* beginning at 48th line of *Resurvey on Chance,* 22 acres; and also part of *Friendship,* 143 acres. Signed by mark. Mary Ellis released dower.

V:111-112. Griffin Johnson recorded deed 16 March 1774 from Joseph Flint and Charity Flint his wife, for £40, *Morgan's Chance,* on west side of Town Creek, about 9 miles from the mouth, 50 acres. Signed before Michael Cresap, George Brent.

V:113-114. Colin Dunlap and son, and company recorded bill of sale 16 March 1774, from Benjamin West, for £51..18..9, assigns one small iron gray horse, 2 cows, 2 sows, 14 pigs, 6 sheep. Signed before Edward Burgess.

V:114-115. Thaddeus Beall, Robert Beall son of James, Edward Fitzgerald and John Higdon recorded bill of sale 17 March 1774, from William Bloyes for £103..17..6, assigns 3 feather beds and furniture, 3 pots and pot hooks, one linen wheel, one woolen wheel, 4 head black cattle, 3 hogs, 3 chairs, 2 tables, one gun, 4000 pounds tobacco, 1 looking glass, 2 augers, 1 drawing knife, 3 iron wedges, 2 axes, 2 grubbing hoes, 5 broad hoes, 2 plows, 2 cider casks, 15 geese, 20 barrels Indian corn, all household furniture and one woman's saddle and one mans saddle, and crop about to be sown. Nevertheless if sum paid on time, sale is void. Signed by mark before Charles Jones.

V:115-116. Alexander Clagett recorded deed 16 March 1774 from Mordecai Boone for £78 Penn., sells two tracts, *The James,* 75 acres and *Addition to the James,* 29 acres.

V:116-117. James Ellis (uncle of Solomon Ellis) recorded deed 16 March 1774, from Solomon Ellis for £22, assigns tract called *Good Luck,* beginning at 48th line of *Resurvey on Chance,* for 22 acres. Margaret, wife of Solomon Ellis released dower.

V:118-119. Joseph Chaney recorded Land Commission 17 March 1774. To Joseph Smith, Thomas Smith, Richard Carter and Charles Swearingen, on *Rents Chance.* Deposition of Charles Chaney about 73 years old, testified about 20 years ago, that he saw a white oak standing on ridge above Beaver Creek, that was the bounded beginning tree of *Rents Chance,* then taken up by John Rent Senr. Samuel Lilly, aged about 30 years, deposed that about 13 years ago, a certain Larkin Peirpoint, showed him a white oak saplin, blowed up by the roots on a ridge on the north side of Beaver Creek as the beginning tree of *Rent's Chance.* Signed March 12, 1774.

V:119-120. Francis Gartrell recorded deed 17 March 1774 from Benjamin Griffith and Rachel his wife, late Rachel Gartrell, relict of John Gartrell, deceased, being possessed of title of dower to tract, *Snowden's Fourth Addition to his Manor,* for £24 quit claim to their title. Signed before David Lynn, Edward Burgess.

V:121-122. Upton Sheridine recorded deed 17 March 1774 from Ephraim Howard for £51..3..9, part of *Duke's Woods,* beginning at 3rd line of *Carmack's Farewell,* to part of a tract called *Middle Way,* containing 22 3/4 acres.

V:122-123. John Kennedy recorded bill of sale 18 March 1774 from Robert Dawe for £129..3..9, one small horse, one gelding two mares, 12 head cattle, 4feather beds, an old wagon, etc.

V:123-124. George Brent recorded deed 18 March 1774 from Joseph Flint for £5, 104 acre part of *Resurvey on Flint's Chance.* Charity Flint released dower.

V:124-127. Thomas Clagett recorded deed of confirmation 18 March 1774 from Col. Henry Brooke (grandson of Clement Brooke). Whereas Mrs. Jane Brooke, deceased, widow of Clement Brooke, did in her lifetime convey to aforesaid Thomas Clagett, 250 acre part of *Dann,* beginning at a bound tree of Col. Henry Darnell's tract, *Forrest,* and there was a deficiency of 25 1/4 acres. Confirms deed for deficit.

V:127-129. Samuel Gates recorded lease 18 March 1774 from Thomas Johnson Jr. of City of Annapolis, for rents and considerations herein, leases 100 acre part of *Three Springs,* adjacent to part of Thomas Spoldinge. To pay annual rents, and plant and maintain orchard of 100 apple trees.

V:129-130. William Lynn recorded bill of sale 19 March 1774 from William Shaw for £15..15 assigns one white cow, one black cow and calf. Signed before John Stull, Joseph Chapline.

V:130 John Dorsey recorded bill of sale 20 March 1774 from John Barnes, son of James of Frederick County, sells to John Dorsey of Ann Arundel Co., merchant for £60, my crop of tobacco made by me in the proceeding year on *Chew Farm,* now in the tobacco house and possession of Joshua Barnes, son of Robert. Signed 19 March 1774, by mark John Barnes, son of James.

V:130-131. John Dorsey recorded mortgage, 20 March 1774, made by Nathan Barnes, son of Robert of Frederick Co., planter for £36 lot #33 on *Chew Farm,* from Samuel Bennett Chew to the said Nathan Barnes of Robert for 100 acres. Signed Nathan Barnes, son of Robert.

V:132-133. Joseph Gordon recorded deed 22 March 1774 from John Logsdon for £89..5 Pennsylvania, sells tract called *Bedford,* adjacent to *Half Moon,* 111 acres. Margaret Logsdon voluntarily gave up her right of dower.

V:133-134. Martin Hoffman recorded deed 22 March 1774, from Edmond Turner for £206, part of *Fletchall's Good Will,* and *Pleasant Hills.* Catherine Turner released dower right.

V:134-136. Bernard Hershberger recorded deed 22 March 1774, from George Striker for £300, tract *Cooperton,* 100 acres; also *Striker's Timber Land,* at 11th line of *Willyard's Lot,* surveyed for Daniel Wilyard for 64 ½ acres. Catharine Stricker released dower.

V:136-138. Christian Miller recorded deed 22 March 1774 from Simon Miller of Virginia, for £40, *Resurvey on Hard Grubbing,* surveyed 2 April 1763 for 127 acres. Signed by mark.

V:138-140. Lazarus Wingert, wheelwright, recorded deed 22 March 1774 from Benjamin Van Pelt of Georgetown, taylor, sells lot #204 in Georgetown. Mary Van Pelt released dower right.

V:140-141. Peter Becraft Jr. Recorded deed 22 March 1774 from Amos Right, for £95, tract called *Becraft's Delight,* on Linganore Creek, 50 acres, on 5th line of *Mount Pleasant,* deed for 18 ½ acre part. Signed by mark. Rachel wife of Amos Right released dower.

V:141-143. Edward Ward recorded deed 22 March 1774 from Nicholas Roads for £24..5, *Ward's Choyce,* part of *None Left,* 24 1/4 acres. Jean Road released dower.

V:143-145. Jacob Dunkell recorded deed 22 March 1774 from Michael Cookus for £650, two contiguous tracts, beginning at *Shear Spring,* 180 acres and part adjacent to land Jacob Snider bought of Valentine Baust, containing 18 3/4 acres. Christiana, wife of Michael Cookus released dower.

V:145-146. Michael Cresap recorded deed 22 March 1774 from Nehemiah Martin of Frederick County, Virginia, for £21..14, *Martin's Choice,* on run called Martin's Mill Run, which empties into the North branch of the Potomack above Sideling Hill, 35 acres. Signed by mark before Thos Waring, Geo Brent.

V:146-148. Jacob Philip Studer recorded deed 22 March 1774, from Anthony Pollhower for £26, tract called *Bad Enough.* Signed by mark.

V:148-150. Henry Hersberger recorded deed 22 March 1774, from Henry Ounger for £370. Three tracts, part of *George's Quarter,* 32 ½ acres; 2nd. Tract conveyed by Wm Fream recorded in P:219-220; and 3d. Part of *Frenchman's Purchase,* P:353-354, 24 acres. Signed by mark. Catherine Ounger released dower.

V:150-153. Ezekial Beatty recorded deed 22 March 1774 from Thomas Beatty for £42, part of 600 acres conveyed to him by John Hall out of *Middle Plantation,* on 4th line of *Discovery,* belonging to Jacob Shell. M&B for 200 acres. Catherine, wife of Thomas Beatty released dower.

V:153-157. Jonathan Rose of the Colony of Virginia, recorded deed 22 March 1774, from Marmaduke Leight, late of Hunterdon County, West Jersey, for £15 sterling, sells *Mount Pleasant,* adjacent to *Boyle's Fancy,* resurveyed by John Myers, beginning at Myers Branch on Potomac. 50 acres. Signed Marmaduke Lights. [pg. 156 is blank.]

V:157-159. Jacob Hoffman recorded deed 22 March 1774 from Joseph Burneston of Frederick Town, for £22, Lot #157 in Frederick Town on main road from Frederick Town to Georgetown, and joins Henry Barton's lot. Ann Burneston released dower.

V:159-161. John Beall recorded deed 22 March 1774 from Alexander Beall for 5 shillings, part of *Trouble Enough,* end of 35th line, to *Resurvey on Long Looked For,* 124 acres. Elizabeth, wife of Alexander Beall released dower.

V:162-163. Michael Reeder recorded deed 22 March 1774, from Thomas Durben for £200 conveys 100 3/4 acres, part of *Resurvey on Lamb's Choice.* His wife (name blacked out) examined released dower.

V:163-164. Joseph Gordon recorded deed 22 March 1774 from John Logsdon for £9 sterling and £30 current money, assigns *Logsdon's Amendment.* Signed before Joseph Wood, Anthony Arnold. Margaret Logsdon released dower.

V:165-166. James Soper recorded deed 22 March 1774, from George Wilson for £200, tract *Difficulty,* 100 acres. Signed by George Wilson by mark. Mary Wilson released dower.

V:167-168. Geo Sharon recorded deed 22 March 1774, from Saml Krabell for 5 shillings, lot #166 in Jerusalemtown, Hannah, wife of Samuel released dower.

V:168-170. Allen Miller recorded deed 22 March 1774 from John Volgamott, sells a small part of *Watersnake,* conveyed by Samuel Volgamot to Christian Wise, and by said wise to John Volgamott, with agreement about use of tail race in present location. 1 acres, 25 perches. Magdalena Volgamott released dower rights.

V:171-172. Salome Lyddane recorded deed 22 March 1774 from James Bradt, brother in law, and Maria Elizabeth his wife, for £38, assigns lot #7, with house in Middletown, purchased of Michael Jesserong. Signed Jacobus Bradt.

V:173-174. Snowdan Sergeant recorded deed 22 March 1774 from Richard Ankrum for £130, 100 acres of *Betsy's Delight,* resurveyed on the *Resurvey on John and Sarah,* granted to John Hook. Signed by mark before John Stull, Edward Burgess. Elizabeth Ancrum released dower.

V:174-176. Mark Harmon recorded deed 22 March 1774, from Henry Leatherman, for £40, *Flyfisher Maidle,* granted him in 1772, 204 acres. Signed in G.S. Margaret Leatherman released dower.

V:176-178. Casper Cramer recorded deed 23 March 1774, from Benjamin Cornell for £200 *Joseph's Chance,* on a branch falling into Alloway Creek, 40 acres. Also part of *Brooks Discovery on the Rich Lands,* 20 1/8 acres adjacent to *Joseph's Chance,* Sarah Cornell released dower. Signed before Joseph Wood, Rachel Wood.

V:178-180. George Jantz recorded deed 22 March 1774,from George Jacob Schley, gunsmith, for £265, lot #44 in Frederick Town, with liberty of passing cart or wagon on land through lot #43, gives lot title from [Daniel] Dulaney to George Michael Jesserang to Jacob Wise to Ludwick Weltner to George Jacob Schley. Margaret Schley released dower.

V:180-182. Philip Rodenpillar recorded deed 22 March 1774. To all Christian people, I Philip Rodenpiller, weaver, for good causes and consideration confirm to the Dutch Presbyterian Congregation, one acre, part of *Second Choice,* near a road leading from the main road to Levenstone's mill, for 6 shillings, for use of church and school house. Signed before Thos Price, Thomas Warring. Acknowledged.

V182-183. Azariah Gatton recorded deed 22 March 1774, from John Harris for £47..10, part of *John's Delight,* by estimation 100 acres. Signed before Sam'l Beall, John Robert Peter. Elizabeth Harris, wife of John, released dower.

V:184-185. Earnest Baker recorded deed 22 March 1774 from Jonathan Hager, made 16 March, for £5, lot #113 in Elizabethtown. Pay annual rents. Signed before Thos Prather, John Stull.

V:186-187. Michael Tasler recorded deed 22 March 1774 from Jonathan Hager made 16 March, for £5, lot #92 in Elizabethtown. Pay annual rents. Signed before Thos Prather, John Stull.

V:188-189. Thomas Reignhart recorded deed 22 March 1774 from Jonathan Hager made 16 March, for £5, lot #74 in Elizabethtown. Pay annual rents. AF paid Wm M. Beall

V:189-191. John Adam recorded deed 22 March 1774 from Jonathan Hager made 16 March, for £5, lot #86 in Elizabethtown. Pay annual rents. Signed before Thos Prather, John Stull.

V:191-193. Henry Funck Sr. recorded deed 22 March 1774 from Jonathan Hager made 16 March, for £5, lot #147 in Elizabethtown. Pay annual rents. AF paid Wm M. Beall

V:193-195. Geo Rinehart recorded deed 22 March 1774 from Jonathan Hager made 16 March, for £5, lot #56 in Elizabethtown. Pay annual rents. Signed before Thos Prather, John Stull.

V:195-197. John Coon recorded deed 22 March 1774 from Jonathan Hager made 16 March, for £5, lot #35 in Elizabethtown. Pay annual rents. Signed before Thos Prather, John Stull.

V:197-199. Isaac Kenedaugh recorded deed from Jonathan Hager made 16 March, for £5, lot #38 in Elizabethtown. Pay annual rents. Signed before Thos Prather, John Stull.

V:199-201. Abraham Troxall recorded deed 22 March 1774 from Jonathan Hager made 16 March, for £5, lot #113 in Elizabethtown. Pay annual rents. Paid alienation fine to Wm M. Beall

V:201-204. Lodowick Young, Martin Harry, Leonard Shryock and Conrad Hogmire for 5 shillings recorded deed 22 March 1774 from Jonathan Hager, made 16 March, granted lot #221 in trust for use as schoolhouse for the Dutch Lutheran Congregation in Elizabethtown.

V:204-205. Thomas Beatty recorded bill of sale 22 March 1774 from John Carn for £40 sells two sorrel horses, one colt, four sheep, one lamp, 28 hogs, all my household goods and plantation utensils. Signed by mark.

V:205-207. Geo Waltz recorded deed 22 March 1774 from Jonathan Hager, made 17 March, for £5, lot #42 in Elizabethtown. Pay annual rents. Signed before Thos Prather, John Stull.

V:207-208. Thomas Dyson recorded bill of sale 22 March 1774 from Thomas Brannon for £20, six head of hogs, one cow. Redemption. Signed before Chs Jones, Geo Briscoe.

V:209-210. Patrick McCardil recorded deed 22 March 1774 from Jonathan Hager made 17 March, lot #53 in Elizabethtown. To pay annual rents. AF paid Wm M. Beall

V:211-212. Adam Salmon recorded deed 22 March 1774 from Edward Dorsey, son of John of Anne Arundel County, for £75, sells interest in *Resurvey on Small Beginning,* on draught of Pipe Creek, containing 50 acres. Signed before Upton Sheridine, Wm Beatty.

V:213-214. Doctor Henry Schnebeley recorded deed 22 March 1774 from George Waddel for £72, tract *Huclebarry Level,* near Conecocheague, near Isaac Baker's, 80 acres.

V:215-216. John Smouse recorded deed from Samuel Chase for £50. *Come by Chance,* 137 acres.

V:216-219. Jacob Zug and Ellen or Alan Miller recorded deed 22 March 1774 from Saml. Wolgamott and John Wolgamott, miller, for £30 assigns all that water that shall not be wanted on Samuel and John Wolgamoths, mills erected and situated on tract called *Resurvey on part of Water Sink,*

V:219. Martin Harry recorded bill of sale 22 March 1774 from Balser Hess, shoemaker, assigns a house and lot in Elizabeth Town, where James Caldwell now lives, to hold for period of two months.

V:220-221. Adam Stewart and Robert Peter recorded deed 22 March 1774 from Ninian Mockbee for £187..10, tract *Good Luck,* 150 acres. Mary, wife of Ninian Mockbee released dower.

V:222. Richard Donaldson, recorded 16 August 1774. James Patterson, Charles Beall and Richard Donaldson confess judgment for £59..11, and 295 lbs tobacco recovered against James Patterson, 3rd Tuesday of March last, debt and costs for use of Mitchell and Gaither.

V:222. Wm Inyard recorded supersedeas 16 August 1774 for 16 shillings debt against George K. McDonald.

V:222. Henry Creager recorded supersedeas 16 August 1774 against David Swank, Jacob Shannenberg and Michael Tice, confess judgment 20 June 1774 for £15..4 and 2/6 costs.

V:222. Edward Cain and John Betts confess judgment 20 June 1774 for £2..17..2 on 14 May 1774 to Christian Grove.

V:223. Thos Richardson recorded 18 Aug. 1774 supersedeas against George Stricker, Jacob Young and Adam Tasker for £86..8..4.

V:223. Mathias Rough, recorded supersedeas 16 Nov 1774 against James Smith, £47..14

V:223. William Hobbs recorded supersedeas 16 Aug. 1774 against Jeremiah Covell, Wm Stevens and Wm Turner, £5..17..11 and 221 lbs. Tobacco recovered 19 March 1774.

V:223 Michael Kirkpatrick, Wm Flint, George Kirkpatrick confess judgment to James Smith, £31..14.

V:223. John Lanhorn recorded supersedeas 16 Aug. 1774 against John Haggerty, Andrew Scott and John Haggerty, Jr. For £15..4.

V:224. Edmon Ingman and Francis Gilbert confess judgment to Jacob Israel £41..6..6 debt.

V:224. Jacob Dunkill, Richard Haffer and Jacob Schley confess judgment to Samuel Beall £96..14..4

V:224 John Lidy, Andrew Link and Jacob Bishop confess judgment for £10..10.

V:224. George Keysinger, J. Young and Isaac Cogar confess judgment for £228

V:224. John Oden, Wm West and Benj Holly confess judgment.

V:224. Walter S. Green, Peter and John Pancoast confess judgment to Thomas Richardson.

V:224. Thomas Dyson, Aaron Harris and Stephen Keyser confess judgment for £77..19..4

V:224. Benjamin Spyker, Andrew Birdsell, John Capert confess judgment to Harry Lazarus.

V:225. John West, John Gilcrest and Andrew Reintzel confess judgment for Hezekiah Boone £40.

V:225. John Hayman Jones, Simon Reeder, Benoni Dawson confess judgment for £99..5.

V:225. Thos Dyson, Clement Beall and Henry O'Neale confess judgment to Thomas Richardson, for £24..10, 17 Aug. 1774.

V:225. Thomas Dyson, Clement Beall and Henry O'Neale confess judgment to William Molleson for £80..1, 17 Aug. 1774

V:225. John Switzer, Abraham Troxell, and Michael Weaver confess judgment to Henry Repple for £212, 18 Aug. 1774

V:225. David Swank, Jacob Shornberger and Michael Tice confess judgment to Jacob Harman, for 14 shillings and 6 pence, 20 June 1774.

V:225. Adam Ox, Peter Hoffman confess judgment for £16 to Paul Zentzigger.

V:225. Conrad Spoon, Wm Bentley, confess judgment for 19 shillings, 2 July 1774.

V:225. Wm Ridge, Benj. Albridge and David Shawhen confess judgment to Samuel Wickham for £1..13, and 2/6 costs. 17 Aug. 1774.

V:226. Sam'l Love recorded supersedeas 20 Aug. 1774 against Thomas Jennings, John Wise and John West, £125..6.

V:226. Thomas Jennings, John West and John Yost confess judgment for £32..13..6 to Cunningham and Co.

V:226. David Showen, Stephen Julian, Abm Miller and Isaac Miller confess judgment to Normand Bruce, £356.

V:226. Peter Fout, John Shelman, Christian Stoner confess judgment unto Henry Willer for £579.

V:226. James Frazer, David Moore and Chs Beatty confess judgment to Henry Ridgely for £10..10 17 Nov. 1774.

V:226. Joseph White, Joseph Magruder and James Haislip confess judgment to Nathaniel Norris for £148. 17 Nov. 1774.

V:226. Thomas Sprigg Wootton, James Perry and Richard Crabb confess judgment unto Stephen Stewart for £33..12, 18 Nov. 1774

V:226. George Hubley, John Unsel and William Baird confess judgment to Jacob Fisher for 5/6 and 2/6, 24 Sept. 1774.

V:226. Peter Disor, Thomas Sims and Nicholas Vernor confess judgment to John Sellers for £2..5 debt and 2/6 costs, 5 Sept. 1774.

V:227. Philip Rodenpiller recorded deed 22 March 1774 with the Dutch Presbyterian and Lutheran Congregations for £9, for use as a church and a schoolhouse, assigns part of *Second Choice,* containing 9 acres. Signed in German script before Thos Price, Thos Warring. 4 ½ pence alienation fine paid by the Dutch Congregation to Wm M. Beall.

V:228. Nicholas Hower and Adam Westerberger recorded deed 24 March 1774, from Thomas Polhouse for £30 one light bay horse and saddle and bridle, saddle bags, one brindle cow, one copper kettle, one table and desk, one chest, one ten plate stove, 9 pewter plates, other housewares, Signed before Thos Price, Michael Trifler.

V:228-229. Andrew McGuire recorded bill of sale 15 April 1774 from Philip Billing to pay sum £25 in 1 year and one month.

V:230. John George Moyer recorded the following, 8 April 1774, from Philip Nollert of Middletown for £0..10 assigns steel kettle and all property for debts. Signed before Wm Coffereth.

V:230-231. John Holmes Junr. recorded deed 26 March 1774, from John Owen for £241..10..6 assigns all his right and interest in *Owen's Resurvey*, where William Owen settled, 138 acres more or less. Signed before David Lynn, Edward Burgess.

V:231-232. Anthony Gossler recorded deed 22 March 1774 from Isaiah Boone for £40 Lot #10 in Georgetown on Potomac River. Hannah, wife of Isaiah released dower. Taken before Robert Peter, Adam Stewart.

V:232. Archibald Dick recorded release of dower 2 April 1774. In Chester County, Pennsylvania, Mary Dick, wife of Archibald Dick, released her rights to John Tompson, to premises recently sold by the said Archibald Dick.

V:232-233. Jacob Gobble recorded 25 April 1774, articles of agreement between Michael Erter, carpenter, regarding a road for wagons through the said Erter's land to Gobble's plantation, on the main road leading from Westminster Town to Frederick Town.

V:233-234. Jacob Nehart recorded bill of sale 25 April 1774, £11..2 from Anthony Prout assigns four head of black cattle, one black horse. If sum paid with interest, sale is void.

V:234 Jacob Zug recorded deed 22 March 1774, from Samuel Wolgamott, part of *Resurvey on Water Sink,* on Great Marsh, part of his Lordship's Manor of Conococheague in to the Potomac River, adjacent to *Chew's Farm;* also part of a tract called *William's Lookout,* adjacent to *Water Sink,* where the mill race is on Jacob Zug's land, across the marsh. Wolgamott keeps the privilege of digging ditch to draw water off. Contains 288 acres. Signed before Sam'l Beall Junr, James Smith. Barbara Wolgamott released dower.

V:238-240. Philip Creighbam, heir at law to his father, Adam Creighbam, recorded deed 22 March 1774, from Casper Huffman for £162, tracts called *Brightwell's Choice,* granted to Jonathan Hager for 50 acres; 2nd, part of tract *Resurvey on Mountain of Wales,* 51 acres; and third, part of tract conveyed in April 1772 by George Gillespie, called *Gillespie's Bargain,* Signed in German script before Thomas Prather, John Stull. Margaret Huffman released dower.

V:241-242. John Stoner recorded mortgage 24 March 1774 from John Orr for £35, part of *The Ovel,* on Sams Creek, near Ullerick Mislers. Signed before Wm Beatty and Henry Barnes.

V:242-243. John Willetts recorded deed 29 March 1774 from Charles Carroll of Annapolis. Whereas John Diggs formerly mortgaged tract called *Hazel Valley,* and the representatives of John Diggs, conveyed same to John Willets for 5 shillings to clear title.

V:243-245. Charles Greenberry Griffith of Charles recorded deed 26 March 1774 from Ludwick Davis. Whereas Ludwick Davis conveyed to his brother Thomas Davis 17 June 1761, two parcels, *Warrenford's Square,* and *Lodowicks Range,* 193 acres. Deed ineffective, and Thomas Davis released property back to Lodowick on condition that he should convey the same to Samuel Mount of Virginia, who gave bond to said Chas G. Griffith, tract on Seneca Creek, 162 acres, and Lodowick's Range. Eleanor Davis wife of Lodowick released dower. Samuel Mounts signed assignment.

V:245-246. John Bean recorded sale 31 March 1774, from Thos Burghe for £80, assigns tract called *Devall's Forrest,* adjoining *Beall's Good Will,* 100 acres. Signed by mark. Elington Burghee, wife of Thomas released dower right, before Thos Price, Wm Blair.

V:247-248. Michael Arter, carpenter, recorded deed 5 April 1774 from Jacob Gobble, *Resurvey on Good Fellowship,* Signed by mark, witnessed by Normand Bruce, Robt Portteus, and Jos. Wood.

V:248-250. Nicholas Fower (or Hower) and Adolph Iler, recorded bill of sale 20 April 1774 recorded bill of sale 20 April 1774 from John Michael Wydmyer and Eleanor Wydmyer for 5 shillings, Negro Nan, about 14 years of age. Signed before Wm Beatty, Henry Barnes.

V:250-251. John Willetts recorded deed 22 April 1774 from Wilfred Neal, Eleanor Diggs, and Raphael Diggs, executors and heirs of Edward Diggs, late of St. Mary's County for £175, tract adjacent to Wm Farquhar's part. Signed before Hanson Briscoe, Henry Rowser.

V:251-252. Peter Crowl recorded deed 24 March 1774 from Peter Kemp for £6..9 sterling, tract *Daniel's Den,* 6 3/4 acres. Signed German Script before Normand Bruce, Peter Logsdon. Sarah Kemp released dower.

V:252-254. James McGuire recorded deed 22 April 1774 from Michael McQuire for *Patient's Care,* adjacent to *Owings Choyce.*

V:254-256. Thomas Stevenson recorded deed 22 April 1774 from Thomas Taylor for £100..10, parcels 67 acre part of *Resurvey on Hazel Thicket,* 53 acres of *Resurvey on Mount Pleasant,* and one acre of *Content.* Metes and bounds given for 121 acres in whole. signed before Sam'l Beall, Junr., Wm. Beatty. Caleb, wife of Thomas Taylor released dower.

V:256-257. Wm Sterling recorded deed from 22 April 1774 from Wilfred Neal and Eleanor Diggs, executors of Edward Diggs, late of St. Mary's County for £40 part of *Brother's Agreement,* on the north side of Ryland's Branch.

V:257-258. Brooke Beall and William Deakins recorded deed 22 April 1774 from John Thompson for £70..6 part of *Conjurer's Outdone,* 35 ½ acres. Signed before Charles Jones, Andrew Heugh. Eleanor Thompson released dower rights.

V:259-260. Michael McGuire Jr. recorded deed 22 April 1774 from Michael McGuire for £10 sterling, part of *Resurvey on part of Patents Care,* 5 acres.

V:260-262. James Downey recorded deed 22 April 1774, from Peter Baker for £250 Pennsylvania, tracts on Antietam, near Province Line, *Departe Spring, George's Fancy*, and *Burkett's Folly.* Christian Baker his wife released dower.

V:262-263. Anthony Roof recorded deed 22 April 1774 from Michael Roof for £10, *Resurvey on Green Castle.*

V:263-264. Lewis Smith recorded deed 22 April 1774 from Henry Weaver for £22 for *Chestnut Thickett,* on south side of Blue Mountain for 21 acres. Signed German Script, Henrich Wieber, Catherine wife of "George" Weaver released dower.

V:264-265. Nicholas Cope recorded deed 22 April 1774 from Michael Haines of Baltimore County, for £100, part of *Range,* patented by Richard Croxall, and sold to Yost Cope of Philadelphia. Tract on south side of Little Pipe Creek. Catherine, wife of Michael Haines released dower.

V:266-267. Thomas McGuire recorded deed 22 April 1774 from Michael McGuire Senr for £100 tract called *Thomas Delight* and part of *Resurvey on Patients Care,* and part of tract called *Ohio,* containing 159 acres.

V:268-269. John Shuman recorded deed 22 April 1774 from Mary and Mathias Lawrence for £21 Pennsylvania, land called *Hoggs Delight,* on Maple Branch, between Ridge and Short Mountain, 55 acres. Signed by mark before John Stull, Saml Beall Jr.

V:269-270. James Miller, merchant of Prince George's county, recorded bill of sale 26 April 1774, from Benjamin Griffith, crop of tobacco, a servant woman, two feather beds and furniture, two horses, pewter dish, pewter basin, one woman's saddle, other items. Signed before Edward Burgess.

V:270-273. George Keller recorded deed 22 April 1774 from Thomas Keller of Cumberland County, Pennsylvania for £100 Pennsylvania, *Resurvey on Ash Swamp,* 77 1/4 acres. Signed before Wm Brice, James Stull. Martha Keller released dower.

V:273-275. George Derr, Henry Leatherman and Valentine Linganfelter recorded deed 22 April 1774, made 29 March 1774 from Andrew Livingston for £500 tract called *Miller's Delight,* on east side of the Mill Branch of Kittoctin Creek, containing 100 acres. Signed before Thos Price, Jacob Miller. Elizabeth Livingston released dower rights.

V:275-278. Nicholas Smith recorded deed 22 April 1774, from Thomas Keller for £45, part of *Prickly Ash Bottom,* 28 acres. Signed Thomas Collar. Martha, wife of Thomas Keller released dower.

V:278-281. Philip Jacob Miller recorded deed 22 April 1774 from Thomas Keller for £45, part of *Ash Swamp*, adjacent to *Prickly Ash Bottom,* Signed Thomas Collar. Martha, wife of Thomas Keller released dower.

V:281-284. Gaspar Frietzsche, skinner, recorded deed 22 April 1774 from Isaac Kenodagh of Elizabethtown, for £35, lot #14 in Elizabethtown to pay yearling 4 shillings, 6 pence. Signed by mark. Elizabeth Kenodagh released dower.

V:284-285. George Custard recorded bill of sale from Gaspar Frietshe for £30 bond, assigns lot #14 in Elizabethtown. If sum paid by due date, sale void.

V:285-286. Barnet Linganfelter recorded deed 25 April 1774 from Abraham Linganfelter for £375, lot #49 in Sharpsburg, and likewise a sugar tree desk and a corner cupboard, provided nevertheless that if sums paid by date, then sale is void.

V:287-289. Abraham Linganfelter recorded Lease 26 April 1774 from Joseph Chapline for yearly rents and covenants, assigns tenement called *Hickory Tavern,* with 8 3/4 acres land, and to maintain buildings for 21 years to pay annually £3..5. Signed by both parties.

V:289-291. Jacob Goble, cooper, recorded deed 28 April 1774 from Edward Lamb. Whereas reference is made to a deed between the parties in 1767, which was defective, for 5 shillings, deed made to correct prior deed for *Resurvey on Good Fellowship,* 109 acres. Eleanor Lamb released dower rights.

V:292. Anthony Noble recorded bill of sale 3 May 1774 from Benjamin Wright for £11..4 all my crop of tobacco, on the ground owned by Cornelius Fitchow, where John Brooner now lives. Signed before Wm Devon Clary, Charles Clinton.

V:292-295. Benjam Stewart recorded lease 5 April 1774 from John Chisholm for part of tract called *Icoburgh Forest,* 100 acres, for term of 18 years, to plant and maintain apple orchard of 100 trees, other covenants.

V:295. Simon and Thomas Nicholls recorded bill of sale 5 April 1774 from John Nicholls for £95, assigns 2 feather beds and furniture, 3 iron pots, Dutch oven, 2 chests, iron pot rack, 4 pewter basins, 6 pewter plates, 2 dishes, 2 tables, one gelding, 2 mares, 2 cows and calves, 2 cows and yearling, 3 2-yr old heifers, 5 sheep, 16 hogs. Signed before Wm Deakins Jr. Thos Sprigg Wootton.

V:296-297. John Clagett recorded deed 5 April 1774, from Mordecai Boone for £300 sells two tracts, *The James* and *Addition to James,* adjacent to part sold to Alexander Clagett by Mordecai Boone, containing 20 acres.

V:297-298. Alexander Clagett recorded deed 5 April 1774 from John Clagett for £5, part of tract called *Butler's Disappointment.* Near Potomac River.

V:298-300. John Moore recorded deed 9 May 1774 from Pearce Lamb for £400 part of *Lamb's Resurvey,* adjacent to *Brown's Plague, Resurvey on Good Fellowship,* and *Father's Care.* Catherine wife of Pearce Lamb released dower.

V:300-302. George Noble Wheeler recorded lease 9 May 1774 from Thomas Darnall for annual rents and considerations herein, leases 100 acres *Hope.* To plant an apple orchard of 100 trees.

V:302-304. Christian Prengle recorded deed 7 May 1774 from Sebastian Derr for 5 shillings, half lot in Frederick Town, #29. Catherine Derr released dower rights.

V:304-305. Christian Prengle of Frederick Town, inn holder, recorded deed 7 May 1774, from Sebastian Derr, 5 shillings for lot #20 in Fredericktown. Catherine Derr released dower rights.

V:305-307. Edmond Riggs recorded deed 10 May 1774, from John Harris for £100 sells part of tract called *John's Delight,* known by name of *Green Briar,* 84 acres. Signed before Wm Luckett, William Brice. Elizabeth Harris, wife of John, released dower rights.

V:307-309. Archibald Allen recorded deed 10 May 1774 from John Harris for £266, part of *John's Delight,* beginning at 35th line, adjacent to Margaret Hickman's part, for 210 acres. Elizabeth Harris, wife of John released dower rights.

V:309-311. Joseph Magruder recorded deed of gift 11 May 1774 from Saml Magruder 3d, for natural love and affection for my son, grants part of tract called *Hensley,* adjacent on 12th line of *Trouble Enough,* 314 acres. Margaret, wife of Samuel Magruder 3d released dower rights.

V:311-312. Renalden Walker recorded release of mortgage 12 May 1774 from Arthur Nelson. Whereas he mortgaged tract *Virgin's Delight,* containing 120 acres, 5 Dec. 1773.

V:312-313. Thomas Bowles recorded bill of sale 13 May 1773 from Elias Barton. In consideration of his being special bail in court case brought by Samuel Irwin, and additional sum of 5 shillings, he assigns one walnut desk, one walnut square dining table, one walnut round breakfast table, one looking lass, 8 pictures, 6 chairs, one pair of hand irons, one walnut chest, two walnut bedsteads, two iron pots, one iron pot rack. Sale void if court appearance met.

V:313-315. Valentine Wing recorded deed 13 April 1774 from John Goble for £45, assigns lot in town of Westminster on Main Street adjacent to Mathias Hook and Enoch Davison. Elizabeth Goble released dower rights.

V:315-318. Alexander Whitacre recorded deed 14 April 1774 from Joseph Jones of Prince George's County for £609 assigns part of *Two Brothers,* originally granted John and Thomas Fletchall, for 200 acres. Also *Coales Purchase,* 120 acres. Signed before Christopher Lowndes, Richard Henderson. Margaret wife of Joseph Jones released dower.

V318. Thomas Waring recorded marks for cattle and hogs on 22 April 1774.

V:318. Paul Road recorded bill of sale 20 April 1774, from John Dull. I make over one black horse, one red cow and calf, and crop of wheat. Signed by mark. Witnesses Massam Dean, Joan Dean by mark.

V:318-320. William Hawker recorded deed 14 April 1774 from Richard Northcraft for £20 sterling, all his interest in tract *Exchange,* standing near Middle Seneca about a mile above Stephen Hampstons, it being the beginning tree of a tract taken up by George Barkharmmer. 100 acres. Verlinda, wife of Richard Northcraft released dower.

V:320-322. Christopher Tefenbach recorded deed 23 April 1774 from Peter Kemp for £5..15 tract called *Kemp's Luck,* containing 3 acres. Signed in German Script. Sarah wife of Peter Kemp released dower. [marginal recording "del'd Paul Defenbaugh, 16 March 1785"]

V:322-324. Christopher Tefenbach recorded deed 23 April 1774 from Peter Kemp for £11..5, tract called *Hard Grubbing,* containing 4 3/4 acres. Signed in German Script. Sarah wife of Peter Kemp released dower. [marginal recording "del'd Paul Defenbaugh, 16 March 1785"]

V:324-326. William Murdock of Carroll's Tract of Pennsylvania, weaver, recorded deed 22 April 1774 from Alexander Orr for £22 Pennsylvania, *Archie's Lot,* on south side of Turkey Run, into Tom's Creek, containing 30 acres. Signed before Norman Bruce, Robt Pottens. Martha Orr released dower rights before Normand Bruce, William Blair.

V:326-328. Peter Crowl recorded deed 22 April 1774 from Frederick Christman for £25, part of *Long Meadow,* 50 acres. Signed before Normand Bruce, Ralph Logsdon. Elizabeth Christman released dower rights.

V:328-330. Thomas Aldridge recorded deed 22 April 1774 from John Owen for £5, part of *Owens Resurvey,* containing 65 acres. Signed before David Lynn, Edward Burgess.

V:330-332. Jacob Snowdenberg recorded deed 22 April 1774 from Ephraim Howard for £200 part of *Spring Garden,* containing 100 acres. Elizabeth, wife of Ephraim released dower.

V:332-333. Gerard Briscoe and Ludwig Yost recorded deed 22 April 1774 from John Mummit, carpenter, for £60, tract called *Trail's Choice,* surveyed for David Trail, containing 50 acres. Signed German Script. His wife came and was examined apart and released dower rights. Name not given.

V:333-336. James Downey recorded deed 22 April 1774, from Peter Baker for £100 tract called *Baker's Fancey,* obtained by conveyance from Christopher Burkett, containing 88 ½ acres. Signed, Christian Baker wife of Peter released dower.

V:336-338. Henry Shaver recorded deed 22 April 1774 from Henry Shriock for £50, *Chance,* beginning at tract called *Long Looked For,* 89 acres. Signed before Thos Prather, John Stull. Catherine Shryock released dower rights.

V:338-340. Jacob Storm recorded deed 22 April 1774 from Henry Shriock for £105, tract on Dry Run, called *Chance,* containing 113 acres. Catharine Shriock released dower.

V:340-341. Sam'l Cookson recorded deed 22 April 1774 from Michael Fouts for £6, tract called *Some Thing,* containing 2 acres. Signed German script before Jos Wood, William Bentley. Barbara Fouts released dower.

V:342-344. John Kinsey recorded deed 22 April 1774 from Jno Crumbacher for £300, part of *Jacob's Pasture,* 27 acres; *Haugh's Branch,* a part of *Michael's Fancy,* beginning at tract called *Black Oak Hill,* 35 acres, and part of *Michael's Fancy* containing 10 acres. Signed before Jos Wood, Normand Bruce. Eve Crumbacher released dower.

V:344-346. Ludwich Iguor recorded deed 22 April 1774 from Joseph Chapline for £6, lot #80 in Sharpsburgh.

V:346-347. Frederick Fox recorded deed 22 April 1774 from Joseph Chapline for £2..10, lot #1 in Sharpsburgh.

V:347-349. Henry Leonheart recorded deed 22 April 1774 from Michael Keller for £170, part of *Resurvey on Den of Wolves,* containing 100 acres. Signed in German Script, Eleanor Keller released dower rights.

V:349-351. Wm Whitmyer recorded deed from 22 April 1774 Joseph Chapline for £8, lot #86 in Sharpsburgh.

V:351-353. Joseph Maier recorded deed 22 April 1774 from Charles Angel for £26..10, part of *Resurvey on Shoemaker's Lot,* containing 53 acres. Signed in German Script [Carl Angel] Ulianna wife of Charles Angle released dower rights.

V:353-355. Geo Michael Haun recorded deed 22 April 1774 from Frederick Sower for £25, tract on draught of Great Pipe Creek, containing 31 acres.

V:355-356. Jacob Feizer recorded deed 22 April 1774 from Michael McGuire Junr., for £75 part of tract *Ohio,* conveyed to him by Samuel Owings, containing 100 acres.

V:357-358. Matthew Pigman recorded deed 22 April 1774 from John Owen for £30 sterling, part of *Owen's Resurvey,* on branches of Seneca. 100 acres.

V:358-360. Joast Runckle recorded deed 22 April 1774 from Peter Kemp for £1..16, part of *Hard Grubbing,* containing 4 1/4 acres. Signed before Normand Bruce, Ralph Logsdon. Sarah wife of Peter Kemp released dower.

V:360-361. Mathias Hook recorded deed 22 April 1774 from Anthony Arnold and Hannah Arnold, of the town of Westminster, for £43, sells lot #30 in Westminster. Hannah, wife to said Arnold released dower rights.

V:362-363. John Young recorded deed 22 April 1774 from Ephraim Howard for shillings, sells part of tract called *Spring Garden,* 92 acres. Elizabeth Howard released dower rights.

V:364-365. Yost Zimmerman recorded deed 22 April 1774 from Henry Shriock for £5, for *Chance,* a part of *Resurvey on Chance,* 13 ½ acres. Catherine Shyrock released dower right.

V:365-366. Frederick Fox recorded deed 22 April 1774 from George Walls of Berkeley County, Virginia for £10, lot #76 in Sharpsburg.

V:367-369. Martin Harry Sr. of Hagerstown, recorded deed 22 April 1774 from Ludwig Young for £35 Pennsylvania, lot #20. Modline Young released dower rights.

V:369-371. Peter Crowl recorded deed 22 April 1774, from Frederick Chrisman for £150 part of *Kelly's Range,* 100 acres. Elizabeth, wife of Frederick released dower rights.

V:371-373. John Lynch recorded deed 22 April 1774 from Christopher Thomas for £30 *Andrew's Folly.* Wife's name left blank in dower release statement.

V:373-375. Patrick Hines recorded deed 22 April 1774, from Charles Angel for £51 *Resurvey on Shoemaker's Lot,* 102 acres. Signed G.S. Carl Engel. Uliana his wife released dower rights.

V:375-377. Arnold Boone recorded deed 22 April 1774 from Josiah Boone for £32..12..6, *Boone's Good Luck,* and part of *Rocky Spring,* for 6 and 12 acres. Hannah Boone released dower.

V:377-379. John Waters recorded deed 22 April 1774, from Christopher Lowndes for £25, for tract called *Turkey's Flight,* on branch of Bush Creek, commonly called Long Branch, originally granted John Prather in 1752. By virtue of an attachment obtained against said Prather in Frederick County court, 17 June 1775, for use of Christopher Lowndes, sold to John Waters son of John. Elizabeth Lowndes released dower.

V:379 Ludwig Yost recorded deed 22 March 1774 [sic] deed made 6 April, from Joseph West Jr for £5..6..10, lot called *Resurvey on Mill Tract,* for 14 1/4 acres. Sarah West released dower.

V:382-385. Ludwig Yost recorded deed 22 April 1774 from David Trail Sr for £294..9..6, tract called *Good Will,* for 100 acres. Margaret Trail released dower.

V:385-386. Christian Steiner recorded deed 22 April 1774 from Jacob Berry for £18, lot # one in Frederick Town.

V:387. James Ray recorded deed 22 April 1774 from Isaiah Boone. For £82 part of *Rocky Spring,* 55 acres. Hannah wife of Isaiah released dower.

V:388-391. Thomas Johnson and Francis Deakins recorded deed 22 April 1774, from Thomas Duckett for £300. *Resurvey on Flag Pond,* 200 acres. Mary wife of Thomas Duckett released dower.

V:391-393. James Simpson and Ninian Mockby recorded deed 22 April 1774 from James Taylor for £191, assigns 191 acres of land called *Thomas and James,* lying on a branch of Great Seneca, signed before Robert Peter and Adam Stewart. Margaret, wife of James Taylor released dower.

V:393-395. George Dill, blacksmith, recorded deed 5 May 1774, from Michael Buff for £100, tract called *Resurvey on Williams Venture,* beginning at tract called *Newry,* containing 256 acres, signed before Jos Wood, John Frazier. Mary Buff released dower right.

V:395-398. Billingsley Roberts recorded deed 22 April 1774 from John Thompson for £195..16..3 part of tract known as *The Conjuror Out Done,* containing 121 ½ acres. Signed before Charles Jones, Andrew Heugh. Eleanor, wife of John Thompson released dower.

V:398-401. Robert Peter, merchant, recorded deed 7 May 1774, from William Douglas, late of Loudoun County, Virginia, merchant, for £500 sterling, tract called *Good Luck,* adjacent to tract taken up by John Bradford, lying near the mouth of Seneca, containing 50 acres more or less; and tract called *Sugar Bottom,* conveyed to William Douglas by Ninian Edmonston, on or about 2 July 1766, containing 300 acres on the Potomac River. Receipt. Acknowledgment. Elizabeth, wife of William Douglas released dower. Wm M Beall received alienation fine.

V:401-404. William Head Sr. Recorded deed 13 May 1774, from John & Elizabeth Julian for £140 *Resurvey on Butler's Lot,* on a small draught of Fishing Creek, 296 acres, all rights except the thirds of Mary Brawner during her natural life. Signed before Jos Wood, Normand Bruce.

V:404-406. Henry Crowell recorded deed 13 May 1774, from Leonard Kitzmiller for £405..5, tract *Ivey Church,* on Beaver Dam Branch of Pipe Creek. 222 acres. Hannah Kitzmiller released dower.

V:406-408. Abraham Kise recorded deed 13 May 1774, from Wilfred Neal and Eleanor Diggs executors of Edward Diggs, for £100, *Bedford,* on south side of Great Pipe Creek, 100 acres.

V:408-410. Christopher Cruse recorded deed 13 May 1774, from Joseph Chapline for £5, an out lot in the town of Sharpsburg.

V:410-412. John Welty recorded deed 13 May 1774, from Charles Carroll for £79, *Resurvey on the Pines and Addition to the Pines,* 181 acres.

V:412-414. John George Flick recorded deed 13 May 1774, from Christ Criss for one shilling, half lot in Sharpsburg. Catherine Criss released dower.

V:414-416. Sam'l Flemming recorded deed 13 May 1774, from John Creal, carpenter, for £29, half lot adjoining George Whitehair, part of lots #199 to 206; same covenants and claims as in deed from Daniel Dulaney to Joseph Hardman, son and heir at law of Joseph Hardman, deceased, for the said half lots. Signed John Creel and Samuel Flemming before Andrew Scott and Thomas Price.

V:416-418. Robert McNutt recorded deed 13 May 1774, from Edward Magruder of Prince George's County, for £80, *Wootton's Discovery,* adjacent to *Long Swamp,* taken up by Jacob Shingutatur[1] for 122 acres.

V:418-420. Flail Pain recorded deed 13 May 1774, from Thomas Gaunt of Prince George's County, part of *Hawkins Merry Peep a Day* for 15 acres, on Potomac River, adjacent to line between Flail Payne and his brother John Payne on tract , part of *Payne's Delight.* Signed before John Cooke, Clement Hollyday.

V:420-423. Melchor Belshoover recorded of Elizabethtown, recorded deed 13 May 1774, from Jacob Rhorar, for £69, five lots of ground adjoining Jonathan Hager, on northwest of Elizabeth Town. Christiana Roarer released dower rights.

V:423-426. John Keller recorded deed 13 May 1774 from John Rowland, for £324, for 100 acres of *Pleasant Spring,* Esther Rowland released dower rights.

V:426-428. Henry Shriock recorded deed 13 May 1774, from Thos Cresap for £5, one half lot #6 in town of Skipton on main street. Signed before Michael Cresap and Thomas Warring. Hannah Cresap released dower.

V:428-429. Leonard Spong recorded deed 13 May 1774, from Joseph Chapline for £1, lot #127 lying in Sharpsburg.

V:430-432. Lucas Fleck recorded deed 13 May 1774, from Robert McNutt for tract on *Long Swamp,* formerly belonging to Jacob Shingletaker, deceased, and by his will and testament conveyed to seat Robert, on northwest side of honey Branch on Monocacy. 100 acres. Mannett McNutt released dower.

V:432-434. John Bowen recorded deed 13 May 1774 from Charles Carroll, on *Resurvey on the Pines and Addition to the Pines,* 60 acres.

V:434-436. Henry Shnebly recorded deed 13 May 1774 from Jonathan Hager for £21 Pennsylvania, lot #112 in Elizabeth Town.

V:436-439. Samuel Paughtley (Beachley) recorded deed 13 May 1774, from Capt. Evan Shelby for £120, tract *Long Bottom,* patented 1 Sept. 1752, on west side of Licking Creek, adjacent to *Miller's Folly,* 126 acres. Lettice Shelby released dower.

V:439-440. Abraham Linganfelter recorded deed 13 May 1774, from Joseph Chapline for £2..10, for lot #71 in Sharpsburgh.

V:441-443. John Storm recorded deed 13 May 1774, from Charles Carroll for £9, part of *Resurvey on the Pines and Addition to the Pines,* 16 ½ acres.

V:443-445. Robert Beatty recorded deed 13 May 1774, from Charles Carroll for £263, part of *Resurvey on the Pines and Addition to the Pines,* 600 acres.

---

[1]Peter Wilson Coldham, *Settlers of Maryland, 1751-1765,* patented in 1760. Name nearly indecipherable in deed, taken from patent record.

V:445-447. Jacob Boyer recorded deed 13 May 1774, from Christopher Lowndes of Prince George's County, for £100, lot #18 in Frederick Town. Elizabeth Lowndes released dower.

V:447-451. John Lawrence recorded deed 13 May 1775, from John Dorsey, son of John for £304..1, parts of *Mount Pleasant,* adjacent to *Good Luck,* and *Friendship.* 306 acres and 150 acres. John Dorsey, son of John signed Deed. Mary Dorsey released dower rights.

V:451-454. Andrew Warman recorded deed 13 May 1774 from Major Henry Ridgely for £325, assigns part of *Partnership,* containing 133 acres. Signed before John Burgess, Basil Burgess.

V:454-456. Thomas Jennings recorded deed 12 May 1774 from Charles Beatty and George Fraser Hawkins, for £36 sterling, lots #278 &279, in Georgetown, on *Knave's Disappointment.* Martha wife of Charles Beatty and Susan Freeman wife of George Fraser Hawkins released dower rights.

V:457-458. Philip Fails recorded deed 13 May 1774 from Philip Coone for £55 lot #13 in Sharpsburg. Signed in German script (Philip Kuntz). Margaret Coone released dower rights.

V:458-459. Thomas Rigdon recorded deed 13 May 1774, from Thomas Jennings for £7..15, lot #175 in Addition to Georgetown, part of *Knave's Disappointment.* Sarah, wife of Thomas Jennings released dower.

V:460-461. William Beatty recorded deed 13 May 1774, from Mary Richey for £200, part of *Dulaney's Lot,* 50 ½ acres.

V:461-463. Mathias Bucke recorded deed 13 May 1774, from Christopher Lowndes of Prince George's County, for £260, part of *Tasker's Chance,* 260 acres. Elizabeth Lowndes released dower.

V:463-466. Abraham Roland recorded deed 13 May 1774, from William Pepple, miller, for £200, part of *The Great Meadow,* adjacent to part conveyed to Peter Pepple by Michael Fouts, 16 1/4 acres. Elizabeth, wife of William, released dower.

V:466-467. George Keefer recorded deed 13 May 1774, from Joseph Chapline for £2..10, lot #35 in Sharpsburgh.

V:467-469. Samuel Butler recorded deed 13 May 1774, from Arthur Beatty for £30, lot #21 in town of Westminster on west side of Main Street. Eleanor wife of Arthur Beatty released dower.

V:469-471. George Custard recorded deed 13 May 1774, from Michael Sheple for tract, *Water Wort,* lying above Krebills Mill, containing 51 acres. Signed by mark. Ann Sheple released dower.

V:471-472. Michael Myers recorded deed 13 May 1774, from Mordecai and Sarah Holm for £70, lot #92 in Frederick Town.

V:473-474. Robert Huffman recorded lease 13 May 1774, from James Chapline, in consideration of yearly rents and covenants, tract *Loss and Gain,* now in possession of James Chapline, 100 acres including messuage or tenement, for 21 years, he is to build a dwelling 24 by 26 feet and a barn, 50 feet by 20 feet, and shall pay the quit rents due.

V:474-476. George Kustard recorded deed 13 May 1774, from Abraham Earlinger for £5, lot #17 in Jerusalemtown. The wife (name left blank) released dower rights.

V:476-479. John Hockman recorded deed 13 May 1774 from Andrew Warman, carpenter, for £150, *Brown's Delight,* on draught of Sams Creek, 50 acres, also *the Peach Orchard,* 8 ½ acres. Signed by mark. Barbara Warman released dower rights.

V:479. Christian Keiser recorded deed 13 May 1774, from Charles Carroll for £61..12, tract *Stony Meadow,* on the south side of Great Meadow Branch, 26 acres.

V:480-482. Jacob Warman recorded deed 13 May 1774 from Ludwig Moler for £100, part of *The Range,* surveyed for Richard Crepell, metes and bounds given for 30 acres. Honor Moler, wife of Ludwick, released dower rights.

V:482-484. Azel Waters recorded deed 14 June, 1774, from Robert Wood for £225, 119 acres, part of *Resurvey on Joseph's Friendship*, Catharine, wife of Robert Wood released dower.

V:484-486. Henry Piper recorded deed 13 May 1774, from Reynoldo Walker and Elizabeth Walker, for £485..16..3, part of *Virgins Delight,* 144 ½ acres.

V:486-487. Peter Haun of Sharpsburgh, recorded deed 13 May 174, from Abraham Linganfelter for £35, lot #9 in Sharpsburgh. Barbara, wife of Abraham released dower.

V:487-489. David Arter recorded deed 13 May 1774, from Jacob Goble cooper, for £50, part of *Resurvey on Good Fellowship.* 49 acres, in two parts. Signed by mark.

V:489-491. Adam Austin recorded deed 26 May 1774, from Robert Peter for 5 shillings. All lands, under trust that Robert Peter may occupy, possess and enjoy said lands and tenements and estates. Elizabeth, wife of Robert Peter released dower.

V:491. Jacob Hess and Christian Line recorded bill of sale 16 May 1774, from Christian Miller, jobber, for £32..13..4, delivered to Jacob Hess and Martin [sic] Line, three cows, other livestock, household furnishings, wheat and crop in ground.

V:492-494. Charles Greenberry Griffith recorded bill of sale, 17 May 1774, from Joseph Hall for £57..10..3, one Negro boy, Phill, 7 years old. Signed before Edward Burgess.

V:494-495. Edward Tansey recorded deed 17 May 1774, from Alexander Magruder for £30, *Resurvey on Johnson's Folly,* previously mortgaged by Edward Tanzy to Alexander, Magruder, and now paid back. Susannah Magruder released dower.

V:495-496. Thomas Contee recorded bill of sale 18 May 1774, from Edward Wheeler for £36..16..4, Negro man Greig and man Richard about 16 years old.

V:496-497. William Molleson recorded bill of sale 18 May 1774, from Henry Atchison for £38..13..3, one bay mare, one white horse, one cow and one yearling, two beds and furniture. Signed by mark before Adam Stewart, Alexander Contee.

V:497-499. Solomon Turner recorded deed 16 May 1774, from Henry Hall of Anne Arundel County, in compliance with the court and in agreement with Henry Hall, deceased, and for 5 shillings, conveys 100 acres of *Partnership,* signed before Richard Harwood Sen., Thos Watkins Junr.

V:499-501. James Beatty recorded deed 19 May 1775, from Thomas Beatty for £42, tract called *Middle Plantation,* containing 200 acres. Signed before Wm Beatty, Henry Barnes.

V:501-503. Thomas Durbin recorded deed 20 May 1774, from John Rister of Baltimore County, for £600, part of *Resurvey on Locust Neck,* 580 acres. Signed German script before Normand Bruce, Robert Porters. Margaret Rister released dower rights.

V:503-505. Ephraim Howard recorded deed 22 May 1774, from Upton Sheridine, for £5..12, tract called *The Gore,* on dividing line between them, and part of *Howard's Range.* 2 ½ acres.

V:505-507. Peter Beale recorded deed 24 May 1774, from Henry Nicodemas for £75, tract *Mountain Stage,* adjacent to *Fell's Retirement,* 77 acres. Mary Nichodemas released dower.

V:507-509. Devalt Willyard and David Smith recorded bill of sale 24 May 1774, from Nicholas Hoke for 5 shillings, assigns one black horse, and one cow, nevertheless if he satisfies a debt to a certain Fielder Gant, with costs and interest, this sale is void.

V:509-511. Andrew Poulson recorded deed 24 May 1774, from Henry Nichodemas for £138..15, tract *York Company's Defence,* to end of second line of *Poulson's Chance,* to *Resurvey on Stony Batter,* 111 acres. Mary Nicodemas released dower.

V:511-514. Henry Nichodemas recorded deed 24 May 1774, from Wm Buchanan, for £508..11..3, part of *Mountain Stage,* and *York Company Defence,* adjacent to *Fell's Retirement,* and *Rich Meadows,* to Joseph Murray's part. 544 acres. Signed before Wm Spears, Andrew Buchanan of Baltimore County.

V:514. Charles Greenberry Griffith recorded bill of sale 24 May 1774, from Aaron Lee for £25, one gray mare, other livestock, furniture and kitchen ware. If paid by 1 June next with interest, sale is void.

V:515-516. John Molone, Sr. of Marsh Hundred, and Jno McKay of Sharpsburgh, recorded bill of sale 24 April 1774, from James McKay of Sharpsburgh, one black gelding, three cows; if sum paid by 1 Nov. Sale is void.

V:516-517. Robert Wood recorded deed 26 May 1774, from Jacob Collar for £43..6, part of *Den of Wolves,* 17 acres 52 perches. Magdalena Collar released dower.

V:517-520. Robert Wood recorded deed 26 May 1774, from William Beall for £425, *Woods Defense* and *Friendship,* granted William Murdock. 291 acres.

V:520-522. Peter Hawn recorded deed 29 May 1774 from John Creager for £135, part of *Third Addition,* 85 acres.

V:522-524. Elias Groshank recorded deed 29 May 1774 from John Creager for £290, part of *Third Addition,* 138 acres.

V:524-526. Adam Shroiner recorded deed 29 May 1774 from John Creager for £185, part of *Third Addition,* 102 acres.

V:527-528. William Farmer recorded deed 28 May 1774, from Sarah Farmer, widow and Samuel Farmer, for £10 sterling, assigns all their claim to part of tract called *Samuel's Chance,* at head of Hawlings River, containing 61 acres.

V:528 George Brent recorded mark of cattle 2 June 1774.

V:528-530. Martha Crom recorded bill of sale for land 20 May 1774, from Peter Stoup for £40, for part of *Stouder's Look Out,* on 2nd line of *Good Luck,* containing 50 acres; but if sum paid, then sale is void.

V:530-533. Richard Haff recorded deed 24 May 1774, from Edward Tansey for £100, part of *Johnson's Neglect,* 15 acres, and also part of *Resurvey on Johnson's Folly,* 85 acres. Wife to Edward Tansey, not named, came and released dower.

V:533-535. William Weston and Samuel Miles of the City of Philadelphia, recorded mortgage 3 August 1774, from Martin Harry under bond of obligation for £1296..9 Pennsylvania, and sum of £648..4..10, to be paid by 1 August 1776, to secure loans, assigns lot #1 in Elizabeth town.

V:535-537. James Simpson and Ninian Mockbee recorded deed 30 May 1774, from Nicholas Seybert, miller, for £135, part of tract called *The Pleasant Fields,* containing 78 3/4 acres. Signed before Robert Peter, Adam Stewart.

V:537-540. James Simpson and Ninian Mockbee recorded deed 30 May 1774 from Abraham Boyd and Barbara Boyd his wife; Richard B. Hall and Margaret Hall, for £350 tract called *the Lost Jackett,* containing 200 acres. Margaret, wife of R. B. Hall released dower rights, and Barbara Boyd released dower rights.

V:540-542. Mordecai Beall recorded deed 30 May 1774, from Robert Wood for 5 shillings, gives 100 acres of land, 90 ½ ac res of part of *Woods Design,* and 9 ½ acres part of *Den of Wolves.* Catharine, wife of Robert Wood released dower.

V:542-544. Moses Rawlings recorded deed 20 June 1774, from Leonard White and Mary his wife for £65, *Richard's First Choice,* on the Town Creek, 88 acres. Signed before Michael Cresap, Thos Warring.

V:544-546. Thomas Beatty recorded deed 3 June 1774 from John Beatty for £40 part of tract near Frederick Town, called *Rocky Creek,* 18 34 acres, conveyed to John Beatty by a John Beatty of Ulster County, New York, 15 June 1759. Sarah wife of John Beatty released dower.

V:546-549. Thomas Beatty recorded deed 3 June 1774 from William Beatty and Henry Cook, executors of Ezra Beatty, deceased; Ezekiel Beatty, and Elijah Beatty. Whereas Ezra Beatty by his will instructed his executors to convey over all lands, and whereas Edward Beatty, possessed in fee part of tract called *Rocky Creek,* from purchase from George Beatty, and having contracted for sale two other parts of the same tract from John Kimball and Agnes his wife, and the other from a certain John Beatty; the two last parts being conveyed by will dated 3 Feb. 1755 and devised unto the child with which his wife was then bigg, and all that part purchased of George Beatty. This tract went to Edward Beatty, the son of Edward Beatty the testator, being the child with which the testator's wife was then big, and whereas he died 15 Aug. 1768, and his three brothers Ezekial, Ezra and Elijah inherited the same. Now for £530, sells tract to Thomas. Christiana, wife of Ezekial Beatty released dower rights.

V:550-551. Samuel Volgamott (Wolgamott) recorded deed 3 June 1774, from John Volgamott for £300, part of *Water Sink,* 40 acres. Signed by mark. Modelaner, wife of John released dower.

V:551-554. John Beatty recorded deed 3 June 1774, from Thomas Beatty for £72, part of *Middle Plantation,* 74 acres. Catharine wife of Thomas Beatty released dower.

V:554-556. Christian Prengle, innholder, recorded deed 3 June 1774, from Thomas Beatty for £192, part of *Rocky Creek,* 40 acres. Catharine wife of Thomas Beatty released dower rights.

V:556-559. Abraham Lighter recorded deed 3 June 1774, from Doctor Henry Schnebely for £80, part of *Resurvey on Rich Barrens,* now called *Forrest.* Beginning at a stone 8 perches from Lightner's spring or well. 142 acres. Elizabeth Schnebley released dower.

V:559. John Lang recorded bill of sale 3 June 1774, from Henry Leydey, for £26..10..2, anvil and bellows, two beds and furniture.

V:560-562. Josias Harrison recorded deed 3 June 1774, from Orlando Griffith for £30, tract called *Benjamin's First Beginning,* at end of the third line of *Cow Pasture.*

V:562. John Hall of the City of Annapolis, attorney at law, recorded bill of sale 13 June 1774, from Benjamin Dorsey for £360 assigns the following Negro slaves: Deborah, Fanny, Arry, Phil, Lid, Poll, Nan and Will; together with their increase, for the use of Rachel Ridgely, now the wife of Henry Ridgeley. Signed Benjamin Dorsey before H. Ridgely, Polly Ridgely.

V:563-564. Lucas Fleck recorded deed 14 June 1774, from Robt McNutt for £100, *Watkin's Discovery,* on 6th line of *Long Swamp,* taken up by Jacob Shingletaker, 122 acres. Hanna McNutt released dower rights.

V:565. Colin Dunlop & Sons, merchants of Glasgow, recorded bill of sale 15 June 1774, from George Sharrah for £85, house and lot in Jerusalemtown, with all improvements.

V:566. Edward, son of John Dorsey, and Nicholas, son of Henry Dorsey, recorded bill of sale 15 June 1774, from Benjamin Dorsey for £180 sterling, four cows and calves, two steers, 30 head of sheep, 70 hogs, one roan mare, and two white servant men, Timothy Collins and Charles Ashmore, rye, corn and wheat in the ground, six large tablespoons, and all household furniture. Signed before Jacob French and Joseph Dorsey.

V:567. Ezra Beatty recorded release of dower 16 June 1774, from Catharine Beatty, the same being on the back of deed from Thomas Dorsey, recorded in Liber T, folio 184.

V:567-568. Leonard Davis recorded bill of sale 4 July 1774, from William Davis Senr. for 1301 lbs. Crop tobacco, and 5 shillings, delivers one Negro man Jack, one Negro boy Harry, and Negro women named Hannah, Jeannie, and Calilie, and girls named Peg and Charity. Also two feather beds and bedsteads and furniture, one oval table, two square tables, one corner cupboard, two chests, five chairs, two house irons, two iron pot racks, one pair of fire tongs, one box iron and heaters, three cows and calves, and one steer. Signed before Robert Peter, Robert Ferguson.

V:568-569. Thomas Gantt Jr., recorded deed 5 July 1774, from Barton Philpott for £10 part of tract called *Merryland,* which Philpott bought of Adam Stewart, Thomas Montgomery and Cumberland William, land called *Coxon's Rest,* containing 10 acres.

V:569-570. Lawrence O'Neale recorded bill of sale 22 August 1774, from James Knox for £25, two bay horses, 8 years old, one sorrel horse, 10 years old, one roan horse, 10 years old; and one wagon.

V:570-571. Mordecai Boon recorded deed 4 August 1774, from Thomas Beall for £210 tract called *Beall's Chance,* near a large Rocky Spring, the beginning of *Nelson's Folly,* taken up by Arthur Nelson, laid out for 100 acres. Ann, wife of Thomas Beall, released dower.

V:572-573. Jacob Christ recorded deed 14 June 1774, from Robert Wood for £76..17., 30 3/4 acres of tract *Wood's Design,* Catharine, wife of Robert Wood released dower.

V:573-576. Jacob Young recorded deed 14 June 1774, from Valentine Motter for 5 shillings, called *Smith's Mistake Rectified,* 138 acres. Signed German script. Catharine Motter released dower.

V:576-578. Joseph Evey recorded deed 14 June 1774, from Jacob Root for £5 sterling, part of *Resurvey on First Choice,* on waters of Antietam, granted to Thomas Powell for 282 acres, out of which he deeded to Root, 137 ½ acres, this part begins at tract of land called *Scotch Lot,* to first line of Bealer's part, deed for 5 acres. Barbara Root released dower rights.

V:578-580. Martin Rhorer recorded deed 14 June 1774, from Ignatius Perry of Prince George's County, for £200 assigns part of *Brother's Request.* 100 acres. Margery Perry released dower.

V:580-582. Christopher Trapp, weaver, recorded deed 14 June 1774, from Jonathan Hager for £10 Pennsylvania, lot #273 in Elizabeth Town.

V:582-584. Jacob Root recorded deed 14 June 1774 from Joseph Evey for £5 sterling, *Scotch Lot,* on Beaver Creek, a draught of Antietam, adjacent to *Resurvey on First Choice.* Eve, wife of Joseph Evey released dower.

V:584-586. Frederick Rhorer, tavern keeper, recorded deed 14 June 1774, from Jonathan Hager for £10, lot on NW side of Christopher Trapp's lot, on south side of alley, lot #272 in Elizabeth Town, to pay annual rents.

V:586-587. Baltis Fout recorded deed 14 June 1774, from Thos Beatty for £250, land near Frederick Town called *Rocky Creek,* 45 acres. Catharine Beatty released dower.

V:588-589. Peter Youtsey recorded deed 14 June 1774, from Jacob Young for £100 part of *Smith's Mistake Rectified.* Eleanor, wife of Jacob Young, released dower.

V:590-593. Joseph Avey recorded deed 14 June 1774 from John Gerhart for £20, part of tract *Mount Merry,* 48 ½ acres. Gertraut, wife of John Gerhart released dower.

V:593-596. Jacob Keplinger recorded deed 14 Jun3 1774, from Geo Leonard Peckenpaugh for £__[blank], parcel called *Shaw's Barrack,* at Half Mile Branch, a draught of Kittoctin Creek, adjacent to *Resurvey on Turkey Range,* 58 acres, plus part of the *Resurvey,* 32 acres. Signed German Script, Anna Mary Beckenbaugh, wife of George Leonard released dower.

V:596-598. Catharine Beatty, the wife of Thomas Beatty, recorded deed 14 June 1774, from Thoms Beatty, for love and affection for his wife, and 5 shillings, assigns part of *Rocky Creek,* for 50 acres. Signed before John Middagh, Elijah Beatty.

V:599-601. John Stoner recorded deed 14 June 1774, from Edward Dorsey, son of John of Anne Arundel County, for £637, part of *Small Beginnings,* adjacent to *Friendship,* for 311 acres.

V:601-603. Stephen West of Prince George's County, recorded deed 14 June 1774, from Orlando Griffith for £89, part of *Benjamin's Second Beginning,* for 80 acres.

V:603-605. Frederick Steidmyer of Elizabethtown, recorded deed 14 June 1774, from Jacob Rhorar for £40, lot on Northwest side of Elizabethtown, #12, 13, 14, 15, & 16. Christiana Rhorar released dower rights.

V:605-607. Jacob Sibert recorded deed 14 June 1774 from Allen Killough for £60, part of tract called *Resurvey on the Three Cousins,* containing 72 acres. Signed before Wm Baird, John Stull.

V:607-609. Michael Tom recorded deed 14 June 1774 from Thomas Davis, son of Ephraim, a minor about 6 years old, and William Gaither, guardian of said Thomas, and Elizabeth, wife of said Ephraim, by order of the Chancery Court, sells tract *Stony Ridge,* containing 73 acres for£61..4 paid previously and £11 since the death of said Ephraim. Signed by Thomas Davis, William Gaither, and Elizabeth Gaither. Elizabeth Gaither released dower rights. Signed before David Lynn, Edward Burgess. [Yes, it was recorded that Thomas Davis signed as well as his guardian - step-father.] Alienation fine paid Wm M. Beall

V:609-611. Conrad Hogmire recorded deed 14 June 1774, from Thomas Johnson Jr. and Samuel Chase of the City of Annapolis, for £9 part of the *Gleanings,* for 20 acres. Ann Johnson, and Ann Chase, wives of Thomas and Samuel released dower.

V:611-613. James McAllister recorded deed 14 June 1774, from Thos Gott Junr. for £45, part of *Hawkins Merry Peep a Day,* on Potomac River, adjacent to *Merry Land,* and *Payne's Delight,* 15 ½ acres. Signed before Jno Cooke, Clement Hollyday.

V:613-614. William Beatty recorded deed 14 June 1774, from Thomas Beatty for £20, part of *Middle Plantation,* 66 acres.

V:615-618. Martin Kersner, miller, recorded deed 14 June 1774, from Doctor Henry Schnebeley for £5..10, part of tract called *Pleasant Hills,* 22 acres. Elizabeth Schnebeley released dower.

V:618-620. Henry Smouse recorded deed 14 June 1774 from Samuel Thomas for £26, *Resurvey on William's Neglect,* on Sam's Creek, 18 1/4 acres. Salomy, wife of Samuel Thomas released dower.

V:620-622. Peter Stoup recorded deed 14 June 1774, from Christian Stover for £40, *Stover's Lookout,* on second line of *Good Luck,* 50 acres. Signed before Joseph Wood, Catherine Wood. Barbara Stover released dower.

V:622-625. Jacob Avey recorded deed 14 June 1774 from John Gerhart for £10 sterling, *Mount Misery,* 30 acres. Gertraut, wife of John Gerhart released dower.

V:625-627. Melchor Belahoover, butcher, recorded deed 14 June 1774 from Jonathan Hager for £10 Pennsylvania, lot on NW side of Lutheran Church Lot, lot #285 in Elizabeth Town, to a corner, of a certain Jacob Rohrer's lot.

V:627-629. William Beatty recorded deed 14 June 1774 from Ezekiel Beatty for £45, 26 acres of *Dulaney's Lot,* conveyed by Susannah Beatty to her son Ezekial Beatty, now deceased. He bequeathed to his son Ezekiel Beatty in two parcels. Christenah Beatty, wife of Ezekial, released dower.

V:629-632. Jacob Sibert recorded deed 14 June 1774 from George Shaver for £620, four tracts containing together 219 acres: part of *Good Neighbor,* 106 acres; *Stony Hill,* 16 acres; *Germany,* 66 acres; and part of *Resurvey on Mountain of Wales,* 31 acres. Wife not named, released dower.

V:632-634. Stephen West recorded deed 14 June 1774, from Josias Harrison for £30, *Resurvey on Locust Bottom,* 30 acres. Elizabeth Harrison released dower.

V:634-636. Luke Mudd recorded deed 14 June 1774, from Richard Lilly for £138, *Resurvey on the Dolphin,* and *Hampton Forrest,* called *Good Luck. 138 acres.* Signed before Wm Beatty, Henry Barnes. Alienation fine paid Wm M Beall.

V:636-637. Frederick Rhorar of Elizabethtown, recorded deed 14 June 1774, from Jacob Rhorar for £25 Pennsylvania, lots on NW side of Elizabethtown. Christiana Rhorer released dower.

V:639-641. Joseph Norris of Frederick County, recorded deed 14 June 1774, from Francis Turner of Baltimore County, collier, for £240 sells *Kelly's Purchase,* part of *Piles Delight,* 125 acres.

V:641-644. John Stone recorded deed 14 June 1774, from John Cary, made 28 May 1774, for £246, part of a tract called *Smith's Mistake Rectified,* containing 246 acres. Signed John Carey. Mary Carey released dower rights.

V:644-646. Valentine Motter recorded deed 14 June 1774, from Jacob Young for £11.. Part of *Four and one half Gallons of Rum,* 11 acres. Eleanor Young released dower.

V:646-649. Mathias Saler recorded deed 14 June 1774, from Ignatius Perry for £48, part of *Brother's Request,* 24 ½ acres. Margery, wife of Ignatius released dower.

V:649-653. Saml Finley, surveyor, recorded deed 14 June 1774, from Jacob Rhorar for £51..10, part of *Bristal Corner,* adjacent to Melchior Belshaver, Jonathan Hager, and Jacob Rhorar, to line sold to Michael Fackler, containing 4 acres. Christenah Rhorer released dower.

V:653-655. John Cary recorded deed 14 June 1774, made 28 May 1774, from Valentine Motter for 5 shillings, tract described in V:641-644. Signed Valentine Motter, Catharine Motter released dower.

V: 655-658. Stephen West of Prince George's County, merchant, recorded deed 14 June 1774 from Henry Griffith for £250, tract called *Cow Pasture,* beginning at *Locust Levels,* 150 acres; for 2nd part beginning at *Virgin's Lott,* to west line of Greenberry Griffith's part of *Cow Pasture,* containing 260 acres. Signed before David Lynn, Edward Burgess. Ruth, wife of Henry Griffith released dower.

V:658-661. Samuel Finley, surveyor, recorded deed 14 June 1774, from Jonathan Hager lot #220 on south west side of the Lutheran School House lot in Elizabethtown.

V:661-663. Jacob Sibert recorded deed 14 June 1774 from Daniel Campbell for £60, *White Oak Ridge,* on 14th line of *Green Bottom,* laid out for 50 acres. Signed before John Stull, Wm Baird. Jean, wife of Daniel Campbell released dower rights. Alienation fine paid Wm M Beall.

V:663-665. Zach Maccubbin recorded deed 22 June 1774, from Walter and Clement Beall for £365, tract called *Charles and Benjamin,* 67 acres. Part of tract called *Labyrinth,* adjacent to *Charles and Thomas,* to *Clean Drinking.* Susanna wife of Walter Beall, and Priscilla wife of Clement Beall released dower. V:665-666. Whereas Simon Sheffer on 25 July 1770, mortgaged within two tracts for £81..6, and the said Walter Beall and Clement Beall have paid same with legal interest, Thomas Cramphin signed release of mortgage to Zachariah Maccubbin

V:666-668. George Plummer recorded deed 27 July 1774, from Abraham Crum for £20 Pennsylvania, part of tract called *Matre Beginning,* on Plankstone's Branch, containing 42 acres. Abraham Crum, widower, acknowledged deed.

V:668-670. John Bark recorded deed 27 July 1774 from Mathias Stull for £150 tract called *Turkey Hills,* adjacent to tract called *Saturn,* taken up by Dr. Scott, containing 100 acres. Signed by mark before Saml Beall Jr., John Stull. Dorrithy, wife of Mathias released dower rights.

V:670-672. James Smith recorded deed 27 July 1774, from Thomas McCloskey, son and heir of William McCloskey, late of Frederick County, deceased, for £15, assigns lots #167 and #170 in Frederick Town.

V:672-674. Nicholas Hildebrand recorded deed 27 July 1774, from Adam Croass for £8..10, lots #177 & 178 in Frederick Town, between John Rose and the said Adam Grose. Signed by mark. Elizabeth Crows wife of the said Adam Gross, released dower rights.

V:674-676. Peter Erb recorded deed 27 July 1774, from Easil Casdon for £40 part of parcel called *Rattle Snake Den,* near a branch called Little Bair Branch that falls into Great Pipe Creek, containing 50 acres more or less. Signed Azal Condon before Benjamin Beans, Ruxton Gray.

V:676-679. Frederick Reamer recorded deed 27 July 1774, from George Goul for £350 part of *Resurvey on Ill will,* granted to George Gaul 22 April 1775, starting at original beginning tree of *Ill Will,* [2] for 111 acres. Also tract called *Gillespies Bargain,* containing 40 acres. Signed George Gall before Thos Price, John Stull. Elizabeth Goul released dower rights.

V:679-681. William Willson, son of George, recorded deed 27 July 1774, from Jonathan Nixon for £10, part of *Resurvey on the Farm,* 26 1/4 acres. Mary, wife of Jonathan Nixon released dower.

V:681-682. Jacob Evey recorded deed 27 July 1774, from Jacob Sallsgaver for 5 shillings, certain water privileges from Jacob Sallsgiver's mill dam.

V:682-684. George Custard recorded deed 27 July 1774, from Mathias Smithley for £20 tract called *Stony Bottom,* containing 54 acres, which tract was granted unto a certain Sunsey Smithey, now deceased on 5 Oct. 1759, and Matthias Smithley is heir at law.

V:685-686. John Wise recorded deed 27 July 1774, from Thomas Jennings for £30, lot #278 in Georgetown on the Potomac River. Sarah, wife of Thomas Jennings released dower.

V:686-689. John Wilcoxon recorded deed 27 July 1775, from Benjamin Harris for £125, part of the *Hermitage,* adjacent to south line of *Winexburgh,* to parcel laid out for Henry Watson, now in the possession of Benedict Calvert, then to lands of James Sayer, now in possession of Thomas Cramphin, then to Benjamin Perry's land. 116 acres. Sarah Harris released dower rights.

---

[2]Ill Will was granted to George Gillespie, 7 Dec. 1769. Did not see patent for Resurvey in Peter Wilson Coldham, *Settlers of Maryland, 1766-1783.*

V:689-690. John Fasnaught recorded deed from 27 July 1774, Joseph Evey for 5 shillings, privilege to take water from Sallsgaver's saw mill from Saturday to Sunday, from April to August.

V:690-692. Elisha Hoskinson recorded deed 27 July 1774, from Jonathan Nixon for £10, *Resurvey on the Farm,* 11 3/4 acres. Mary Nixon released dower rights.

V:692-694. Valenine Boroff recorded deed 27 July 1774, from Thomas Jennings of Georgetown, for lot #89 in Georgetown. Sarah, wife of Thomas Jennings released dower.

V:694-696. Stophel Miller recorded deed 27 July 1774, from Joseph Nearon for £30, tract called *Fruitful Valley,* on a draught of Great Pipe Creek, containing 20 acres, a tract called *Rock Spring.* Signed before Wm Beatty, Henry Barnes. Mary Nearon released dower rights.

V:696. Frederick Missell recorded lye bill 27 July 1774, from Catherine Row, wife of John Rowe. Whereas I Catharine, in passion, abused and freely aspersed Mary, wife of Frederick, calling her a thief and a whore, for which I sincerely repent and I acknowledge t be a false and notorious lye.

V:697-699. Christn Shriock and John Smith, trustees of the Lutheran Church, and George Zimmerman and Charles Baltzell, trustees of the Presbyterian Church, recorded deed 27 July 1774, from Fred Holtzman for £5..17 sells part of tract called *Partnership,* adjacent to tract called *Mill Place,* containing six acres for use of school house and chapel. Signed in German Script. Eve Margaret Holzapfel released dower rights.

V:699-701. Richard Beall of Sam'l recorded deed 27 July 1774, from Jonathan Nixon, assigns part of *Hills and Dales,* adjacent to *Fenwick,* and *Charles and William,* adjacent to Henry Clark's land bought of Ignatius Perry, containing 4 acres. Receipt for £14. Mary Nixon released dower.

V:701-702. Christian Adichon, widow, recorded deed 27 July 1774, from Valentine Morton for £55, lot in town of Sharpsburgh. Catharine, wife of Valentine Morton released dower rights.

V:703-704. James Johnson and Roger Johnson recorded deed 23 December 1772 from Samuel Lewellen, for £90 sells tract *Buck's Resort,* 100 acres. Signed before Jos Wood, Catherine Wood. Hannah wife of Samuel Lewellen released dower.

V:704-706. Robert Peter and Andrew Heugh recorded deed 20 November 1773 from William Needham, for payment of his debts and for 5 shillings, assigns tract called *King Cole,* of which Sarah Needham, deceased, was seized; along with part of *Labyrinth,* lying between Charles Jones and his tract called *Forest,* also one other tract, *Needham's Discovery,* 11 acres. Also all the Negroes, goods and chattels, providing that if debts paid, sale is void. Signed before Charles Jones, Adam Stewart.

END OF LIBER V

LAND RECORD ABSTRACTS, LIBER W:

1-8. Stephen Newton Chiswell and Nathaniel Newton recorded letter of attorney 21 April 1774. John Charter, formerly of Kilvington in the County of Nottingham, but now of Marston in the County of Lincoln in the Kingdom of England, labourer, only surviving brother and heir of Thomas Charter, formerly of Kilvington, aforesaid, taylor, and late of Old Seneca in the Province of Maryland, planter, deceased, intestate. Whereas by certain indenture of lease and release on or about 24 February 1755 between John Charter and Stephen Newton Chiswell of Old Seneca, sells tract called *The Henry* containing by estimation 197 acres. Information in affidavits attested to by Notary's in England, and letter of instruction, dated Horncastle 9 Jany 1754 to Mr. Chiswell, Received your of 17th September and immediately gave to my brother John, who joins with us in our hearty thanks, ... instructs that he is to take into his possession whatever plantations and other effects in Maryland, and to act on our behalf, John and Matthew Charter. Followed by affidavit that John Charter is now only son still living of Robert and Ann Charter, and brother of Thomas, in 1759. A portion of the Parish Register was also recorded indicating that Thomas was the son of Robert and Ann Charter, baptized January 20, 1687.

W:8-10. Ben McKinley recorded deed 24 May 1774, from Catharina Willson, formerly wife of John McKinley and executor of his will appointed with Benjamin McKinley, assigns two patents[3] to Benjamin McKinley, listed as recorded in 1765 in Liber P no 5, folio 238, and Liber BCGS 42 fol. 151, in consideration that he will provide for other heirs of the will.[4] Deed witnessed by William Blair, Elizabeth Blair.

W:10-11. John Daly recorded deed 29 July 1774 from Thomas Jennings for £200, lot #89 in Addition to Georgetown. Sarah Jennings released dower.

W: 11-13. Nicholas Beard recorded deed 28 July 1774, from Samuel Chase and Thomas Johnson, of the City of Annapolis for $50, *The Gleanings,* 102 acres. Signed & acknowledged. Ann, wife of Thomas and Ann wife of Samuel, released dower before Dann of St. Thos Jenifer.

W:13-16. John Fasnaught recorded deed July 1774 from Joseph Eavy, for £500, tract on Beaver Creek, a draught of Antietam, part of *Scotch Lot,* at a point between Joseph Evey's dwelling house and Jacob Saltsgivers, to Bealer's land, to 2nd line of Jacob Root's containing 103 ½ acres; mentions saw mill on adjacent lines, also part of *Resurvey on First Choice,* 5 ½ acre; and part of tract called *Mount Misery,* 48 ½ acres. Signed before Sam'l Beall Jr., Eleanor Beall. Eve, wife of Joseph Evey released dower right.

---

[3]*Settlers of Maryland, 1766-1783,* by Peter Wilson Coldham lists the two patents: John McKinley, Frederick County, *Transylvania,* 120 acres, 10 Dec. 1772 and Catherine MacKinley and her son Benjamin, executors of John Mackinley, 120 acres, 3 March 1773, Transylvania.

[4]*Maryland Calendar of Wills,* Vol. 13, pg. 180. Will of John McKinley of Marsh Creek Settlement, Piney Creek Hundred dated 13 Jan 1767, presented for probate, April 1767. Names wife Catherine, son Benjamin, son Andrew one whole share, balance to be divided equally between wife and all children. (Not named).

W:16-17. Jacob Reister recorded bill of sale 1 August 1773, from Thos Brannon of Georgetown, for £28, a free born mulatto boy, Jacob Lizer, aged 5 years, to serve until he is 21 years old.

W:17-20. John Trammell recorded deed 12 Aug. 1774 from Stephen Richards for £1800, *Resurvey on Spring Garden,* signed before Thos Price, Christr Edelen. Elizabeth Richards released dower.

W:20-21. Dominic Bradley recorded deed 12 Aug. 1774 Steven Richards for £12 assigns tract originally patented by Adam William Young, 9 June 1770, BC&GS #41, called the *Poplar Spring*, beginning at a poplar tree standing at spring on east side of the mountain, on last course of *Resurvey on Saplin Ridge*, laid out of Jacob Mathias, 29 acres Signed by mark. Elizabeth Richards released dower.

W:21-23. Sam'l Chase and Thomas Johnson recorded 12 August 1774, from Peter Hoover, for 5 shillings, part of tract called *Gleanings,* 87 acres. Signed GS. Cloe Hoover wife to Peter released dower.

W:23-24. Eleanor Allison recorded bill of sale 16 August 1774 from Henry Allison to his daughter, for diverse good causes, and also a promise made to my father, natural love and affection, and 5 shillings, I give to Eleanor a Negro woman named Eleanor. Signed Hendry Allison in presence of Aneas Campbell, Aneas Campbell Jr.

W:24-26. Charles Chance recorded deed 15 August 1774, from Henry Clance for £50 lot #20 lying in Taney Town. Signed GS before Joseph Wood, Catherine Wood.

W:26- 28. [Marginal note, delivered to Saml Bogg of S.] Samuel Boggess recorded deed 14 August 1774, from Ben Dorsey for £233..8..8 tract called *Sams Luck*, adjacent to *Resurvey on Pleasant Valley,* the 98th course of tract called *Partnership,* containing 202 acres. Signed before William Beatty, Upton Sheridine. Sarah, wife of Benjamin Dorsey released dower.

W:28-30. Theobold Eachberger recorded deed 19 August 1774 from Andrew Haberly, agreement in 1772, for lots #233 & #234. in Frederick Town, Elizabeth Haberlin wife of Andrew Haberlin released dower rights.

W:30-31. Benjamin Summers recorded bill of sale 29 August 1774. I Thomas Summers, for £90 assigns all my right to the lease executed by Danl Carroll in Frederick County, for 150 acres, and one Negro boy named Nathaniel, 3 horses one mare and colt, 8 head of cattle, 9 head of sheep, 10 head of hogs, 3 feather beds & furniture, 4 tables, one square table, 11 chairs, 3 iron pots, 3 dishes, one dozen plates, 3 basins, 1 looking glass Signed before Thos Price, Val. Shriner. Receipt.

W:31-33. John Smith recorded deed 25 Aug. 1774 from Philip Trine, part of tract called *Virgin's Delight,* 196 acres. Signed by mark before Wm Beatty, Upton Sheridine. Susannah wife of Philip Trine examined apart released dower rights.

W:33-35. Francis Beall recorded lease 17 Aug. 1774 from George Willson, part of tract of land called *Difficulty,* 100 acres for term of 21 years, to plant 50 good apple trees. Signed before Wm Deakins Jr., William Luckett.

W:35-36. Frederick Fox recorded deed 17 August 1774 from Valentine Matter for £7..10, lot in town of Sharpsburgh, to pay Joseph Chapline, his heirs, 5 shillings rent. Catherine wife of Valentine Motter released dower.

W:37. William Head recorded deed 17 August 1774 from Robert Wood for and in consideration of his having a chapel and school house built near him, gives 1 ½ acres, on part of tract called *Wood's Design,* at a small hill, by the side of a draught that leads into Hunting Creek.

W:38 Wm Luckett recorded bill of sale 9 Nov. 1774 from John Linch for £72..10 sells 3 beds and furniture, 2 pots, 30 barrels of Indian corn, 1000 weight of pork, 10 bushells of wheat, 4 barrells of beans, 5 pewter basins, 13 pewter plates, 2 tables, 6 knives and forks, other farm items and livestock. Signed by mark before Wm Luckett Jr., Ann Maddoe by mark.

W:38-41. Christopher Welsley recorded deed 17 August 774 from Martin Shoup. Whereas, Liber F: 968, deed made 19 March 1760 between the same parties, for additional sum of 5 shillings, makes correction, assigns 69 acres of *Resurvey on Mankin.* Signed German Script by both parties.

W:41-43. George Bear recorded deed 12 August 1774 from Benjamin Johnson of Frederick Town, Silversmith and Susanna his wife, part of tract called *Rocky Creek,* containing 150 acres.

W:43-44. James Burgess recorded bill of sale 17 Aug. 1774 from William Bright for £20 one old black horse, one dark brown cow & calf, one feather bed and furniture, one large iron pot, one skillet, one frying pan, one black walnut table, 3 pewter dishes, dozen pewter plates, one small iron kettle and two spinning wheels. Signed Wm Bright before Wm Blair.

44-46. Christian Orndorf & others [George Keefer, John Middlecalf, Conrad Hayberger, trustees appointed by the Calvinist Congregation, in and about Sharpsburgh] recorded deed 17 Aug. 1774, made 2 April 1774 between Abraham Linganfelter

46-47. Peter Erb recorded deed 7 Aug. 1774 from Richard Brown of Bedford Co., Pennsylvania for £40 tract called *Howars Delight Resurveyed,* metes and bounds for 100 acres.

W:48. Leakin Dorsey recorded bill of sale 8 Sept. 1774 from Henry Barnes Sr of Frederick County, for £34 one sorrel mare, signed before Richard Davis, Rezin Davis.

W:48-50. Benjamin Harris recorded deed 8 Sept 1774 from Thomas Butler for £23 part of tract called the *Hermitage.* Elizabeth Butler released dower rights.

W:50-52. Thomas Fletcher recorded deed 6 Sept. 1774 from Andrew Scott for £3 assigns lot #65 in Georgetown, a part of *Knave's Disappointment.*

W:52-53. John Michael, mason, recorded deed 12 Sept. 1774 from Jacob Michael of Frederick Town, Mason, assigns lot #229. Catherine Michael released dower right before Thos Price, Wm Beatty witnesses.

W:53-54. Teter Wise recorded deed 12 Sept. 1774 from Joseph Chapline for £2 for lot #57 in Sharpsburgh.

W:54-56. Jacob Schley recorded deed 8 Sept 1774 from Charles Beatty & George Fraser Hawkins for £6, for lot #200 in Addition to Georgetown. Susanna Freeman wife of George Fraser Hawkins released dower rights.

W:56-58. Joseph Lovejoy recorded deed 12 Sept 1774 from Baltis Fouts for £100 tract called *Duvall's Forrest,* containing 100 acres. Signed before Thos Price, John Baker.

W:58-59. John Phillips recorded deed 12 Sept. 1774 from Joseph Wood Jr. For £60, sells part of *Resurvey on Welch Cabbin.* Ann Wood released dower rights.

W:59-61. Francis Cullom recorded deed 12 Sept 1774 from Ludwick Davis, the son of William, for 5 shillings, all his interest in a certain tract of land called *The Hazard,* that falls into Bennett Creek, containing 60 acres. Signed before Thos Sprigg Wootton, David Lynn. At same time Benjamin Harris and Clary his wife released their right of dower within the said land.

W:61-62. Martin Walse recorded deed 12 Sept 1774 from Charles Chase and Thomas Johnson Junr., attorneys at law of Annapolis, Maryland, for £35, assigns part of *The Gleanings,* 100 acres.

W:62-64. Basil Beall recorded deed 12 Sept. 1774 from Jacob Shuh for 5 shillings, assigns, part of *Resurvey on Anchor and Hope,* containing 8 acres. Barbara Shuh released dower rights.

W:64-66. Casper Eader recorded deed 12 Sept 1774 from Joseph Wood Jr. For £38 part of tract called *Round About,* 23 acres. Anne Wood released dower rights.

W:66-68. Nathan Browning recorded deed 12 Sept. 1774 from George Cullom for 5 shillings, all his interest in part of *Resurvey on Timber Neck,* containing 113 acres. Margaret, wife of George released dower rights.

W:68-69. Henry Crose of Lancaster County, Pennsylvania, recorded deed 12 Sept 1774 from Jacob Snowdenberger for £100, part of *Spring Garden,* Margaret Snowdenberger released dower.

W:69-72. George Spangler recorded deed 12 Sept. 1774 from Rafael Neale of St. Mary's County, for £564.19 land on Great Pipe Creek, called *Bedford*, bought of Edward Diggs and Normand Bruce, 31 October 1767, except for 167 acres sold to William Pidgeon, and 150 acres sold to John Berryon and 150 acres sold to Henry Coonce, laid off by John Logsdon but not yet conveyed. Signed before Jeremiah Jordan, J.P., St Mary's County.

W:72-74. Jacob Shuh recorded deed 12 Sept. 1774 from David Miller for £400, part of *Resurvey on Anchor and Hope,* containing 80 acres. Elizabeth, wife of David Miller released dower.

W:74-75. Jacob Eppracht recorded deed 12 Sept. 1774 from Thomas Jennings, for £15, lot #54 in Georgetown on the Potomac River. Signed before Wm Stewart, Wm Deakins, Jr. Sarah wife of Thomas Jennings released dower.

W:75-76. Townley Bruce recorded bill of sale 28 Sept. 1774 from Charles Cooper of Colchester, Virginia, for £63, sells mulatto man named Will. Signed before Wm Bayley, Jr.

W: 76-78. William Barroll of Philadelphia City, recorded mortgage 25 September 1774 from John Coopersmith, whereas he is bound for £333 to discharge, assigns tract in Frederick County, called *Resurvey on Timber,* for 120 acres. If sums paid sale is void.

W:78-79. James Jameson, surviving partner of a firm in trade, recorded bill of sale September 1774, from Charles Saunders, who is justly indebted in several sum of money, and from a suit in Charles County against him as executor of the last will and testament of Jane Doyne, deceased, he sells and assigns the following Negro slaves, Negro Charles 40 years old, boy Absolam 15 years, woman named Charity 20 years old and her child Nan, about 6 years of age. Witness David Lynn, Joshua Sanders.

W:79 Nathan Burdette recorded his cattle mark 6 Oct. 1774.

W:79. Basil Johnson recorded his cattle mark, 12 Oct. 1774.

W:80-82. George Swingle recorded deed 29 Sept. 1774 from Michael Kirkpatrick. Waterways rights on 100 acres, part of *John's Lot,* on Antietam, and *Dickenson's Pleasure,* for use of George Swingle's mill. Signed before John Stull, Wm Blair.

W:82-87. Samuel Moore recorded deed 25 August 1774 from William Risk of Hamilton Ban Twp., York Co., Penn. and Mary Ann his wife, and Amos McGinley of Carroll's Delight and Hamilton Ban Twp., and Ann his wife; and Samuel Stone of Carroll's Delight, Whereas Daniel Carroll, late of Duddington Manor in Prince George's County, by his will assigned to his sister Mary, one half of 10,000 acres lying on the Monocacy in Frederick County, part of *Carroll's Delight,* and *Carrollsburgh,* and he did authorize Charles Carroll to sell the same, and he sold part of William Rusk, and to Amos McGinley, the remaining parts, which now Amos McGinley and Ann his wife for £100 paid by Samuel Moore, assigns part of *Carroll's Delight,* formerly in Frederick County, but now in Hamilton Ban Twp., in York County in Pennsylvania, being also the same tract which was granted to William Rusk by Charles Carroll, adjacent to lands of Hugh Dunaway and Andrew Hart, to lands of William Waugh, containing 216 acres plus 150 perches and an additional quantity of 16 acres and 100 perches. (Metes & bounds given). Signed William Risk, Mary Ann Risk, Amos McGinley, Ann McGinley before Wm Blair, Normand Bruce.

W:88-90. George Scott recorded commission and depositions. 20 Aug. 1774, to Joseph Smith, Christian Orendorf, Abraham Linganfelter and William Good, tract *Saturn.* Richard Dean, 73 years old, deposed regarding bound tree of land taken up by Doctor Andrew Scott, near Richard Dean's plantation. 30 July 1773. Thomas Dean, 33 years old attested to tree belonging to Doctor Scott, and deponent saw William Dent, surveying the land.

W:90-91. Charles Perry, Simon Nicholls and Isaac Strider recorded land commission, certificate and depositions 22 August 1774 to Doctor Thomas Sprigg Wootton, Samuel West, William Robertson and Joseph Willson, on tract called *The Pynes.*

W:92-94. Christian Eversole and John Middlecalf recorded commission and depositions 22 August 1774, on Resurvey on part of *Spriggs Delight.* George Moore, 46 years stated that he heard William Moore Sr. Say stone at head of spring in gully in a bottom by the Potomac was the boundary between William Moore and Henry Roan who then lived on the lower part of *Sprigg's Delight.* Daniel Robbins, age 46 years, says that William Moore Sr. showed him said stone. John Moore, age 73 years deposed to stone. Signed by mark.

W:94-99. Thomas Cramphin recorded commission and depositions 26 August 1774 to David Lynn, Zadok Magruder, Thomas Owen Williams and William Robertson, on part of tract *Hermitage.*

Benjamin Harris, 60 or thereabouts, deposed at a white oak near Watry Branch which falls into Rock Creek, touching his knowledge regarding bounds of tract sold by Thomas Butler and Jeremiah Stympson, part of *Hermitage,* states that 30 or 40 years ago he went with Jeremiah Stympson to said tree and was told it was the beginning of his land. At a bound hickory in Mrs. Elizabeth Perry's plantation, about 100 yards from the branch, tract sold by Thomas Butler to Benjamin Perry, 33 years before in company with Thos Butler, Benj. Perry and James Edmonston (the surveyor), and said hickory was the beginning of Perry's land. Regarding bounds of parcel sold to William Davis, 30 to 40 years ago, he was in company with Butler, Edmonston and said Davis, and sapling was beginning tree. William Condon, aged 56 years deposed regarding bound tree of William Davis' tract, and identified hickory as the NE corner of part of tract sold to his father, Richard Condon. John Wilcoxon, aged 40 years, attested to the bound of tract sold to Benjamin Perry and also the NE corner of Condon's land. Alexander Clagett, 30 years old, deposed regarding a resurvey on Perry's land 6 years before.

W:99-103. Robt Beall, Alexander Beall, Robert Owen and George Roberson recorded land commission and depositions, 25 August 1774. Petitioned to perpetuate the bounds of *Batchelor's Forest.* Commission issued to Thomas Cramphin, Allen Bowie, John Wilcoxon and Richard Berry. Depositions taken 4 May 1774 of Thomas Swearingen, age 46, showed bound white oak tree at first corner of plantation of George Robertson, where he now dwells and said John Swineford deceased about 17 years ago, and Nicholas Baker about 15 years ago, likewise showed him tree as the bound tree of *Batchelor's Forest.* James Brooke, between 60 and 70 years old, solemnly declared that about 50 years ago, Nicholas Baker deceased showed him said tree as the beginning tree of *Batchelor's Forest.* John Lacklin, 50 years old, or thereabouts, deposed that 16 years ago Benjamin Beall showed him the said bound tree as the beginning of land where John Swineford then lived, called *Batchelor's Forest,* and about 14 years ago Nicholas Baker, deceased identified same tree. Archibald Edmonston, aged 60 years or thereabouts, stated that 37 years ago, he believes his brother James Edmonston told him that the white oak was the beginning tree. Nathaniel Crawford, 46 years, deposed on white oak.

W:104-106. Zachariah Beall, son of Samuel, recorded deed 7 August 1774 from Thos Johns for one shilling, tract, *Resurvey on Piney Grove,* granted Thomas Johns, for 600 acres. Signed before Adam Stewart, Wm Deakins Junr. 24 shillings Alienation fine paid Wm M. Beall.

W:106-108. Charles Pen recorded deed 7 August 1774 from John Owen for £80, *Rich Plains,* 81 1/4 acres. Signed before David Lynn, Edward Burgess. [Marginal note, delivered Charles Pen 6 August 1784].

W:108-110. Jacob Cassell recorded deed 7 August 1774 from Martin Winter for £25 for *Stocksdales Hills,* 25 acres. Signed before Charles Jones, Wm Blair. Mary wife of Martin Winter released dower.

W:110-112. Jacob Fullwider recorded deed 12 August 1774 from Adam Coil for £65 sells tract, *The Gap,* beginning at Wardrop's land, called *Cary's Old Place,* signed in German script, before Thos Price, Fr. Warring. Elizabeth, wife of Adam Coil released dower.

W:112-113. Michael Weaver recorded deed 149 Aug. 1774 from George Diffenbaugh who makes over one lot #237 in Frederick, house still to be built. Signed by mark. Magdalena, wife of George Diffenbaugh released dower rights.

W:113-115. Joseph Tomlinson Jr recorded deed 17 Aug. 1774 from Joseph Tomlinson Sr., for tract called Fifth lot of Wills Town, beginning on 21st line of tract on Wills Creek, near mouth of Gladstone's Run. 280 acres. Signed before Thos Price, Normand Bruce.

W:115-117. Henry Rinegar recorded deed 17 August 1774 from Leonard Miller for £300, part of *Brooke's Discovery on the Rich Lands,* on line sold to John Schoolfield. Signed by mark before Normand Bruce, Robt Potters. Catharine wife of Leonard Miller released dower.

W:117-118. Jacob Fullwider recorded deed 26 August 1774 from Adam Coil for £50, on tract *Wood and Worse,* on east side of South Mountain, on main road from Frederick Town to Fort Frederick. Elizabeth Coil released dower right.

W:119-120. Thomas Beall, son of George, recorded deed 19 Aug. 1774, from Mordecai Boone for £451, tracts *The James* and *The Addition to the James,* containing 226 acres. Signed before David Lynn and Jane Threlkeld. Acknowledged before David Lynn and Wm Deakins, Jr.

W:120-121. Greenberry Ridgely of Anne Arundel County, recorded bill of sale 7 August 1774 from Solomon Turner for £12, three cows and three calves, two feather beds and furniture. Signed by mark before Chas Jones, Chas Griffith.

W:122-123. Andrew Hyne recorded deed 17 August 1774, [made 20 Aug. 1774] from William Bright tract granted 20 Oct. 1769 to James Barrance, beg. At tract called *The Flag Patch,* granted to Jacob Duckett. 75 acres. Sarah Bright released dower.

W:123. Walter Beall recorded bill of sale 1 Sept. 1774 from Anguish Shaw for £42, sells one bay horse, one white horse, one brindle cow and calf, one brindle cow, 3 year old heifer, 2 yearling heifers, one sow and 7 pigs, 8 shoats, 2 beds and furniture and all household furniture and plantation utensils. Signed before Adam Heugh, Sarah Heugh.

W:124-126. John Weller recorded deed 17 Aug. 1774 from Henry Firor. Whereas Philip Knavel deceased by his last will dated 23 Oct. 1773 appointed Henry Firor executor, he thereby sells tract *Buck's Horn,* for £35, metes and bounds given containing 13 acres, originally conveyed by John Yost to Philip Knavel deceased.

W:126-128. Dederick Henninghauser recorded deed 25 August 1774 from Samuel Buzzard for £3..10, for lot #20 in Middletown.

W:128-129. Francis Gilbert recorded bill of sale 28 August 1774 from Edward Engman (or Ingmar) for £7..18, sells one dun horse, one feather bed, 1 doz pewter plates, two large dishes, my cow and grain on the land of Francis Gilbert and Musgrove Simpson. Signed by mark.

W:129-131. Gilbert Kemp recorded deed 17 August 1774, from Martin Shoup for 5 shillings, deed to correct metes and bounds on prior deed for *Resurvey on Marken.*

W:131-133. Christian Weaver recorded deed 26 August 1774 from Jacob Beyer (or Bier) for £80, lot #18 in Frederick Town conveyed by Francis Dorsey of Anne Arundel County in March 1770, recorded in Liber P:636. Signed G.S. Jacob Beyer. Mary Bier released dower rights.

W:133-135. George Zimmerman, Michael Lauer and Balser Tutter recorded deed 25 Aug. 1774 from David Fortney, gunsmith, for £38, tract called *Resurvey on Limestone Rock,* 21 ½ acres, adjacent to tract *Deer Spring.* Signed David Fortney. Elizabeth Fortney released dower.

W:135-136. Anthony Stock, well digger, recorded deed 26 August 1774 from Joseph Burnesten, shoemaker, lots #186 & 187 in Addition to Frederick Town, conveyed in 1764 by Daniel Dulaney. Ann Burneston released dower.

W:136-137. Ursula Little and Michael Little recorded marriage contract 25 August 1774 with Stephen Ramsburgh, agreeing on settlements of estate prior to marriage to Ursula. Signed before Otho H. Williams, Jacob Klein.

W:138-139. Henry Lampright and Nicholas Schappart recorded deed 25 August 1774 from John Cary for £7..5, assigns lot #214 in Addition to Frederick Town. Mary Cary released dower rights.

W:139. Charles Doll recorded bill of sale 27 August 1774 from Simon Reeder for £7, one Negro boy, William, about 9 years old.

W:140-142. Christopher Selfly recorded deed 25 August 1774, from Gilbert Kemp. Whereas by deed of conveyance made 19 August 1760 and recorded in Liber F, folio 951 &c. a certain Martin Shoup conveyed to Gilbert Kemp, 94 acres of *Resurvey on Mankin,* originally granted Martin Shoup, and on 10 March 1767, conveyed part. Now assigns 14 acres.

W:142-145. Charles Hedges recorded deed 25 Aug. 1774 from Martin Keplinger for £600 two tracts, *Leeds,* at head of Tobias Branch, at the foot of Kitoctin Montan, 50 acres, and part of *Resurvey on Johnson's Lot,* on 3rd line of aforesaid tract, *Leeds,* 150 acres. Signed. Elizabeth, wife of Martin Keplinger released dower.

W:145-147. Francis Thomas recorded deed 25 August 1774 from Wm Deakins Jr. for £36..18, part of tract formerly called *Pork and Potatoes,* 82 acres.

W:147-149. Joseph Wood Jr recorded deed 25 August 1774, from Henry Reed for £350, part of tract *Link together,* containing 325 3/4 acres. Jane, wife of Henry Reed released dower.

W:149-150. Philip Smith recorded deed 25 August 1774 from Theobold Eachberger for £5..10, lot #234 in Additional Lots of Frederick Town. Maria Eachleberger released dower rights.

W:150-152. Benjamin Tomlinson recorded deed 25 August 1774 from Joseph Tomlinson for £200 Pennsylvania, sells the *Fourth Lot*, of Wills Town, lying on the East side of Wills Creek, containing 250 acres.

W:152 Michael, Peter and Joseph Little recorded agreement 25 August 1774 with Ursula Little, in preparing for marriage with Stephen Ramsbugh, agrees with three sons that they may occupy the plantation of Peter Little deceased. Signed before Otho Williams, Jacob Klein.

W:153-154. William Holmes recorded deed 25 August 1774 from Edward Doran, in consideration of debt due to William Holmes, assigns part of *Bear Bacon,* excepting 100 acres already sold to Samuel Waters. Signed by mark, Edward Doran (or Dern) before John Holmes and Nancy Holmes.

W:154-156. William Trammel recorded deed 18 August 1774, from Aden Pancoast and Abigail Pancoast his wife, made 11 August 1774, for £25, sells part of tract called *Darby Island,* in Potomack River, below the mouth of Seneca Creek, adjacent to part conveyed to Thomas Johns.

W:156-157. Anthony Noble recorded bill of sale 10 August 1774, from Joseph Renaldo for £14..9 Pennsylvania, one bay mare, 14 hands.

W:157-158. Leonard Troutman and Ann Troutman his wife, recorded lease 10 August 1774, from Peter Troutman for £20, lets during their natural lives, 12 ½ acres, part of *Resurvey on Miller's Chance,* reserving the right of Peter Troutman to dig a ditch through the meadow to carry water from Fishing Creek, to his meadow.

W:158-160. Mathias Strubb recorded deed 25 August 1775, from Adam Shroiner for £220, part of *Third Addition*, 202 acres. Mary Shroiner released dower.

W:160-161. Thomas Beall recorded deed of gift 16 August 1774 from George Beall in consideration of love and affection for my son, Thomas, lot in Georgetown on Potomac River, on Water Street, to include building now rented to Mr. John Ferguson for a lumber house and counting room. Signed before Adam Stewart, Wm Deakins Jr.

W:162. Robert Peter recorded bill of sale 22 August 1774, from William Talbott for £132, slaves, Negro woman Kate, man Joe, and boy Harry, together with her increase. If sum paid by 1 August next, sale is void.

W:163-164. Samuel Tomlinson recorded deed 25 August 1774 from Joseph Tomlinson Senr. [remarks in margin: Deed del'd to John Tomlinson, for the heirs of Sam'l his brother, in presence of C.H. Barrett, 22 Aug. 1778.] for £100 assigns the third lot of Wills Town on west side of Wills branch, 88 acres.

W:164-166. Christian Keefer recorded deed 21 October 1774 from William Diggs Junr of St. Mary's County, whereas he executed a deed to Nicholas Orey for 100 acres, part of *Diggs Lot,* on 14 Nov. 1754, recorded in Liber E:608 & 609, and some of the lines were erroneous, corrects metes and bounds for 100 acres. Signed before Richard Barnes, Henry Reeder.

W:166-167. Alexander Thomas Hawkins recorded mortgage 21 Oct 1774 from John Hawkins for £634..11..2 assigns Negroes, Basil, Frank, boy Sam, women Lucy and Dida, one mullato girl Lydia, Negro girls Fibia, Henny and Rachel, boy Leander, and 20 head of sheep, four feather beds and furniture; provided always, that if the said John pay the full sum by 1 November 1775 with lawful interest, sale is void.

W:168-170. Adam Troup and Catherine his wife, recorded deed 21 Oct. 1774 from Henry Funk and Susannah his wife, Ludwick Young and Magdalena his wife, and Samuel Barkley and Anna Maria his wife. Whereas Isaac Simmons, late of Frederick County, deceased, father of said Susannah, Catharine, Magdalen and Anna Maria, died intestate and was seized of a tract called *Simmons Rocket,* by common agreement make division. Metes and bounds given for part. Signed by all parties.

W:170-172. Henry Funk and Susannah his wife recorded deed 21 Oct. 1774 from Adam Troup and Catherine his wife, Ludwick Young and Magdalena his wife, and Samuel Barkley and Anna Maria his wife. Whereas Isaac Simmons, late of Frederick County, deceased, father of said Susannah,

Catharine, Magdalen and Anna Maria, died intestate and was seized of a tract called *Simmons Rocket,* by common agreement make division. Metes and bounds given for part. Signed by all parties.

172-174. Samuel Barkley and Anna Maria his wife, recorded deed 21 Oct 1774, from Henry Funk and Susannah his wife, Adam Troup and Catherine his wife, and Ludwick Young and Magdalena his wife. Whereas Isaac Simmons, late of Frederick County, deceased, father of said Susannah, Catharine, Magdalen and Anna Maria, died intestate and was seized of a tract called *Simmons Rocket,* by common agreement make division. Metes and bounds given for part. Signed by all parties.

W:175-176. Michael Huffman recorded deed 21 Oct 1774 from Jacob Funk for 1 shilling for lot #176 in Jerusalemtown. Ann, wife of Jacob Funk released dower.

W:176-177. Major Angus McDonald of the Colony of Virginia, recorded deed 1 Sept 1774, from John Harris for £5 sterling, *John's Delight,* surveyed by him 6 June 1769, metes and bounds given for 45 ½ acres. Signed before Wm Luckett, Wm Bowie. Elizabeth, wife of John Harris released dower.

W:178. Richard Hagen recorded bill of sale 20 Oct. 1774 from Ignatius Hagen for 964 lbs tobacco and 5 barrells of Indian corn paid by my son, Richard Hagen, have bargained and sold one young Negro boy named Sam, he being the child of my Negro woman, Rachel.

W:178-179. Jacob Funk recorded bond 20 Oct. 1774, from George Swingle, for £2000 Pennsylvania, to indemnify him from any damage or trouble from a water course running through *Marsh Head,* and *Walnut Grove,* given to Joseph Krebel by aforesaid Jacob Funk.

W:179-180. Mathias Coller recorded deed 21 Oct. 1774, from Lawrence O'Neale, sheriff of Frederick County. Whereas in pursuance of an act of assembly for relief of certain prisoners in the several goals, he sells real and personal estate of Nicholas Alspaugh, who was in custody of Lawrence O'Neale for debt of £80..9.. 8, he sells lot #19 in Elizabethtown.

W:180-182. Samuel England recorded deed 21 Oct. 1774, from Alexander McGee, for £110, tract called *Stony Hollow,* taken up by Nicholas White on 7th line of *Arnold's Choice.* Eleanor, wife of Alexander McGee releases dower.

W:182-184. Thomas Cramphin recorded deed 21 Oct. 1774, made 5 Day 1774 from Maddoc Dyson for £25, part of *Resurvey on Non Eaten,* 225 acres, beginning at line of a deed from John Veirs and William Veirs to said Dyson. Signed and acknowledged before David Lynn, Edward Burgess.

W:184-185. Leonard Shriock recorded deed 21 Oct. 1774, from Henry Shriock for £25 Pennsylvania tract called *Today,* 5 acres. Catharine, wife of Henry Shriock released dower rights.

W:186-187. Henry Snider recorded deed 21 Oct. 1774 , from Martin Hockerlin for £5 lot #85 in Jerusalemtown. Signed by mark.

W:187-190. Henry Clark recorded deed 21 Oct. 1774, from Ignatius Perry of Prince George's County, for £267..15, part of *Charles and William,* by the line of tract conveyed by Charles William and John Beall to Charles Perry to tract called *Kilmarnock,* 218 ½ acres, and also tract called *Fenwick,* about 19 July 1735 conveyed by Ninian Tannehill to Charles Perry for 36 ½ acres. Signed before David Crawford, Jeremiah Magruder. Margery wife of Ignatius Perry released dower.

W:190-191. William Hall of Prince George's County, recorded sale 21 Oct 1774 from George Selman, for £9, sells one dark gray mare, one dark colored cow and black calf and red heifer. Signed before Edward Burgess.

W:191-193. Christopher Shroeder recorded deed 21 Oct. 1774, from Frederick Zacharias for £100, tract called *Pallentine,* on Barren Branch of Great Pipe Creek. Anna Maria Zacharias released dower.

W:193-194. Henry Snyder recorded deed 21 Oct. 1774, from Jacob Funck for one shilling, lot #32 in Jerusalemtown. Anna Funk released dower.

W:194-196. John Swank recorded deed 21 Oct. 1774, from Jacob Funck for one shilling, lot #75 in Jerusalemtown. Anna Funk released dower.

W:196-197. John Peltz (Beltz) recorded deed 21 Oct. 1774, from Adam Crose (Gross) for £9, lots #177 & 178 in Frederick Town. Elizabeth wife of Adam released dower.

W:198-200. William Selby recorded deed 21 Oct. 1774, from Samuel Baker for £208..13, tract *Snowden's Mill Land,* conveyed by Richard Snowden to John Baker on the Paint Branch of the Eastern Branch of the Potomac for 273 acres. Sarah wife of Samuel Baker released dower.

W:200-201. Samuel Baker recorded deed 21 Oct 1774 from William Holmes of Anne Arundel County for £37 tract called *Snowden's Mill,* Signed before David Lynn, Edwd Burgess

W:201-203. Jacob Rowland recorded deed 21 Oct 1774, from Jacob Funck for £20 Pennsylvania, part of tract called *White's Lot,* containing 4 acres. Signed before Wm Baird, John Stull. Anna Funk released dower rights. Alienation fine paid Wm M Beall.

W:203-204. Jacob Petry recorded deed 21 Oct 1774, from John Depew for £200 tract, *Addition to Good Luck,* containing 117 acres. Catharine wife of John Depew released dower right. Signed before Wm Baird, John Stull. Anna Funk released dower rights. Alienation fine paid Wm M Beall.

W:205-206. Henry Cline recorded deed 24 Oct 1774, from Jacob Koontz, Junr., blacksmith for £50, lot #36 in Taneytown. Mary wife of Jacob Koontz released dower right.

W:206-207. John Galloway and William Cochran of Carrollsburgh recorded agreement 21 Oct. 1774 regarding 200 acres lying on Toms Creek.

W:207-209. Henry Clark recorded deed 21 Oct 1774 from Jonathan Nixon. Part of *Hills and Dales.* Mary wife of Jonathan Nixon released dower rights.

W:209-212. James Johnson recorded deed 21 Oct, 1774 from Richard Waters made 20th Oct 1774 for £355..5 sells tract called *Wheat's choice,* beginning at a draught of Buck Lodge Branch, containing 53 acres. One other tract called *Resurvey on William's Tryal,* containing 165 acres. Signed by Richard Waters before David Lynn, Edward Burgess. Elizabeth wife of Richard Waters released dower rights.

W:212-213. John Shirock Jr recorded 21 Oct 1774 made 6 Oct 1774 from John Shriock Sr of York Co., Pennsylvania and John Shriock Jr of Elizabeth Town in Frederick County, lot in said town.

W;213-215. Ninian Beall, son of Ninian, recorded lease 22 Oct 1774 made17 Oct 1764 between Greenberry Belt two tracts on Ten Mile Creek, called *Farewell,* the other called *Resurvey on Friend in Need* containing 100 acres. He will find 200 apple trees, to plant in a regular orchard. Signed by both parties.

W:215-216. Peter Angle recorded bill of sale 20 Oct 1774, from John Angles for £9..10 sells one brown mare, provided always that if sum paid, sale is void.

W:216-218. William M Beall recorded deed of confirmation 20 Oct. 1774, made 28 Oct between Joshua Benton - reference made to U:96.

W:218-220. Samuel Hanson recorded deed 11 Nov 1774, made 12 Oct 1774 from Thomas Kirk Jr. For £36, tract called *Red Oak Level.* Signed before Wm Beatty, Ezekl Beatty. Elizabeth Kirk released dower rights.

W:220-221. John Solomon Miller recorded deed from George Barkhart 14 Nov 1774, for £150 tract called *Slydman's Lick*, on Conococheague Creek. Signed German script before William Baird, John Stull. Gertraut wife of George released dower rights.

W:222-224. Handel Barrick recorded deed 14 Nov. 1774 from William Clark, *Resurvey on Creager's Alley.* Rosannah, wife of William Clark released dower.

W:224-225. John Kennedy recorded deed 29 June 1775, made 28 June 1775, from Joseph Wood Jr for £100 tract *Round About,* 140 acres. Ann, wife of Joseph Wood Jr., released dower.

W:225-227. John Buchanan recorded deed 12 Nov. 1774 from Andrew Shroyer and Minyard, his wife. Whereas Raphael Taney conveyed lot #12 in Tawney Town, now for £40. Signed in German script, and by mark, ? Reynard Shroyer.

W:227-228. Richard Blacklock recorded deed 12 Nov. 1774 from Thomas Blacklock for £100, tract called *The Remains,* and *Addition to the Remains,* 100 acres.

W:228-229. Alexander Thos Hawkins recorded deed 13 Nov. 1774 from Geo Frazer Hawkins, executor of John Stone Hawkins, for £45, one half moiety of tract *John and Priscilla.*

W:230-231. Andrew Levenstone recorded deed 14 Nov. 1774, from Peter Bateman of Hampshire County, Virginia, for £30 Pennsylvania, tract called *Ramble by Quaker Tricks,* 48 ½ acres. Mary Bateman released dower.

W:231-232. Andrew Levenstone recorded deed 14 Nov. 1774, from Peter Bateman of Hampshire County, Virginia, for £126, tract called *Second Choice,* 126 ½ acres. Mary Bateman released dower.

W:233-234. Andrew Levenstone recorded deed 14 Nov. 1774, from Peter Bateman of Hampshire County, Virginia, for £4, tract called *Stoney Hall,* 4 acres. Mentions deeds of Peter Fisher and William Humbert. Mary Bateman released dower.

W:235-236. Samuel Miller recorded 14 Nov. 1774 from Michael Stoker for part of lot #82 in Frederick Town. Elizabeth, wife of Michael released dower.

W:236-237. William Clink recorded deed 14 Nov. 1774 from John Hammond for £7, *Resurvey on Good Neighborhood,* 7 acres. Margaret wife of John Hammond released dower.

W:237-239. [Marginal note: ex'd & dld Ann G. Wronick, excr of grantee, 30 July 1797.] Ludwick Young and Magdalena his wife, recorded deed 14 Nov 1774, from Henry Funk and Susannah his wife, Adam Troup and Catherine his wife, and Samuel Backley and Anna Maria his wife. Whereas Isaac Simmons, late of Frederick County, deceased, father of said Susannah, Catharine, Magdalen and Anna Maria, died intestate and was seized of a tract called *Simmons Rocket,* by common agreement make division. Metes and bounds given for part. Signed by all parties.

W:239-241. David Kennedy recorded deed 14 Nov. 1774, from Richard Beard for £50, part of *Carroll's Delight,* adjacent to division line with John Crawford, to a corner of William Rusk's part. Metes & bounds for 55 acres. Catharine wife of Richard Baird released dower.

W:241-242. Ooley Crumpacker recorded deed 14 Nov. 1774, from Michael Urner, [Marginal note: Exam'd & del'd to John Crumpacher, son of Ooly Crumpacher, who hath sold the land to Martin Woolf, 7 May 1783]. For £3, Martin Urner sells tract called *Martin's Corner,* on the 9th line of *Chance,* surveyed by Allen Farquhar, lying on Sams Creek, a draught of Pipe Creek, for 30 acres.

W:242-244. Mathias Smeisser recorded deed 14 Nov. 1774, made 9 Oct. 1774 from Rinehart Replogle for £500, *Resurvey on Smith's Lot.* 150 acres. Barbara Rappleigle, wife of Rinehart, released dower rights.

W:244-245. Walter Fundenbergh recorded deed 14 Nov. 1774, from Charles Beatty of Frederick Town for 5 shillings, tract granted Charles Beatty called *I'll Try for It,* adjacent to *Pleasant Valley,* containing 17 acres. Martha Beatty released dower.

W:246-247. John Ebert of Baltimore County recorded deed 14 Nov. 1774 from Samuel England, for £220 Pennsylvania, sells tract *Brother's Inheritance,* 111 acres. Prudence England, released dower.

W:247-249. Peter Krout recorded deed 14 Nov. 1774, from Stephen Ullerick of a certain part of America known by the name of Back Woods, for £50 sells part of tract called *Stephen's Hope,* beginning at tract called *Much Grumbling,* for 141 acres. Signed German Script. Susannah Ullerick, his wife, examined apart released dower right.

W:249-250. Paul Rineacre recorded deed 14 Nov. 1774, from Mathias Hook for £55, lot #31 in Westminster, to pay William Winchester annual rents of 7 shillings, 6 pence. Catharine, wife of Mathias Hook released dower.

W:250-251. Christian Deakins recorded deed 17 Nov. 1774, from George Silver for £12 sterling, tract *Resurvey on Little Worth,* 65 acres. Signed in German Script. Margaret, wife of said George released dower.

W:251-252. Thomas Schley of John recorded deed 14 Nov. 1774 from David Beckel, for £25, lots 191 & 192 in Frederick Town, to pay rents due Daniel Dulaney. Signed German script, Catharine wife of David Beckle released dower.

W:253. Michael Null recorded deed 14 Nov. 1774, from William Digges of Saint Mary's County, for £3, part of *Resurvey on Brother's Agreement,* containing 4 acres, 20 perches. Catharine Digges released dower right.

W:254-255 Plan of Georgetown, addition thereto as described in deed recorded in 254a.

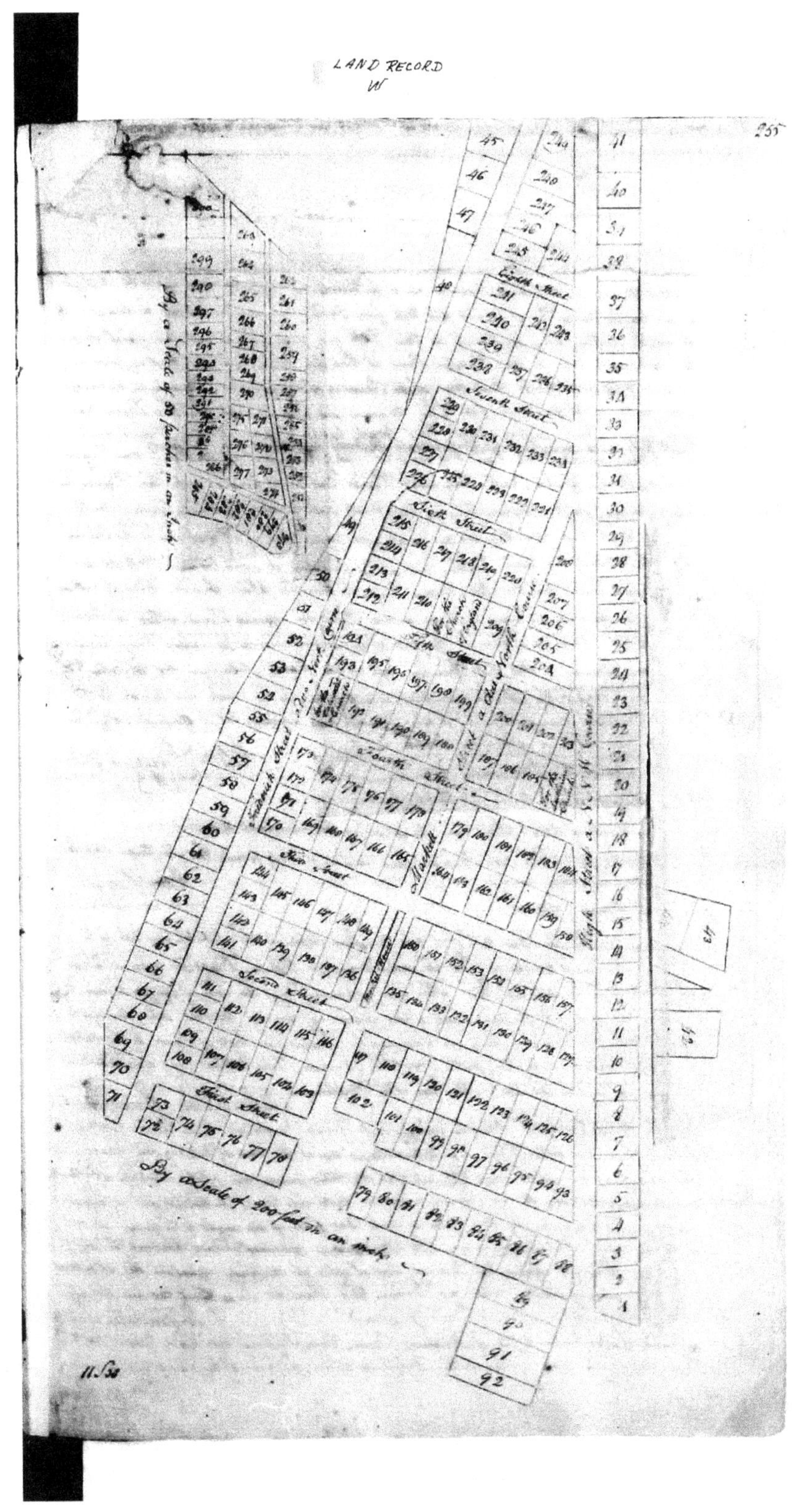

W:254-254(a). Benjamin Ricketts recorded deed 14 Nov. 1774 from William Dent of Guilford County, North Carolina, for £23 part of tract *Granby,* on Rock Creek, to John Kennedy's line. 15 acres. Clarlata (?), wife of William Dent released dower.

W:254(a). Charles Beatty and George Frazer Hawkins recorded 9 May 1770, Having purchased part of tract of land called *Knave's Disappointment,* formerly the property of George Gordon, deceased, late of Frederick County, and for the pubic benefit have laid off the said tract into 304 lots or parcels of, ground. Four of the lots are given to public use, to wit, one for building a church for the use of the Church of England, one for a Calvinist Church, one for a Lutheran Church and the other and one other. Drawn in the presence of Adam Stewart, Thomas Johns, William Deakins Jr. and Zephaniah Turner, trustees and managers.

W:256. Normand Bruce recorded deed 14 Nov 1774 from William Diggs of St. Mary's County for £40..10, part of *Resurvey on Diggs Lot,* 92 acres. Catharine Diggs released dower rights.

W:257. William Shaw, Thos Swearingen and Samuel Swearingen recorded bill of sale 16 Nov. 1774 from John Tannehill for £72..6..5, 3 calves and yearlings, 2 heifers, a horse, 4 feather beds and furniture, 4 sows and 4 shotes, a crop of tobacco, a desk, chair, 3 pots. Agreed to pay ½ of the amount by last day of August 1775, and balance by last day of August 1776, then bill of sale is void. Signed before Adamson Tannehill, James Keen.

W:257-258. John Paxton of York Co., Penn., recorded 16 Nov. 1774 from Richard Brooke, two tracts, *Hobson's Choice* 16 ½ acres and *Addition to Hobson's Choice,* 17 ½ acres, beginning at end of 59th line of *Addition to Brooke's Discovery on the Rich Lands.*

W:258-259. Benjamin Ogle Jr., recorded deed 16 Nov. 1774 from Richard Butler, son and heir of Peter Butler, seized of lot #96 in Frederick Town.

W:259-260. Richard Brooke recorded deed 16 Nov. 1774 from Matthias Pigman for £17..12, part of *Pleasant Plains of Damascus,* 100 acres. Dorcas, wife of Matthias released dower.

W:260-261. Jacob Stier recorded deed 17 Nov. 1774 from George Silver for £12 sterling, sells *Resurvey on Little Worth,* granted said Silver 21 Jan. 1774, beginning at a tract called *Father's Gift.* Signed German script. Wife (not named) released dower right.

W:261-262. Saml Blackman recorded release of dower from Mrs. Elizabeth Peter. On back of deed recorded in Liber U, folio 295, the following endorsement was made. Mrs. Elizabeth Peter, wife of Robert Peter released dower.

W:262-263. John Lawrence Hawkins and Elizabeth his wife recorded deed 7 November 1774, from William and Susana Fraser Bayley. Whereas they are jointly seized in a tract called *Contention,* containing 472 acres on Capt. John Run; beginning at tree of Col. Darnall's land called, the *Forrest,* they made deed of partition in two parts. Signed by all four parties.

W:263-266. (Includes a blank page) John Wayman of Anne Arundel County, recorded deed 17 Nov. 1774, from Zachariah Linthicum, for tract *Rich and Level,* on side of Snowden's River for 67 acres, and also part of *Gaither's Forrest,* containing 23 acres. Signed by mark before William Deakins Jr., Adam Stewart. Sarah Linthicum released dower.

W:266-267. Robert Jameson recorded deed 16 Nov. 1774 from Richard Brooke for £20, *Addition to Brooke's Discovery on the Rich Lands,* beginning at Piney Creek, and 5th line of tract called *Wattson's Delight,* to tract made over my James Brooke to Gerard Wilson for 75 acres. Signed before David Lynn, Edwd Burgess.

W:267-268. Doctor Henry Schnebeley recorded mortgage 17 Nov. 1774 from Christr Lighter for £53..1..7, tract called *Christian's part,* beginning at *Poe's part of Well Taught,* containing 107 acres. Provided Nevertheless if sum paid with interest by designated dates, sale is void and of no effect.

W:268-270. John Alspaugh recorded deed 6 May 1774 from Lawrence O'Neale for £67..5..5. Whereas a certain Bernard Eichelberger at suit for debt against David Alpaugh, had issued a writ of fi fa for his lot #5 in New London Town, with improvement to £160, offered at public sale, but had no buyers, at that price. John Alspaugh became high bidder for £106. Lot sold by sheriff Lawrence O'Neale to John Alspaugh for £106. Signed by both parties.

W:270-271. Christian Keefer recorded deed 20 Nov. 1774, from Lawrence Creager for £400, part of *Resurvey on Digges Lot,* adjacent to 100 acres conveyed by William Diggs to Nicholas Ory, containing 50 acres; made over to Lawrence Creager in 1773 from William Diggs; and 2nd part sold by John Diggs heir of John Diggs to Lawrence Creager in Oct. 1773 for 108 acres. Signed by both parties in German Script. Mary Elizabeth, wife of Lawrence Creager released dower.

W:271-273. Joseph Brewer, blacksmith, recorded deed 20 Nov 1774 from Nicholas Van Nimmon, for £962, *Resurvey on Moldy Pone,* granted said Nicholas, adjacent to Jacob Grigg's part of 291 acres. Signed by mark. Mary Van Nammen released dower.

W:273-275. Christian Keefer recorded deed 20 November 1774 from Conrad Hockersmith Senr for £400, tract patented to Uncle Uncles called *Chance Medley,* 32 acres; on drought of Tom Creek, another tract containing 50 acres, and others containing all together 142 acres. Signed by mark. Mary wife of Conrad Hockersmith released dower.

W:275-277. Adam Shriver of Pennsylvania, recorded deed 20 Nov. 1774 from Dan'l Spangler for £750, tracts *Shear Spring,* 100 acres; *High Spring,* 46 acres; and also *Wells Forrest,* 10 acres, plus part of *Waggoner's Fancy,* and Resurvey 18 acres, whole quantity 175 acres. Mary Spangler released dower.

W:277-278. Adam Tawney recorded deed 20 Nov. 1774 from Anthony Arnold for £18, part of *Resurvey on Last Shift,* 24 acres. Margaret wife of Anthony released dower.

W:278-280. John Aster (Oster) recorded deed 24 Nov. 1774 from Henry Shriock for £52, Pennsylvania, lot #97 in Elizabethtown, adjacent to John Miller's house and lot. Catrinah Shriock released dower.

W:280-281. Adam Tawney recorded deed 24 Nov. 1774, from Michael Hibner for £475, *Resurvey on Good Fellowship,* and part of *Father's Care,* 108 ½ acres. Catherine wife of Michael Hibner released dower.

W:281-282. Charles Beatty recorded deed 20 Nov. 1774 from John Hinton for £64, *Resurvey on Saplin Ridge,* 56 acres. Signed by mark.

W:283. [marginal note: Examined & del'd to Walter Harding, husband of the said Mary Harding, 19th May 1779.] Mary Harding recorded deed 17 Nov. 1774 from Daniel Dulaney. Whereas Mary is daughter and heir at law of Philip Murphy who agreed to purchase lot from Dulaney, but died before conveyance was made, in consideration of 40 shillings, lot #85 in Frederick Town now conveyed.

W:283-285. John Jacob Young recorded deed 24 Nov. 1774 from Joseph Kephart for £50, 50 acre part of *Stony Ridge,* adjacent to *Resurvey on Pool's Delight.* Catherine Kephart released dower.

W:285. Andrew Fleck recorded deed 24 Nov. 1774 from William House for £40, lot #27 in Sharpsburgh, signed German Script, William Hauss.

W:286-287. Godard Trossel recorded deed 24 Nov. 1774 from George Fleck tract called *Three Springs*. Elizabeth Fleck released dower.

W:287-288. Thomas Barr recorded deed 24 Nov. 1774 from Raphael Taney and William Diggs for £50, part of *Resurvey on Brother's Agreement.* Eleanor Taney and Catherine Digges released dower before Justices of the Peace in St. Mary's County.

W:288-289. Jacob Fisher recorded deed 24 Nov. 1774 from Michael Hibner for £4..10, part of *Resurvey on Good Fellowship,* 1 ½ acres. The wife of Michael Hibner (name not recorded) released dower.

W:289-290. John Ridout of Annapolis, recorded deed 24 Nov. 1774 from Bernard Johnson for £39, tract *Chatham.* 130 acres. Signed Barnet Johnson.

W:290-292. Mary Owen and others (Robert Carlisle Owen, Edward Carlisle Owen and David Owen, heirs of Edward Owen, deceased) recorded deed 24 Nov. 1774 from Lawrence Owen, part of *Resurvey on Friend's Advice,* 100 acres. Receipt: Received of Edward Owen Jr. In his life time £115. Sarah Owen released dower.

W:292-293. Samuel Snowden and John Snowden of Prince George's County and Ann Arundel County, recorded deed 17 Nov. 1774, from Charles Andrews, indebted to the estate of Richard Snowden Senior, of Patuxent Iron Works, for £102..6, sells parcel called *Rich Land,* in Frederick County, containing 100 acres. Signed by mark before Edwd Burgess, Upton Sheridine. Elizabeth Andrews, wife of Charles released dower.

W:293-294. Lancelot and Basil Willson of Prince George's County, recorded bill of sale 17 November 1774 from Joseph Willson, son of Lancelot, for 5 shillings, sell one Negro woman, named Sue and her three children, a boy called Cesar about 5, a girl Phillis, about 3 years old and a boy, Ellick about 1 year old. Signed before David Lynn, Philip Casey.

W:294-295. Balser Culp recorded deed 27 Nov. 1774 from Danl Culp, for £100 all his share of lot in Elizabeth Town. Esther Culp wife of Daniel released dower rights.

W:295-296. John Stull and Jonathan Hager recorded bill of sale 17 Nov. 1774 from Dan'l Culp for £550 assigns one Negro woman called Nancy, about 18 years of age; one horse, clock, three feather beds, and furniture, but provided nevertheless if sum paid, mortgage or bill of sale is void. Signed by all three parties before William Baird and Otho Williams.

W:296-298. Wm Roby Owen recorded deed 26 Nov. 1774 from Matthew Pigman for £90 conveys part of *Pleasant Plains of Damascus,* containing 667 acres. Dorcas wife of Matthew released dower.

W:298-299. Charles Angle and Christopher Erb recorded deed 28 Nov. 1774 from James McGuire for £100. Part of *Resurvey on Patience Care,* and part of a tract called *Ohio,* containing 190 acres conveyed to the said James McGuire by Michael McGuire.

W:299-300. Charles Angle and Christopher Erb recorded mortgage 30 Nov. 1774, from Thos McGuire for £100 tract of land called *Ohio,* and part of *Resurvey on Patience Care,* for 159 acres

W:300-302. Peter White recorded deed 25 Nov. 1774 from Samuel Armitt of Pennsylvania, gentleman, and Mary Ann Charity Abigail his wife, for £10 sterling assigns, lot #33 in Frederick Town.

W:302 Michael Cresap recorded deed 30 Nov. 1774, from Thomas Cresap for £100 part of *Resurvey on Good Hope* for 4 acres. Signed before Thos Warring and Wm Beatty

W:302-303. Spiers, French and Casper, of Glasgow, merchants, recorded bill of sale 16 Nov 1774 from John Barnes, son of James Barnes on *Chews Manor*, for £61..11.. 7 all my crop of tobacco made in 1774 and cured in my tobacco house, built on the plantation I now live on, seized and sold to Hugh Finley, their factor, supposed to contain 5000 weight, as also the lot of land containing 100 acres, held by me from Saml Chew Esq. For 21 years. Signed by mark, John Barnes, son of James. Before Rich'd Davis, John Stull, and Blanchaner Shocker by mark.

W:303-305. Adam Steuart, merchant of Georgetown, recorded deed 20 November 1774 from Nathaniel Offutt, son of Samuel, for £286..10..9 part of tract called *Younger Brother,* being that tract that was willed to the said Nathaniel Offutt by his father, Samuel Offutt, Signed by Nathaniel Offutt, son of Samuel, before David Lynn, Robert Peter. Elizabeth, wife to the said Nathaniel Offutt, examined apart released right of dower.

W:305-306. John Dorsey son of John recorded deed 3 November 1774, from Benjamin Clary of Baltimore County, for £20, part of *Resurvey on Moab,* 447 3/4 acres. Eleanor Clary released dower.

W:306-307. Robert Carrell recorded bill of sale 15 Nov 1774, from Philip Pitting for £12, crop of wheat now growing to make up sum of £12 plus interest owing to him. Signed Philip Bitting, before Thos Price.

W:307-308. Richard Northcraft recorded deed 21 Nov 1774 from William Hawker and Elizabeth his wife, for £20, part of *Buxton's Delight,* 100 acres.

W:308-309. Thos Watters recorded deed 20 Nov. 1774, from John Hall of Annapolis, part of *Middle Plantation,* beginning at 1st line of part conveyed to William Willson, now Nathan Magruder's, containing 102 acres.

W:309-311. George Chrisman recorded deed 20 Nov. 1774, from Thomas Logsdon, for £495, part of *Good Fellowship,* to 1st line of *Cobbs Choice,* adjacent to William Durbin's land. 170 acres. Signed by mark. Mary, wife of Thomas released dower.

W:311. Jos Wilson on behalf of John and Thomas Hartley, of Whitehaven, merchants, recorded bill of sale 17 Nov. 1774, from Danl Stevenson for a considerable debt of £81..13..9, one Negro woman Sue, 23 years old and her two children, Caesar, 3 years old and Phillis, 14 months.

W:311-313. John Row recorded deed 20 Nov. 1774, from Adam Cross (or Gross) for £6, lot #127 in Frederick Town. Signed by mark. Elizabeth Cross wife of Adam released dower rights.

W:313 Margaret Smith Butler and Ann Darnall Butler, recorded deed of gift 28 Nov 1774, from Elizabeth Butler, for natural love and affection for my daughters. To Margaret, Negro girl Nell, one feather bed; to daughter Ann, Negro girl Alice, and one feather bed and furniture, one cow and calf. Signed before Andrew Heugh, Elizabeth Heugh.

W:313-315. John Ferguson recorded deed 20 Nov. 1774 from Samuel Ferguson, to his son, John, for £20 part of *Addition to Brooke's Discovery on the Rich Lands,* 100 acres. Signed by mark. Elizabeth, wife of Samuel Ferguson released dower.

W:315-316. Jacob Sturtsmen recorded deed 20 Nov. 1774, from Lawrence Creager for £30, sells 8 ½ acres of *True Friendship.* Signed in German Script. Mary Elizabeth Creager released dower.

W:316-317. Charles Wells of Baltimore County, recorded deed 30 November 1774, from Benjamin Hall for £80 tract *Find it If You Can,* beginning at 5th line of *Resurvey on Gilboa,* 100 acres of land. Rebecca Hall released dower before David Lynn, Joseph Wells.

W:317-318. Jacob Spurtsmen recorded deed 21 Nov. 1774, from Lawrence Creager for £15 for 10 acres of land called *True Friendship,* adjacent to *Resurvey on Middle Choice,* signed in German script, Lorentz Krieger, and Elizabeth Creager released dower before John Stull, Wm Beatty.

W:319-320. Daniel Spurtsmen recorded deed 21 Nov. 1774, from Lawrence Creager for £100, for 100 acres of tract called *True Friendship.* Signed in German script, Lorentz Krieger, and Elizabeth Creager released dower before John Stull, Wm Beatty.

W:320-321. John Magruder recorded bill of sale 22 Nov. 1774, from Theo Marcus for sundry sums of money, debt due to William Stellers of £20 and to George Read for £7, assigns to John Magruder, 15 barrels of corn, 15 head of hogs, all my fodder, one grey horse, one cow and one gray mare, and household goods. Signed Theo Marcus before Andrew Heugh.

W:321-322. William Hardy recorded deed 24 Nov 1774 from William Barrick for £312, assigns tract *Rays Venture,* on Little Monocacy, 30 acres. Signed by mark before Adam Steuart, Wm Deakins Jr., Mary wife of Wm Barrick released dower.

322. John Ferguson, recorded certificate of marks for cattle and hogs, 10 November 1774. At same time, Josias Ferguson recorded his marks.

322. Thomas Cresap recorded bond 21 Nov 1774. I Southall Bayley, gentleman, am bound and agree to pay £20 with legal interest by 1 May next. Signed before Christopher Sims, Charles Morrow.

W:323-324. David Kennedy of Cumberland County, Pennsylvania, recorded deed 20 November 1774, from Allen Killough for £660..5, assigns part of a *Resurvey on the Three Cousins,* Patented in Maryland, but since running the boundary line, now in Pennsylvania. Metes and bounds given for 226 acres. Signed before John Stull, William Baird. Hannah Killough released dower.

W:324-325. Zachariah Offutt and Eleanor his wife, recorded deed 25November 1774 from Ninian Beall, in consideration of Zachariah Offutt being married to his daughter, 99 acre part of *William and John,* and part of *Beall's Desire,* 254 acres; and part of *William and Ann,* 350 acres. Signed Ninian Beall, son of Ninian. If land is sold, proceeds to be used for support of Eleanor and lawful children of her. Mary Beall released dower rights.

W:326-327. Jacob Fisher recorded deed 20 November 1774, from Anthony Arnold for £18, part of *Resurvey on Last Shift.* Signed by mark before Joseph Wells, Wm Winchester. Margaret wife of Anthony Arnold released dower.

W:327-328. Joseph Boyer recorded deed 20 Nov 1774 from Joseph Kephart, house carpenter, for £80 part of *Stony Range,* 80 acres. Signed by mark. Catharine wife of Joseph Kephart released dower.

W:328-329. Mathias Stallcap recorded deed 20 November 1774, from Charles Warfield for £10 tract called *Sylvia,* 100 ½ acres; Signed before Upton Sheridine, Joseph Wells. Elizabeth Warfield released dower.

W:329-331. Adam Stewart and Robert Peter, merchants, recorded deed 20 November 1774, from Joseph Stallings Junior, for £30, *Grove's Hunting Lot,* to part conveyed to Zachariah White. Signed before Andrew Heugh, William Deakins, Junr.

W:331-332. Frederick Missel recorded deed 20 November 1774, from Samuel and Catherine Miller for £250, lot #109 in Frederick Town.

W:332-333. Jacob Miller recorded deed 20 November 1774, from Michael Wine for £23..8, *Second Brother,* originally made over by Henry Griffith to Joseph West Junr., on draught of Israel's Creek, 210 acres. Susannah, wife of Michael Wine released dower.

W:334-336. Jacob Michael recorded deed 20 November 1774, from Ann and Wm Burneston, executors of the last will and testament of Joseph Burneston, late of the county aforesaid, shoemaker. Whereas Joseph Burneston in his lifetime, for a valuable consideration sold to William Slicer, one lot, and Jacob Michael purchased from William Slicer said lot. Now William and Ann Burneston for 5 shillings, currency, part of additional lots of Frederick Town, lots #156, 157 on Patrick Street. Signed before Jos Wood, Andrew Heugh.

W:336-337. Jacob Michael recorded release of dower from Ann Burneston, widow of Joseph Burneston, on lots above.

W:338-339. James Campbell, Aeneas Campbell Junr., Esther Campbell, Lydia Campbell and Ann Campbell, recorded the following deed 24 November 1774. From Eneas Campbell of Frederick County, for diverse good causes and considerations, and the natural love and affection, confirms to James Campbell his son, mulatto slave named Chloe; to son Eneas, Negro girl named Mill, also one feather bed and furniture, one cow and last spring's calf and part of his lease that he the said Eneas Campbell had of Mary Elmendorf called *Frozen Level,* confirms unto Esther Campbell, one mulatto woman called Christian, and mulatto girl named Kersey; to daughter Lidia Campbell, one mulatto girl named Nell and her increase, one feather bed and furniture, one cow and calf; give and confirm to my daughter Ann Campbell one Negro girl called Eve, and one Negro boy named Phil; one bed and furniture; one lame sorrel mare and her colt; and if too many, they are to be sold, and money put at interest until she arrives at age 16. If any of the children die before they are of age, then items to be divided among the remaining children. Signed before Wm Blair, Edward Burgess.

W:340-341. William Boone recorded deed 25 November 1775, from Samuel Boone, for £10, lot #32 in Georgetown, part of uppermost corner lot. Signed before Edward Burgess, David Lynn. Jane Boone, wife of Samuel released dower.

W:341-343. Adam Morningstar recorded deed 28 Nov. 1775, from John Paul Cruise for £624, part of *Spring Garden.* Mary wife of John Paul Cruise released dower.

W:343-344. Charles Coats records land commission and deposition 29 Nov. 1775. The Right honorable Henry Harford, Esq., issued commission to Mssrs Jonathan Willson, Elisha Williams, Eneas Campbell and Stephen Newton Chiswell, to perpetuate memory of the bounds of tract called *Daniel's Discovery.* Alexander Pearre, aged 52 years deposed that 19 years before he lay out bounds for Charles Coats. Elisha Williams, aged 40 years deposed, regarding a bound tree.

W:345-346. Jacob Sinn recorded bill of sale 6 Dec. 1775, from Paul Gornar (or Corner) for 5 shillings, assigns a house and 2 acre lot, in Baltimore County, whereon a certain John Price now lives, the milch cow and two calves; one iron kettle a parcel of pewter and other household items enumerated. Signed before Jacob Young. Nevertheless if sums paid by 27 November next, sale is void.

W:346-348. Samuel Swearingen recorded deed 9 Dec. 1775, from David Ross, Richard Henderson and Samuel Beall Jr., partners in the Frederick Forge, for £93..4, tract called *Boston,* 386 acres. Ariana Ross, Sarah Henderson, Eleanor Beall released dower rights.

W:348-349. William Lee and Thomas Brooke recorded lease 11 Dec. 1775, made 22 June, between Michael Kirkpatrick and George Kirpatrick, his son, for yearly rents and covenants, lets parcel *Dickenson's Pleasure,* adjacent to William Hill's field, and James Kirkpatrick's fence.

W:350-351. Edward Browning Junr recorded deed 14 Dec. 1775 from Benja Wigfield for £20, parcel called *Fancy* on Middle Bennett Creek, containing 30 acres. Mildred Wigfield, wife of Benjamin released dower rights before Edwd Burgess, Wm Blair.

W:352-353. Jacob Miller recorded deed 14 Dec. 1775, from Thomas Dorsey of Anne Arundel County, for 5 shillings, 27 3/4 acres of *Resurvey on Miller's Chance.* Signed before Caleb Dorsey junr., and Nicholas Dorsey.

W:353-354. Michael Karnhart recorded deed 16 Dec. 1775 from Henry Karnhart for 5 shillings, part of *Fountain Low,* 174 acres. Susannah Karnhart released dower.

W:355-356. David Mitchel and Chas Finley recorded deed 20 Dec. 1775, from Michael Cresap for £60, tract called *Betty's Blessing,* patented to him for 70 acres. Mary Cresap released dower.

W:356-358. Basil Beall recorded deed 6 May 1776 from Henry Hunter for £710, tract called *Castle Henry,* adjacent to *Resurvey on Leonard's Good,* for 284 acres. Ann Hunter released dower.

W:358-359. George Ramsburgh recorded deed 10 August 1776, from Jacob and John Michael of Fredericktown, for £150, part of *Resurvey on George's Discovery,* for 188 acres. Catharine wife of Jacob Michael and Elizabeth, wife of John Michael released dower.

W:359-361. Martin Long recorded deed 8 Nov. 1776 from Michael Eckenberger and Catharine his wife for £130 Pennsylvania, tract called *Hard Fortune,* a part of *Resurvey on Part of Park's Hall*, conveyed to a certain Andrew Grim by Peter Corner, who on 28 June 1773 conveyed to Michael Echenberger. Signed by both.

W:361-362. Henry Hoge recorded deed 13 January 1777 from Peter Creager for £300, tract called *Batchelor's Hall,* 132 acres. Signed by mark before T. Bowles, George Scott. Mary Creager released dower.

W:362-363. Peter Shots of York County, Pennsylvania, recorded deed 17 May 1777, from Ludwick Moler for £1600 part of *The Range,* on Little Pipe Creek, 230 acres. Signed by mark before Upton Sheridine and Tabitha Richardson. Anna, wife of Ludwick Moler released dower.

W:363-365. [marginal note, del'd to Elie Williams, 10 May 1779] Abraham Naff recorded deed 9 May 1776, from Benjamin Musselman for £500, two tracts. *Addition to Catharine's Part,* which fell to Catharine Simmons from Isaac Simmons her father, for 57 acres and part of *Locust Bottom,* 36 acres and improvements. Signed in German Script. Mary Musselman released dower.

W:365-366. [marginal note as above] Abraham Naff recorded deed from Adam Troup and Catharine, his wife, for £600, tract called *Simmons Back,* 101 acres. Signed in G.S., and by mark.

W:366-368. [Exam'd & del'd Zadock Wheat per order 21 May 1779] Alion Miller recorded deed 28 Dec. 1776 from Jacob Zugg, for £269..12, *Resurvey on part of Water Sink,* to have use of water falling on said 75 acres to water meadows on Monday and Tuesdays, to recover same from Samuel Volgamuth. Elizabeth Zugg released dower.

W:368-369. Henry Alsbaugh recorded deed 4 April 1776 from Ethan Loveall of Baltimore County, for £13, lot #44 in town called New London. Signed Ethan Loveall, before Upton Sheridine, Eleanor Sheridine. Mary wife of Ethan Loveall released dower before Upton Sheridine and Joseph Wells.

W:369-370. Michael Trautman recorded deed 21 Nov. 1776 from James Flemming for £75, 172 acres, part of *Resurvey on Stoney Level,* Signed before Thomas Beatty and Charles Beatty. Ann Flemming released dower.

W:370-371. Henry Tutwiler recorded deed 18 June 1776 from Jacob Warrenfeltz for £195, lot #99 in Elizabeth Town. Covenants with Jonathan Hager recorded. Susanna Warrenfeltz released dower.

W:372-374. Abraham Lakins recorded deed 14 Dec. 1776 from Fielder Gannt. Whereas indenture and sale made in 1772, metes and bounds recorded for part of *Fielderia Manor,* beginning at 2nd line of tract *Widow's Rest,* granted to William Matthews, to tract *Spicer's Mill,* then to *Cooper's Hole,* then to *John and Sarah Resurvey* for Richard Ancrum, continuing to tract called *Chaney.* Signed by both parties before Jacob Young, George Scott.

W:374-378. James Higgins recorded deed and record of indemnification from John Lee of Essex County, Virginia, son of Corbin Lee, late of Baltimore County, deceased, and Joseph Sim of Prince George County and Lettice, his wife, formerly Lettice Lee, sister of Hancock Lee, deceased, also the widow of James Wardrope, deceased, and widow of Adam Thomson, deceased of one part. Whereas the said Corbin Lee and Lettice in the lifetime of said Corbin, while the said Lettice was the widow of the said Adam Thomson, being seized in fee as tenants in common of tract called *Addition,* for 350 acres, sold to James Higgins for £612..10, and James Higgins paid Corbin Lee £243..2..3 in part of his share and to the said Lettice, before her marriage to Joseph Sim, £306..5, there is now due to John Lee, heir of Corbin, £40..6..8, now for the said sums, deed is made beginning at Rock Creek Branch, near a bound tree of land formerly surveyed by Thomas Butler, to given line of tract called *Dann,* metes and bounds given containing 363 1/4 acres. Signed John Lee, Joseph Sim, Lettice Sim, before David Crawford, Alexander Symmes, of Prince George's County. Eleanor Lee, of Harford County, widow of Corbin Lee, for £40 released right of dower. Bond of John Lee to James Higgins, indemnifying him for dower rights of Susannah, which she may at any time hereafter claim. Signed before J. Rogers, Thos Sim Lee.

W:378-379. Jacob Myer recorded deed 4 April 1776 from Bernard Hershberger for £500, *Coopertown* on Broad Run of Abraham's Creek, 100 acres and *Timberland,* adjacent to *Willyard's Lott,* surveyed for Dewalt Willyard, 64 ½ acres. Signed in German Script, before Archibald Boyd, Jacob Young. Elizabeth Harshberger, wife of Bernard, released dower.

W:379-380. Jacob Myer recorded deed 26 June 1776, from Michael Boyer on tract called *Crane,* adjacent to *Coopertown,* containing 39 acres. Signed before Bart Booth, Jacob Young.

W:380-381. [Del'd Mr. Richard Jones Waters, 9 Sept 1780]. Josephus Burton Waters recorded deed 26 August 1776, from Edward Doran for £30, part of his 214 acres of *Bear Bacon.* Metes and bounds given for 130 acres.

W:381-383. George Burkhart Sr. Recorded deed 4 April 1776 from Jacob Hope, executor of Christian Sholl, deceased. For £624 Pennsylvania, sells *Resurvey on Plummer's Delight,* containing 9 ½ acres. Signed before Archibald Boyd, Jacob Young.

W:383-384. [Exam'd & del'd to Nicholas Feaser, 26 Oct. 1780.] Jacob Feaser of York County, Pennsylvania, recorded deed 14 Oct. 1776 from Samuel Owings of Baltimore County, for £30, part of tract *Ohio,* adjacent to Adam Buse's part, containing 100 acres. Signed before John Moale, Bale Randall of Baltimore County. Deborah wife of Samuel Owings released dower.

W:384. Francis Pierpoint recorded 3 Sept. 1775 discharge of the following Negroes from service: Isaac Jones, and his wife Jane Jones to be free immediately, and Negro girls Nancy to serve for 13 years, Negro girl Arey to serve for 16 years and 2 months, and girl Cate to serve for 18 years, and then to be free. Signed before Jacob Young.

W:385. Henry Lighter recorded power of attorney23 December 1775, from John Plumb and Rachel his wife of Hampshire County, Virginia.

W:385-388. Andrew Smith recorded deed 23 Dec 1775 from Henry Lighter of Virginia, John Lighter, Henry Lighter the younger, John Lighter the younger of Maryland, John Plumb and Regina, alias Rachel, his wife of Virginia, Frederick Stemple and Esther his wife, Michael Rohr and Mary his wife, and Salome Lighter, widow of Melchior Lighter, deceased of Maryland. Whereas Melchior Lighter in his lifetime on 24 June 1771, had resurveyed tracts called *Loving Brother* containing 100 acres and *Widow's Design,* 50 acres, plus added vacancy into tract called *Middletown,* surveyed for 171 acres. He died, leaving issues, sons Henry, John, Henry the younger and John the younger, and four daughters, Regina alias Rachel, Esther, and Mary parties to the above, and Elizabeth wife of Andrew Smith. Signed by all parties before Thos Cresap, Bartholomew Booth.

W:388-389. [Ex'd & del'd Henry Leatherman, 6 Dec. 1781] George Coster recorded deed 23 Dec 1775 from Mathias Smithley, heir of Limely Smithley, deceased, fuller, for £52 Pennsylvania, *Stoney Bottoms,* 54 acres. Alienation fine paid Wm Murdoch Beall.

W:389-390. John Jeremiah Jacobs recorded deed 18 Dec. 1776, from Lawrence O'Neale for £21, *Prospect,* near Old Town, to Town Creek, between tracts surveyed for Michael Cresap. 53 acres. Henrietta O'Neale released dower.

W:390-391. Jacob Staley recorded lease 20 Feb. 1776, from Philip Angleberger for £212, part of tract *Whinnpenny Felt*, for term of five years.

W:392-393. Adam Isenmyer recorded deed 26 June 1776 from Adam Everley and Peter Jesserong, for £60, tract called *Cherry Chance,* on 10th line of tract *Smithfield.* Christian Everly and Eve Catherine Jesserong, wives of above, released dower right.

W:393-395. Adam Isenmyer, heir of the last will and testament of Frederick Isemonger, deceased, recorded deed 21 Nov 1776 from John Stone. Whereas John Stone and Frederick Isemonger had bargained for part of tract called *Fox Hole,* for £4..10, from the main road, down to said John Stone's dwelling house. Signed by mark. Elizabeth wife of John Stone released dower.

W:395-397. Jacob Myer of Lancaster County, Pennsylvania, recorded deed 11 June 1776 from Nathaniel Nesbett for £100, part of tract called *Hazard,* metes and bounds given for 674 acres. Frances Nesbett released dower.

W:398-399. Michael Troutman recorded deed 21 Nov. 1776 from Peter Seller for £140, part of *Trifle,* beginning at tract called *Miller's Chance,* containing 21 1/4 acres; also part of *Resurvey on Miller's Chance,* containing 21 ½ acres, and another 7 ½ acres, containing in all 49 acres. Catharine Seller released dower rights.

W:399-400. Michael Trautman recorded deed 26 Nov. 1776 from George Castle for £75, part of *Little Friendship,* adjacent to tract called *Muddy Spring,* on a draught of Kitoctin Creek, taken up by John Johnson, containing 50 acres. Margaret, wife of George Castle released dower.

W:401-402. Michael Null recorded deed 5 August 1776, from Andrew Sharar for £100, lot #14 in Taneytown. Margaret, wife of Andrew Shearer released dower.

W:402-403. Adam Ott recorded deed 4 August 1776, from Casper Fritzche, for £70, lot #14 in Elizabethtown. Susanna, wife of Casper Fritzche released dower.

W:403-404. Jacob Pence recorded agreement 30 March 1776, from Philip Sinn, agreed with each other to cut a canal through the upper part of Phillip Sinn's land to convey water to each meadow, to be cut at the expense of Jacob Bence. Signed by mark, by Philip Sinn. Elizabeth, wife of Phillip Sinn released dower right.

W:404-406. Peter Oller recorded deed 23 Dec. 1775, from John Wellday for £35, part of *Piney Grove,* and *Resurvey on the Pines,* and *Addition to the Pines.* Barbara, wife of John Wellday released dower.

W:406-407. James Beatty recorded deed 18 Sep 1776 from Mary Ritchie, widow, tract called *Dulaney's Lot,* to last line of William Beatty's 50 ½ acre part conveyed to him by Mary Ritchie.

W:407-408. Martin Coonce recorded deed 16 Sep. 1776 from Peter Beaver, tract called *Christie's Folly,* adjacent to *Cool Spring,* 3 ½ acres. Signed in German script. Elizabeth, wife of Peter Beaver, released dower.

W:408-401. David Bear recorded deed 6 March 1776 from John Howser for £800 Pennsylvania, part of *Resurvey on Patrick's Lot,* tract called *Middle Barrack,* and the *Resurvey on Middle Barrack,* and *Wackerham*[5] and *Cracket,* all contiguous, containing 236 acres. Signed.

W:410-411. Bardell Keefer recorded deed 14 Oct. 1776, from Samuel Owings for £100 part of tract called *Ohio,* 154 acres. Deborah, wife of Samuel Owings, released dower.

W:411-412. George Miller recorded deed 11 Oct. 1776, from Samuel Owings for £40, part of tract called *Ohio,* 100 acres. Deborah, wife of Samuel Owings released dower.

W:412-414. David Gillespy recorded deed 8 Sep 1776 from Nicholas Rowe for part of *Addition to Sly Fox.* Signed by mark. Elizabeth, wife of Nicholas Rowe released dower.

W:414-415. Philip Smith recorded deed 1 April 1776 from Christena Andichon for £58 paid to her, for lot #36 in Sharpsburgh. Signed by mark before Sam'l Beall Jr., John Stull. Receipt, acknowledgment.

W:415-416. Peter Orndorf recorded deed 21 Nov. 1776, from Henry Smith for £500 part of *Brother's Agreement,* 320 acres. Anna Maria, wife of Henry Smith released dower.

W:416-418. Nicholas Powles recorded deed 10 Sep 1774 from Philip Tune, Susanna Tune his wife, and George Stricker, executors of the last will and testament of Jacob Powlas, deceased. In his lifetime he made a bond to sell to Nicholas Powlas tract called *Content,* on 4 Nov. 1766, 175 acres for £50, except his mother's thirds as long as she lives. In will he directed deed to be made to his brother Nicholas Powlas, and appointed his wife Susanna, and George Stricker, executors. Metes and bounds given for tract.

W:418-419. Matthew Galt recorded deed 19 March 1776, made same date from Matthew Galt Senior for £200, tract called *Peters Park* on south side of Piney Creek, 216 acres. Also part of *Resurvey on Brother's Agreement,* adjacent to *Peter's Park,* 35 acres, and part on wagon road from Frederick Town to York Town, 26 1/3 acres. Signed before Jacob Young, Archibald Boyd.

W:420-421. Christian Dement recorded deed 14 Oct. 1776, from Samuel Owings of Baltimore County, for part of tract *Ohio.* Metes and bounds given for 110 acres. Deborah wife of Samuel Owings released dower.

W:421-423. Jacob Zimmerman recorded deed 16 Sept. 1776 from Henry Delawter for £20, part of *Resurvey on Isaacs Range,* 90 acres, to be held during the nonage or minority of Jacob Delawter, a minor brother of said Henry Delawter, paying sum of £8 share and share alike to the sisters of the said Henry Delawter, and at the time the said Jacob Delawter shall arrive at proper lawful age, to pay sums for the use of Catharine Delawter and Charlotte Delawter, when they arrive at lawful age.

---

[5]John Houser patented *Wackram,* 29 Sept. 1766, and *Heidelburgh Workerham* 22 Oct 1772 for 177 acres. Peter Wilson Coldham, *Settlers of Maryland, 1766-1783.*

W:423-424. John Winders recorded deed 5 Sept 1776, from Francis and William Deakins Junr., for £49..10 tract *Pleasant Mount,* surveyed for Samuel Hughes adjacent to *Resurvey on Discontent,* 49 ½ acres.

W:424-426. Thomas Darnall recorded deed 1 May 1776, made 20 April, from John Darnall. Whereas John Darnall, father of the said John Darnall, devised to John the dwelling plantation that he make deed to his other sons, Thomas and Henry Darnall, dividing the tract *Resurvey on Hope*. For 5 shillings, he deeds, 1392 acres, part of *Resurvey on Hope,* to Thomas Darnall, metes and bounds, gives division line with Henry Darnall.

W:427-429. Henry Darnall recorded deed 1 May 1776, made 20 April, from John Darnall. Whereas John Darnall, father of the said John Darnall, devised to John the dwelling plantation that he make deed to his other sons, Thomas and Henry Darnall, dividing the tract Resurvey on Hope. For 5 shillings, he deeds, 1392 acres, part of *Resurvey on Hope,* to Henry Darnall, metes and bounds given.

W:429-430. Edward Osmond of Anne Arundel County, recorded deed 20 Dec. 1775, from William Maccubbin of Anne Arundel County, for £222..10, part of tract *Moab,* and *Resurvey on Moab,* resurveyed by Benjamin Clary, for 200 acres. Mary, wife of William Maccubbin released dower.

W:430 Francis McDonald, blacksmith, recorded deed 20 Dec. 1775, from Edward Osmond of Anne Arundel County, for £222 part of *Resurvey on Moab,* 200 acres.

W:432-434. James Smith recorded bill of sale 20 Dec. 1775, from Edward Harden, for covenants herein and 5 shillings, assigns servant girl, Barbara Gordon with 2 years yet to serve, 2 milch cows, two dry cows, 2 calves, 8 hogs, one feather bed and bedding, one rug, three blankets, various farm tools, and kitchen implements, shoemakers tools, gun, pistol and powder horn, a quantity of butter, potatoes and pumpkins, spinning wheels, flax, thread and spun yarn, James Smith is to pay the creditors of Edward Harden. Signed by mark before John Barrow, John Mainwood. "Delivers servant girl, Barbara Gordon, in the name of livery and seisen of the whole goods, cattle and chattels within mentioned."

W:434-437. Jacob Humbert recorded deed 23 Dec. 1775, from Adam Loy for £636..15, 42 1/4 acres, part of *Tasker's Chance,* beginning at a mill stone, lying near the mill dam on said land, to given line of Loys 213 acre part of said tract, to include water courses.

W:437-439. Cornelius Willson recorded deed 23 Dec. 1775, from Edward Perryn, John Perryn and Joseph Perryn, executors of John Perryn, Senior, tract called *Two Springs,* 100 acres. Signed by Edward Perrins, John Perrins, Joseph Perrins. Ann Perryn, wife of Edward released dower rights.

W:440-442. Jacob Lawrence recorded 23 Dec. 1775, from Peter Stuck, house carpenter, lot #2 in Middletown. Hester Stuck released dower.

W:442-444. Thomas Contee and Doct. Leonard Hollyday of Prince George's County, recorded deed 23 Dec. 1775, from Thomas Warring for £150 sterling, tract *Warington,* on bank of Potomac River, across from Swan Pond Bottom in Virginia, containing 270 acres more or less.

W:445-446. Thomas Johns recorded deed 23 Dec. 1775 from William Boon, brother and heir at law of Mordecai Boon, for £46, part of *Darby's Island,* in Potomac River. Signed before Edward Burgess, David Lynn.

W:446-449. George Kneable recorded deed 23 Dec. 1775, from John Midscar for £180, part of *Stony Ridge,* beginning at red oak, 1 ½ miles from Stephen Onion's house, containing 100 acres. Also 40 acre part of *Good Neighbor.* Signed Johannes Metzgar. Cathrin, wife of John Metzgar released dower.

W:449-451. Leonard Storm recorded deed 23 Dec. 1775, from Harman Yost, made 21 June 1775, for £8, ½ lot #4 in Middletown, to pay annual quit rents of 3 shillings to Conrad Coonce. Signed Johan Herman Yost. Mary Yost released dower rights.

W:451-452. Christian Lower of Berks County, Pennsylvania, recorded deed 23 Dec. 1775, from Benjamin Stryker of Georgetown, for £100 sterling, lot #78 in Georgetown on the Potomac. Signed before John Stull, Upton Sheridine.

W:452-456. John Ridout recorded deed 23 Dec. 1775, from Joseph Flint for £104..4 Pennsylvania, part of *Resurvey on Darling's Delight,* 62 acres, and part of tract *Force,* 8 acres. Signed before Thos Cresap, and Thos Waring. Charity Flint, wife of Joseph, released dower. Alienation fine paid Wm Murdock Beall.

W:457-459. Peter Shoemaker, tinker, recorded lease 23 Dec., 1775, from Thomas Welsh, land surveyor, for yearly rents and covenants, leases lot #1, part of tract called *Goose Cap,* for term of 21 years, beginning at side of mill creek on the Great Road from Frederick to Elizabethtown, to end of line of *Goose Cap,* conveyed by Nicholas Finch to Thomas Welch for 66 acres. Lot contains 10 acres. Annual rent of £2, or dollars at 7 shillings, 6 pence each. Signed by both parties, and acknowledged before Jacob Young, Archibald Boyd. Hannah Welch, wife of Thomas, released right of dower.

W:459-462. Jacob Dutterow, weaver, recorded lease 23 Dec., 1775, from Thomas Welsh, land surveyor, for yearly rents and covenants, leases lot #2, part of tract called *Goose Cap,* now in Duterrow's possesseion, for term of 21 years. Lot contains 10 acres. Annual rent of £2, or dollars at 7 shillings, 6 pence each. Signed by both parties, and acknowledged before Jacob Young, Archibald Boyd. Hannah Welch, wife of Thomas, released right of dower.

W:462-464. Michael Shaneburger, cordwainer, recorded lease 23 Dec., 1775, from Thomas Welsh, land surveyor, for yearly rents and covenants, leases lot #3, part of tract called *Goose Cap,* for term of 21 years. Lot contains 10 acres. Annual rent of £2, or dollars at 7 shillings, 6 pence each. Signed by both parties, and acknowledged before Jacob Young, Archibald Boyd. Hannah Welch, wife of Thomas, released right of dower.

W:464-467. Phillip Nollert, baker, recorded lease 23 Dec., 1775, from Thomas Welsh, land surveyor, for yearly rents and covenants, leases lot #4, part of tract called *Goose Cap,* adjacent to Jacob Biser's part of tract, for term of 21 years. Lot contains 10 acres. Annual rent of £2, or dollars at 7 shillings, 6 pence each. Signed by both parties, and acknowledged before Jacob Young, Archibald Boyd. Hannah Welch, wife of Thomas, released right of dower.

W:467-470. Jacob Dutterow, weaver, recorded lease 23 Dec., 1775, from Thomas Welsh, land surveyor, for yearly rents and covenants, leases lot #5, part of tract called *Goose Cap,* for term of 21 years. Lot contains 8 acres. Annual rent of £2, or dollars at 7 shillings, 6 pence each. Signed by both parties, and acknowledged before Jacob Young, Archibald Boyd. Hannah Welch, wife of Thomas, released right of dower.

W:470-471. Thomas Morrow recorded deed 2 Jan. 1776 from John Beane. For £100 Continental money of United Provinces of North America, tract called *Hard Fortune,* beginning at Dry Spring on south side of Antietam, containing 50 acres. Signed by mark, and acknowledged before Upton Sheridine, Jacob Young.

W:471-472. Hugh Kennedy recorded bill of sale 2 Jan. 1776, from Richard Lowe, for £9..10, a bay horse between 12-13 hands high, 12 years old, a star on his forehead, a cow and yearling, with Henry Burris's mark, one old feather bed and rug, one dish, 6 plates, one good gun and iron pot, one Dutch oven and lid, onc good portmantua saddle. Signed before Jacob Young.

W:472-475. Cunningham Findley & Company, merchants of Glasgow, recorded mortgage from Joseph Willson for £176, tract called *Beall's Seat,* 100 acres, conveyed to Joseph Wilson by Nicholas Jackson, 21 Sept 1769, with all dwelling houses, out houses, fences, orchards, etc. Sale void if sum of £176..4..10, plus costs of recording and interest are paid by 30 October. Signed before David Lynn, Edward Burgess.

W:476-477. Joseph Gwynn recorded deed of trust 23 Jan. 1776 from Robert Bruce for 5 shillings, assigns Negro man Dick, and Negro boy Harry, to hold in trust for my brother Townly Bruce, to be conveyed after my death, should I die before my return from Boson in New England. Provided nevertheless, should I return safe from Boston then this present deed is null and void.

W:477-479. Archibald Orme recorded deed 23 Jan. 1776, from Samuel Boone for £47..5, tract called *Montrose,* and part of *Resurvey on Rich Meadow,* 31 ½ acres. Jean Boone, wife of Samuel examined apart and released dower rights.

W:479-482. Michael Rohr recorded deed 3 Feb. 1776, from Peter Jesserong, blacksmith, for £100 lot #24, in Middletown, to pay town proprietors annual rents of 7 shillings, 6 pence on 3 March every year. The wife of Peter Jesserang, examined apart, released dower.

W:482-484. Richard Sheckles recorded deed 3 Feb 1776, from Thomas Miles Roberts of Prince George's County, for £50, tract of land called *Stint,* on draught of Seneca Creek, laid out for 50 acres. Signed before Alex Symmes, Wm Loch Weems of Prince George's County. Wife released dower.

W:484-487. Richard Sheckles recorded deed 3 Feb 1776, from Thomas Miles Roberts of Prince George's County, for £250, tract called *Mount Pleasant,* beginning at tract called *Kent,* taken up by Jacob Meek, containing 262 acres.

W:487-488. Robert Wood recorded power of attorney, 12 Feb. 1776, from Sarah Shaw, relict of Joseph Ogle of Frederick County, deceased, appoints Robert Wood her attorney to act on her behalf to make deeds or lease 450 acres, and one Negro man Bob, granted to her during her natural life. Signed by mark.

W:489. Robert Wood recorded lease 12 Feb 1776, from Sarah Shaw, leases one Negro man Jacob, willed to her during her life. Signed by mark.

W:489-490. Thomas Powell recorded lease 15 Feb. 1776, from George Powell, leases lot #1 for 50 acres, of tract called *Hopewell,* to his brother Thomas Powell, for term of original lease, adj. To Martin Lidcher, about 20 yards from tract *Race Ground.*

W:490-493. Charles Beatty and Richard Lilley, recorded deed of trust, 16 Feb 1776, from Sarah Shaw, widow, for 5 shillings, sterling, all the lands, tenements in Frederick County, and delivers and assigns all Negroes, servants, black cattle, horses, hogs, sheep, plantation utensils and household furniture in trust, that he will sell same, except the dwelling plantation and lands where she now lives, being about 500 acres in which she has only a life estate. Signed by mark before Archibald Boyd, Thos Price.

W:493-495. William Deakins Jr recorded deed 18 Feb. 1776, from Richard Thomas for £60, part of *Thomas Discovery,* containing 20 acres.

W:495-496. Jacob Staley recorded bill of sale 20 Feb. 1776, from Philip Angleberger. In consideration that Jacob Staley and Peter Shaver, having passed their bond to Henry Shaver for £59, for my debt and for 5 shillings, sterling, I sell two brown mares, two leather collars with the harness and two pair of iron traces. Signed by mark before William Ritchie, and in German script, Henrich Schaeffer.

W:496-498. Philip Angleberger recorded release of mortgage 20 Feb. 1776, from Henry Shaver. Whereas by deed of mortgage 12 Dec. 1774, recorded in Liber BD1, folio 4, for £100, release signed in G.S. by Henrich Schaeffer, before Peter Schaeffer (G.S.) and Wm Ritchie.

W:499-500. John Gough recorded bill of sale 22 Feb. 1776 from Roger Gough for 5 shillings sterling, assigns one bay mare.

W:500-501. John Glassford & Co., merchants of Glasgow, recorded bill of sale 24 Feb. 1776, from Thomas Pearle, for £186..6..6, one Negro man named Jeffrey and one Negro girl, Jane; and one bright mare, about 6 years old. Signed by mark.

W:501-502. Wm Murdoch Beall recorded bill of sale 26 Feb 1776 from Thomas Aldridge, for £140. Assigns two Negroes, one a boy named Harry, about 14 years old, and a girl named Margery, about 11 years old. Signed before Archibald Boyd, Joseph Beall.

W:502-507. Zachariah Linthiucm recorded deed 27 Feb. 1776, from Walter Baker of Berkeley County, Virginia, for £830 Pennsylvania, tract of land called *Pigg Pen,* on Seneca Creek, 50 acres; 2nd, a tract called *Woolf Pitt,* adjacent to *Buck Bottom,* containing 50 acres; 3d, *Resurvey on Woolf Pitt and the Pigg Pen,* to beginning tree of tract called *Seneca Hills,* taken up by Col. Joseph Belt, containing 384 acres, including 1st and 2nd tracts. Also 4th tract called *Baker's Chance,* on south side of Seneca, 31 acres. Signed before David Lynn, Edward Burgess. Elizabeth Baker, wife of Walter Baker released dower.

W:507-508. Mathias Coones, shoemaker in Sharpsburgh, recorded bill of sale 27 Feb. 1776, from Thomas Morrow for £12..7, one brown mare, two cows; provided nevertheless that if he pays some with interest, sale is void.

W:508-511. John Glassford & Co., merchants of Glasgow, recorded mortgage 28 Feb 1776 from Simon Reeder for £235..12, tract called *Conclusion,* adjacent to 1st line of Richard Hoggin's part, and tract called *Pork and Potatoes,* 248 acres. Signed before Archibald Boyd, Thomas Bowles.

W:511-513. John Garrett recorded deed 4 March 1776 from Peter Kline, of red Stone, for £400, part of tract called *Brother's Good Will,* 200 acres. Catharine wife of Peter Cline released dower.

W:513-516. Joseph Ogle recorded bill of sale 14 March 1776 from Leonhard Campbell for £34..7..2 for one wagon and geers, two cows, one heifer and two bull cows, one chestnut sorrel mare, five hogs, five sheep, grind stone, chest of drawers, cross cut saw, pair still yards, one iron pot hook, two spinning wheels. If sum is paid with legal interest by 29 November, sale is void.

W:516-518. John Glassford & Co., merchants of Glasgow, recorded mortgage 20 March 1776 from Samuel Saffell for £33..6..3, part of parcel located in fork of Seneca, called *Fellowship,* for 100 acres; provided that if sum paid with interest before 1 August, sale is void.

W:518-519. William Cochran of York County, Pennsylvania, recorded bill of sale 20 March 1776 from John Troxall for £100 a Negro man named Will, about 26 years. Signed by mark before Wm Blair, Wm Shields.

W:519-522. Normand Bruce and Susanna Bruce his wife (daughter of Philip Key Esq., late of St. Mary's County) recorded deed of partition and release 21 March 1776, made 2 Oct. 1775 between John Ross Key of Frederick County, son and heir of Francis Key Esq., late of Cecil County, deceased. Whereas Philip Key died seized in fee of a tract called *Resurvey on Terra Rubra,* in Frederick County, which tract was devised by the will of Philip Key unto his son Francis Key, father of the said John Ross Key, and Susanna Bruce to be divided between them. Metes and bounds given for division of tract.

W:522-523 William Beckwith recorded 21 March 1776, from Leonard Belt and Rebecca his wife for £400, tract called *Dan,* beginning at 6th line of tract formerly conveyed to William Dent. Metes and bounds given for 191 acres, except for one piece out of above sold to Benjamin Gittings for 25 acres, and one piece sold to William Coxon for 25 acres; being conveyed to them by Rebecca Brooke. Signed Leonard Belt, Rebecca Belt, before David Lynn, Edward Burgess.

W:524-526. Leonard Belt recorded 21 March 1776, from William Beckwith and Lucy his wife, for £400, part of Dan, same tract as above with same exceptions.

W:526-528. John Daley recorded deed 24 March 1776 from Valentine Boroff of George Town, Frederick County, for £67..10 a lot #89 in Addition to Georgetown on the Potomac River, adjacent to lot made over to John Daly by Thomas Jennings, 15 Feb. 1774. Mary wife of Valentine Boroff released dower rights.

W:528-529. Simon Bowman and Henry Wiggle recorded bill of sale, as security for Peter Haute, to secure them, 21 March 1776. Peter Hanto, farmer, for £7 bound by writing obligatory for £7 to Yost Cline, assigns all the winter grain crop. Signed by mark, Peter Hout. Witness John Stull, Michael Ott.

W:530-533. George Bright recorded mortgage 21 March 1776 from Thomas Morrow for £80 tract called *Hard Fortune.* 50 acres.

W:533-536. William Offutt Magruder recorded deed 24 March 1776 from Joseph White Junr for £300 tract called *The Rich Land,* 250 acres. Signed before David Lynn, Edwd Burgess.

W:536-537. Negro Thomas Altow and Negro Jacob Bacon, discharged from service as of 22 March 1776. from Richard Richardson, manumission. Witnessed by Archibald Boyd, William Richardson.

W:538. Negro Nathaniel Matthews, received release from service 22 March 1776, from Wm Richardson, manumission - to be discharged on 20 November 1779, and may pass and repass as if born free. Witnessed by Archibald Boyd.

W:539-541. William Waters recorded deed 22 March 1776, from Robert Owens Jr for £35 land called *William and Mary,* 51 acres. Rebecca wife of Robert Owen released dower.

W:541-542. Thos Willson recorded bill of sale 26 March 1776 from George Jacob Smedley for £9 sells one yoke of oxen, one brindle, one black & white; one bay mare, two cows, one black & white, the other a red; and a young bull brindle colored; 11 ewes with their lambs, one plow, one stack of wheat, my lease, and all the wheat in the ground, and all my goods and chattels with the rye in the ground. Signed before Richard Wood, and in G.S., Michael Coop (?).

W:542-544. James Winders Jr. Recorded deed 26 March 1776, From Thomas Sims, for £2 lot #84 in Jerusalemtown

W:544-547. Daniel Stutsman recorded deed 29 March 1776, from Jacob Stutsman for £10. Part of *Middle Choice.* 3 acres. Wife of Jacob Stutsman, not named, examined apart released dower rights.

W:547 -549. Henry Prince recorded deed 2 April 1776, from Goodheart Tressler for £30 tract called *The Three Springs.* 50 acres. Signed by mark before John Stull, H. Bowles. Catherine, wife of Goodheart Tressler, willingly relinquished her right of dower.

W:549-551. Denton Jacques late of the City of Annapolis, but now of Frederick County, iron master, recorded deed 4 April 1776, from Col. Thomas Cresap of Frederick County, for £175 parts of *Chance* and *Resurvey on Chance,* containing 323 acres.

W:551-552. [marginal note: Doctor John Shortt the present holder, 25 June 1795] Mary and John Kelly recorded release 4 April 1776. Whereas Mary and John Kelley died on 22 August 1771 lease for term of 500 years; and in consideration of £52..11..7, do sell and assign for the term aforesaid, provided they do not pay the aforesaid sum, with other conditions in lease mentioned, and since the lease was obtained a certain Thomas Simms of Hagers Town, did purchase the aforesaid land, and paid me £67.. I James Verdein of Bartley County, Colony of Virginia have released them. Signed in presence of Moses Chaplin, John Rutherford, Jno W. Ferguson.

W:552-555. Henry Wickham recorded 4 April 1776, from Samuel, John and Thos. Snowden of Prince Georges and Ann Arundel Counties, for valuable considerations made by a certain Nathaniel Wickham, and the further sum of 5 shillings, signed before Basil Burgess, H. Ridgely.

W:555-558. Valentine Morten (Felty Morton) recorded deed 4 April 1776 from Martin Keplinger, for £400 two tracts, *Non Such,* and *Philadelphia.* Elizabeth, wife of Martin Keplinger released dower.

W:558-559. Thomas Simms recorded deed 4 April 1776 from Mary Kelly and John Kelly of Frederick County for £190 tract called *Dry Fountain,*

W:561-563. James Ford recorded deed 4 April 1776, from Thomas Ford for £52 part of *Rocky Neck,* excluding al iron ore and metallic stones on the said 100 acres, reserved in deed unto Thomas Johnson Junr., Lancelot Jacques and Denton Jacques, 23 March 1775.

W:563-566. Philip Crouse, blacksmith of FC, recorded deed 4 April 1774, made between Jacob Crouse of Philadelphia County, Pennsylvania. Whereas Jacob Crouse, as heir at law of his deceased brothers Wendle Crouse and Frederick Crouse, became seized in fee of two sundry tracts, part of *Addition to Brooks Discovery on the Rich Lands,* conveyed unto them by a certain Andrew Park and Abraham Hayter, 3 April 1767, for £172.10 paid to Jacob Crouse he releases his rights. Cristenah Crouse wife of Jacob released dower rights. Witnesses: Wm Beatty, Wm Blair.

W:567-570. Joshua Hobbs recorded deed 4 April 1776 from Joseph Hobbs for £215, tract *I Have Got it All,* Ann, wife of Joseph Hobbs released dower rights.

W:570-572. Peter Myers recorded deed 4 April 1776, from John Kinzey for part of *Jacob's Pasture,* 1 1/4 acres. Wife acknowledged dower release. Amount left blank, lawful money of Pennsylvania.

W:572-574. John Kinzey recorded deed 4 April 1776, from Jacob Myers for £38 Pennsylvania, tract *Kinzey's Neglect,* adjacent to *Michael's Fancy,* 21 ½ acres.

W:574-577. Jacob Shearman recorded deed 4 April 1776, from Henry Alspaugh for £150. Lots #22 & #23, in Westminstertown, adjacent to tract called *White's Levels.* Signed before Upton Sheridine. Mary Alsbough released dower.

W:578-580. Jacob Shearman of York County, Pennsylvania, recorded deed 4 April 1776, from Henry Alspaugh for £50, and the payment of rents and covenants, lot #49 in town of New London on northwest side of Main St., part of *Timber Ridge.* Signed German Script. Mary, released dower.

W:580-583. Griffin Willett of Prince George's County, recorded deed 4 April 1776, from John Villars Pollixen, made 23 Dec. 1775, for £167, tract called *Gore's Adventure Resurveyed,* for 50 acres. Mary, wife of John Villars Pollixen released dower right.

W:583-586. Jacob Gardner recorded deed 4 April 1776 from Peter Jesserong, blacksmith, for £3, part of *Resurvey on Chevy Chase,* on north side of Great Road that leads from Frederick Town to Middle Town, adjacent to *Smithfield,* 56 perches. Wife of Peter (not named) released dower right.

W:586-591. Michael Fackler of Elizabethtown, tavern keeper, recorded deed 4 April 1776, made 24 Feb. 1776, from Jacob Rohrer, for £30 Pennsylvania, sells part of *Resurvey on Hager's Fancy,* and part of *Square,* conveyed by John Rohrer, heir at law of his father Jacob Rohrer, Senr. Signed before Upton Sheridine, Eleanor Sheridine. Christiana Rohrer released dower rights.

W:591-593. Thomas Price recorded deed 4 April 1776, from Thomas Johnson Jr. For £50 tract called *Chestnut Level,* for 300 acres. Signed before Archibald Boyd, Jacob Young. Anne wife of Thomas Johnson, Jr., released dower.

W:593-595. Abraham and Phyllis recorded manumission 6 April 1776, from Israel Thompson. Releases from service, Abraham, age 28 years and Phyllis about 26 years old. Also two female children, Rachel to be free in 1787 and Susy to be free in 1793. For performance of manumission, he gives his bond for £500.

W:595-596. Thomas Contee and John Hanson recorded bill of sale 6 April 1776, from Ignatius Hagan, sells Negro boy named Ben. Signed before Basil Roberts.

W:596-597. Jacob Shaver recorded bill of sale 13 April 1776, from Augustus Leaphart for £100, four milk cows, one steer, one heifer, wagon, plough and iron harrow. Signed in German script before Philip Schmidt, and Henrich Slicer (also GS).

W:597 Richard Sheckles recorded deed 24 April 1776, from Wm Murdock of Prince George's County, merchant, for £246, tract called *Hamburgh,* adjacent to tract, *Snowden's Mill Land,* 3 3/4 acres. Signed before Wm Blair, Edwd Burgess.

W:599-603. [Colonel] James Johnson recorded deed 24 April 1776 from Peter Copeland of Frederick County, farmer, for £600 sells tracts called *Copeland,* 200 acres and *Stoney Bottom,* 30 acres; and *Dear Lane,* 10 ½ acres. Signed by mark by both parties. Witnesses Samuel Wheeler, B. Johnson. Elizabeth, wife of Peter Copeland released dower before Wm Beatty, George Smith.

W:603-604. Wm Molleson of London, merchant, recorded bill of sale 3 May 1776 from Nathaniel Harris for £69..6 one Negro man named Freeman, and one Negro girl named Cloe. Signed before Alex Contee. Receipt. Witnessed by Robert Peter, Justice of the Peace.

W:604-607. Thomas Veatch recorded deed 6 May 1776 from James Gatton for £4..13, part of tract, *Gatton's Good luck,* beginning at end of tract, *Poplar Spring.* Metes and bounds for 23 1/4 acres. Signed before George Scott, Jacob Young. Alienation fine paid Wm Murdock Beall.

W:607-609. Andrew Fleckinger recorded deed 6 May 1776 from George Poe for £100, part of *The Forrest,* 100 acres. Katherine, wife of George released dower.

W:609-611. Peter Cellers recorded deed 6 May 1776, from Jacob Miller for 5 shillings, 27 3/4 acres of *Resurvey on Miller's Chance,* in two parcels, metes and bounds given for 20 ½ acres and 7 1/4 acre parts. Signed before Jacob Young, Wm Beatty. Barbara Miller released dower.

W:612-616. Jacob Hoover and Jacob Harbough recorded mortgage 7 May 1776 from Valentine Shockey for £220, and agreements made herein, tract *Third Resurvey on Sarah's Delight,* for 200 acres. Signed by all three parties.

W:616-618. Ludwick Young recorded deed 9 May 1776, from Adam Troup for £200, lot #43 in Elizabethtown. Catherine Troup released dower.

W:618-621. Anthony Lindsey recorded deed 13 May 1776, from Henry Griffith Dorsey for £450, part of *England's Chance,* to Mathias Stalcup's land, 171 acres. Signed before Upton Sheridine, Joseph Wells. Martha Dorsey released dower.

W:621-625. Adam Ridenour, Junr., John Ridenour, Henry Ridenour and Barnet Ridenhour recorded deed 15 May 1776 from John Haas of Frederick Town, for £180, tract called *Resurvey on Den of Woolf,* for 200 acres. Barbara Haas released dower.

W:625-627. [Marginal note: Examined & delivered Samuel Patterson, 8 April 1783] William Patterson recorded deed 23 May 1776 from Robert Beaty of Frederick County, for £260, sells and assigns parcel, part of *Resurvey on the Pines,* and *Addition to the Pines,* Signed Robert Beaty, before Jacob Young, George Scott. Receipt. Esther, wife of Robert Beaty released dower.

W:627-630. Philip Rodenpiller recorded deed 24 May 1776, from Peter Bright, son and heir of Peter Bregh, late of Frederick County, deceased, for £30, tract called *Lost Bottle,* on south side of hill a quarter of a mile from Philip Bootman's, near the foot of Blue Ridge. 52 acres. Signed, German script before Archibald Boyd, Thos Price.

W:630-632. Phillip Hocker recorded deed 1 June 1776, from James Miller for £35..4..4.. and half penny currency, part of tract called *New Holland,* and part of *Spite Overcome,* 20 1/8 acres. Signed before Christopher Lowndes, Rd Henderson.

W:633-634. Richard Lilley, recorded bill of sale 1 June 1776, from John Collins 8 acres of winter grain, consisting of wheat and rye, growing on the plantation belonging to Christian Stouder, but in the occupation of the said John Collins, one black cow and calf, 10 barrels of flour, one sandy colored sow and six shoats, one pair of iron traces, two pair of harnes, one collar, one set of plow irons and swingle trees, one bed and furniture, one walnut chest, one walnut table, half dozen pewter plates, one pewter dish, one pewter basin, two iron pots, one frying pan, one washing tub, one powdering tub, one hand saw, one drawing knife, two blind bridles. Signed before Upton Sheridine.

W:634-637. William Fout recorded deed 3 June 1774 from John Patterson, for £680 part of *Resurvey on Diggs Lot,* 171 acres. Also tract *Martin's Intent,* on the north side of Toms Creek, that runs into Monocacy, 33 acres. Signed by mark before Jacob Young, George Scott. Margaret Patterson released dower right.

W:637-340. John Lawrence recorded deed 3 June 1776 from Thomas Mullineaux of Anne Arundel County, in consideration of John Mollineaux bond payable to John Dorsey son of John, the said bond being assigned to John Summers, and 5 shillings, assigns tract, *Mullineaux Chance,* 100 acres, in Frederick County. Signed by mark before Edward Burgess, Joseph Wells. Elizabeth Mullineaux released dower.

W:640-644. Thomas Neil, merchant, recorded deed 6 June 1776, from Charles Beatty for £1350 for tract called *Three Partners,* 385 acres. Martha Beatty released dower.

W:644-647. Thomas Neil recorded deed 6 June 1776, from Thomas Johnson Junr., attorney at law, for £1300, tracts *Resurvey on Wild Cat Hill,* 319 acres; and the *Meadows,* 462 acres; and tract called *Convenience,* 219 acres. Ann wife of Thomas Johnson Junr released dower.

W:647-650. Joseph Hobbs recorded deed 6 June 1776, from Charles Carroll for £236..2..6, part of tract called *The Fifth Dividend,* beginning at 5th line of tract *Nothing Venture, Nothing Git,* for 211 acres. Signed before Daniel of St. Thos Jennifer.

W:650-652. Orshe Miller, widow, recorded deed 6 June 1776, from Lawrence Delauter for £33, tract called *Quarrel Hill,* on east side of Mill Run, containing 15 acres. Barbara Delauter released dower.

W:653-655. Mathias Crow recorded deed 6 June 1776 from Peter Hammond for £412 part of *Culloden,* containing 100 acres. Signed in German script, before Saml Beall Junr., John Stull. Sevilla Hammond released dower.

W:656-658. Michael Hibner (Havener) recorded deed 6 June 1776, from George Hivaner, for £150 tract called *Castle Finn,* on Little Pipe Creek, containing 112 acres. Rachel Hivaner released dower.

W:658-661. Henry Landis recorded deed 18 June 1776 from Christian Haas for £965, part of *The Level Glade,* on Little Pipe Creek, and a *Resurvey on the Deeps,* and also part of *Leonard's Range,* in a deed from Abraham Welty to Christian Haas recorded in Liber U:260, together with all buildings, merchant mills, grist mills, saw mills, orchards, gardens and meadows. Signed before Wm Beatty, Upton Sheridine. Margaret Haas released dower rights.

W:662-665. Alexander Warfield recorded deed 18 June 1776 from Francis Simpson of Ann Arundel county, for £200 sterling, part of *Resurvey on Spring Garden* beginning at tract called *Harveys Burrow*, to William Carmack's land, to 18th line of *Resurvey on Winfield's Delight,* metes and bounds for 246 acres. Signed before Caleb Burgess, Nathaniel Ross

W:665-667. [Marginal note: examined and delivered Upton Beall Esq., executor of Grantee, the 17th May 1799] Brooke Beall recorded deed f19 June 1776, from Richard Beall of Samuel, for 10 shillings, tract called *New England Toddy,* 100 acres. Signed before Caleb Burgess, Nathl Ross.

W:667-668. Henry Riddell of Prince George's county, recorded bill of sale 20 June 1776 from William Ridgeway for £36..4..6, one Negro lad called Christopher, about 17 years old. Signed before Robert Peter.

W:668-670. George J. Baltzell, taylor, recorded deed 26 June 1776 from Jacob Baltzell for £14, one half lot #133 in Frederick Town.

W:671-674. George Zimmerman recorded deed 26 June 1776, from Thomas Price of Frederick Town, for £150 sells parcel called *Resurvey on Chestnut Hill,* containing 166 ½ acres by estimation. Mary Price, wife of Thomas Price released dower.

W:674-676. Ogles Heirs bond. At the request of the heirs of Joseph Ogle, the following bond was recorded 26 June 1776. To wit: we, the heirs of Joseph Ogle late of Frederick County, deceased, viz; Guy Elder and Eleanor his wife, Joseph Ogle, Benjamin Ogle, Thomas Ogle, William Ogle, James Ogle and the heirs or representatives of Sarah Ogle, late of Cecil County, and province aforesaid, and one of the heirs of the said Joseph Ogle deceased, are held and firmly bound unto each other in the full sum of £2000 sterling, Whereas Sarah Shaw, executrix of Joseph Ogle late of Frederick County, deceased, has appointed Charles Beatty and Richard Lilley her trustees, by a deed of trust, who are to make a final end of all legacies given, Heirs above signed agreement, along with Thomas Ogle, guardian for the heirs of Sarah Ogle, deceased.

W:676-677. Ogles Heirs bond. Same heirs as above. Except Thomas Ogle listed as child, and James Ogle, signed for the heirs of Sarah Ogle, deceased.

W:677-679. Elizabeth Jewell recorded deed of gift 27 June 1776 from Betty Jewell, widow of Moses Jewell, for 5 shillings and natural love and affection for her daughter, Elizabeth Jewell, daughter of Moses Jewell, a mullato slave named Ross.

W:679-680. Jacob Baltzell recorded release 27 June 1776 from Peter Baltzell, acknowledges I have received full satisfaction for mortgage dated 4 May 1768, for £30 Pennsylvania. Signed before Jacob Young, Geo Scott.

W:680-684. Peter Myers of Loudoun County, Virginia, recorded deed 28 June 1776, from Valentine Myers for £150 for part of tract known as *Resurvey on Black Oak Hill,* for 75 acres, originally granted to Peter Myers by the said Valentine Myers, on 23 January 1758 recorded in Liber F:375-375, this corrects the 3d line, set down wrong, it now being resurveyed, on 8th line of tract called *Friendship.* Signed before David Lynn, Edward Burgess. Martha, wife of Valentine Myers released dower.

W:684-687. Peter Myers of Frederick County, recorded deed 28 June 1776, from Simon Miller of Berkeley County, Virginia, for £30 all his interest in tract known as *Resurvey on Hard Grubbing,* containing 50 acres. Phrany, wife of Simon Miller released dower rights.

END OF DEEDS IN LIBER W

Followed by two blank pages. And then written from back page, 20 pages of the recordings of the Court.

The rear section of Liber W contains the Court Minutes from November 1771. On the Archives Web site, the pagination for this section is 2a-3a-4a, etc. So that when reading deeds on line, if you go to the next page, you will be going back and forth between the land records and the court records.

Page 1. November Term 1771.

Frederick County, Anno Domino 1771. At a county court held at Frederick, on 3d Tuesday of November, being the 19th day, present the Worshipfull: Joseph Wood, Thomas Price, Eanes Campbell, William Luckett, Andrew Heugh, Charles Jones, William Blair, David Lynn, Evan Shelby, Samuel Beall gentleman Justices by his Lordships Commission, for the county aforesaid. Normand Bruce, Esq., Sheriff and Thomas Sprigg, Clerk.

The Sheriff called upon to return his panel of grand jurors, Returns the same out of which the following persons was impaneled, to wit: John Lackland, Stephen Ramsburgh, John Shelman, Basil Beall, Henry Clarke, William Smith Greenfield, Richard Ancrum, William Campbell, Stephen Julian, James Riggs, Thomas Summers, Simon Meredith, John Carmack, John McElfresh, Philip Boyer, Abraham Leakins.

2a.-3a. Being duly summoned and sworn, return to consider and soon after return and present to the court the following presentments, to wit:

We the grand Inquest for the Body of Frederick County do present:

Ann Norris, daughter of William for bearing a base born child of her body contrary to the act of Assembly that case made and provided by the information of Joseph N. Chiswell. William Duvall for beating John Field. James Marshall for assaulting Jacob Hartley. Thos Swearingen for not giving in a taxable to constable. Wm Pearl, son of Daniel for begetting a baseborn child on Susanna Burges. Benjamin Sapp for signing William Duvall's name to an order. Amos Nicholas for begetting child on Hannah Phillips. 3a. Delasmutt Wallin for beating Michael McGraw. Elias Harding for not giving in a taxable by information of Leonard Davis. Nichols for striking Michael Murphey. George Kirkpatrick for beating Michael McGraw. Michael Hafner for not giving in a taxable. Each signed by John Lackland, foreman. Bills of indictment against William Hughes, John Hendrick, Jacob Fleck. Also ordered Paul Hoy of Upper Part Newfoundland Hundred and John Blair constable of Conococheague Hundred to show cause why they did not turn in lists of taxables this present year.

4a. Ordered by the court that summons issue returnable immediately for George Yost to answer the complaint of Nathaniel Tomlinson.

Daniel Regan filed account for payment from county for making one pensioners coffin. Ordered that summons issue for Benjamin Griffin and Rachel his wife, formerly wife of John Gartrell and executor of his estate, to counter secure Samuel Israel Godman and Richard Gartrell who were sureties in testamentary bond.

Lord Proprietary against Edward Garrott, for concealing taxable, and now 3rd Tuesday 19 Nov., in his proper person submits himself to the grace of the Court. Ordered to pay. Middleton Garrett presents himself as Security.

5a. Lord Proprietary against William O'Neale £20, Lawrence O'Neal £10. Security for appearance at next court to answer what shall then be objected against him on behalf of the Lord Proprietary.

Lord Proprietary against William O'Neale £20. Security for appearance at next court to answer what shall then be objected against him on behalf of the Lord Proprietary.

6a. Lord Proprietary against Samuel Cookson, John Cookson £40 and Simon Meredith. £40 that said Samuel Cookson should not keep a sufficient house of entertainment in Winchester Town.

On oath of Jacob Ramsburg, it is ordered by the court here that bench warrant issue against James Miller, Christian Booker and Rudolf Rohrer to answer on not obeying legal process returnable to next court.

Lord Proprietary against Jacob Ramsburg £20, Lucas Flack £20, and appear in court here, acknowledge themselves to stand justly indebted in sums above for personal appearance at next court to testify against Isaac Miller, Christian Booker and Rudolf Rohrer on bench warrant.

On oath of Gillan Strider, ordered by court that bench warrant issue for William Chapline to answer on not obeying Legal process returnable to next court.

7a. Lord Proprietary against Gillion Strider £20, George Wales, £20. Bond to appear in next court as witness.

Lord Proprietary against Edmund Rutter, £40, James Patterson £20, Thomas Winders, £40. Bond on condition that Edmund Rutter should not keep a sufficient house of entertainment according to act of Assembly.

8a. Lord Proprietary against James Mackall, presented for assaulting Wm Taney, and now at this day to court, in his property person, submits himself to the court under protestation of Innocency, Whereupon all and singular being fully understood by the court, it is ordered here that James Mackall be discharged on paying the several officers fees. Thereupon Thomas Richardson became security for the fees.

Lord Proprietary against James Williams, presented for assaulting Edmund Rutter, submits to court under protestation of Innocency. Thereupon the premises by the court here is fully understood, it is ordered that James Williams be fined one shilling and give security for officers fees. Thereupon John Walling became security.

8a-9a. Lord Proprietary against Benjamin Bright, for assaulting Wm Evans Benjamin Bright fined 4 shillings and fees. William Row, became Security.

9a. Lord Proprietary against Jacob Danner, presented for ?. Fined 500 lbs. Tobacco and fees. Robert Wood became security.

Lord Proprietary against George Poe, presented for bastardizing. Fined 30 shillings, and to give security for several officers fees and to keep the child from becoming a charge to the county. Thereupon Isaac Miller became Security.

10a. Lord Proprietary against William Hughes, indicted for assaulting Elizabeth Hughes. William Hughes on the 8th July 1771, with force and arms set forth at Frederick County and within the jurisdiction of this court, an assault on a certain Elizabeth Hughes and make and here then and there beat, wound and treat so that her life was despaired of and other harms is here, then and there did to the great damage of the said Elizabeth and against the peace of the said Lord proprietary his good rule and government. Thomas Jennings, atty genl. True Bill, John Lackland foreman. And the said William Hughes being called appears at the bar of the court here and under the custody of the sheriff of Frederick County – he saith Murphy. he is not in any wise guilty thereof, and for tryal thereof he puts himself upon the court. Jury called, to wit: William Fee, foreman, Isaac Cooper, Mathias and Thomas Fee, Alexander Magruder, John Hopkins, William O'Neale, Charles Jones, Jacob Harman, Conrad Dutterer, John Nels, Arthur Nelson, called and sworn. They found William Hughes guilty. Fined £20. To be kept in close gaol for full term of 12 months, and at the expiration of said term, to enter security for £100 for good behaviour.

11a. Indentures, James Furney aged 14 years, 10 March bound to Matthias Need Junr. by court to age 21 to become farmer. David Furney aged 12 years & 9 months is bound to Henry Shriock, saddler. David Rodgers presented for assault against David Ramsey and three others. 20th November of his Lordship's Dominion. William McClary became security.

12a. Mary Moore, spinster, indicted for stealing, 10 Nov. 1771, of goods and chattels of Thomas Swearingen. Jury called, William Lee, foreman, Isaac Cooper, Matthias Need, Thomas Lee, Alexander Magruder, John Hopkins, William O'Neale, Charles Jones, Jacob Harman, Conrad Duttero, John Hobbs, Arthur Nelson. Verdict, guilty. 13a. Sentence, 5 lashes on bare back. To stand in pillory for 2 minutes.

13a. Abraham Weyart (Reighart) presented for assaulting Mary Wise, placed himself on grace of court. Fined 5 shillings, and required to give security for good behaviour. Michael Shusel became security.

14a. Presented Elias Delashmutt for assaulting Thomas Wells, put himself on grace of court, fined 5 shillings, and gave William Luckett for his security. John Crosier, John Stull and James Verdere, bonded £50 each for keeping a public house of entertainment.

14a-15a. Jacob Flack indicted for stealing. Grand jury says that with force and arms took one snuff box of the value of 20 pounds of tobacco, of the goods and chattels of a certain John Keller; in the custody of the sheriff, a jury was called William Fee foreman, Alexander Magruder, John Cooper, Mathias Need, Thomas Fee, Alexander Magruder, John Hopkins, William O'Neale, Charles Jones,

Jacob Havener, Conrad Duterer, John Hobbs, Arthur Nelson, found not guilty. Jacob Flack gave security for officer's fees by John Brawner.

16a. William Thomas presented for assault, fined 5 shillings, William Luckett became security. Amos Nicholls presented for bastardy, fined 30 shillings, gave security for several officer's fees and to keep child off county. John Casner became security. Conrad Duttero, Philip Boyer and John Carmack bonded for keeping a public house of entertainment.

17a. James Hackman presented commission as High Sheriff of Frederick County. George Allen, age 17, bound to John Unsell to age 21 to learn trade of blacksmith. Michael Runner presented for assaulting Basil Beall, fined one shilling, gave security for several officers fees in William Luckett.

18a. Elias Delashmutt bound in sum of £100 to testify against Daniel Davis. George Kirkpatrick presented for assaulting Michael Magraw. Fined one shilling, Edmond Rutter became security. 18a-19a. Simon Nicholls presented for assaulting Michael Murphey, fined one shilling, Clement Beall became security.

19a. Casper Shaaf bound for £100 to appear in case of Daniel Davis. Charles Hungerford £40, Eanes Campbell £40 and Simon Nicholls £40 for Charles Hungerford keeping a sufficient house of entertainment.

20a. Patrick Breslin petitions the court the following, to wit: humbly showeth that your petitioner being bound to Ignatius Simms by the court for the term of three years and two months, during which time and service was obliged to give your petitioner schooling in the winter time for the said term of three years, and the said Simms has not given your petitioner schooling nor will not yet give him any hopes that your worships will take his case into your consideration as he has neither father nor mother alive nor any friends in this place to see him any justice, and your petitioner duty bound will ever pray .... Upon reading which petition it is ordered that the same be rejected and the Mater pay the fees. James Magrath petitions the court the following.

Recordings abruptly end.

END of LIBER W

Frederick County Deeds, Liber BD1

BD1:1-2. Daniel Dingle recorded deed 1 Dec. 1774 from Mordecai Bean, for 7 shillings lot #169 in Jerusalemtown. Judea wife of Mordecai released dower. [No alienation fines recorded.]

BD1:2-4 James Delaplaine recorded deed 15 Dec. 1774 from James Duley Jr., tract *Duley's Chance,* 34 acres, adjacent to *Reeds Delight.* Signed mark. Elizabeth Duley released dower. Acknowledged before Charles Jones, Andrew Heugh.

BD1:4-6. Henry Shaver recorded mortgage 15 Dec. 1774 from Philip Angleberry, tract called *Whimpenny,* containing 6 acres.

BD1:6 Delitha Taylor, wife of John Taylor, recorded bill of sale 22 Dec. 1774, from Margaret Hickman, widow of Joshua Hickman, confirming gift made to her in 1772, as Delitha Hickman. Signed by mark, before Wm Luckett, Thos Cramphin.

BD1:7-8. Elihu Hickman recorded deed 22 Dec. 1774 from Margaret Hickman, widow of Joshua Hickman, in consideration of natural love and affection and 5 shillings, gives to him tract called *John's Delight,* containing 200 acres. Signed by mark before Wm Luckett, Thos Cramphin.

BD1:9 Michael Eichelberger recorded bill of sale 22 Dec. 1774, from Michael Collier for £26..10, two cows, two heifers, one young black mare. Signed before Joseph Smith, Margaret Reynolds.

BD1:10-11. Archibald Allen recorded deed 19 Dec. 1774, from Edmond Riggs for £45, tract called *John's Delight,* also known as *Green Briar,* signed by mark before Thos Warring, Wm Luckett. Nancy, wife of Edmond Riggs released dower.

BD1:11-12. Valentine Creager, blacksmith, recorded bill of sale 10 Jan. 1775 from Rinehart Waltz, stone mason, for £18..8, roan sorrel horse and one black horse. Signed before Wm Albaugh, Upton Sheridine.

BD1:12. Conrad Doll recorded bill of sale 11 Jan. 1775 from Abraham Patton of Baltimore, County, for £25, one Negro man, Sam, about 23 years old.

BD1:13-14. Mareen Howard Duvall of Prince George's County, recorded bill of sale 23 Jan. 1775 from Cornelius Duvall of Frederick County. Whereas Mareen Howard Duvall has become security in several bonds in Prince George's County, to Francis Bird, Singleton Wootton and John Sprigg, he assigns goods and chattels, Negro boy Toby, and Negro girls Jenny and Flora, together with livestock, horses, cattle and hogs. Signed before Thos Price, Michael Boyer.

BD1:14-15. John Shaver Jr., recorded bill of sale from John Shaver, Sr., for love and affection he has for his son, he assigns one dunn gelding, one cow and calf, two hogs, wagon, gears and plough, one harness. Signed German script, before John Kuhn, George Strickler.

BD1:15-16. John Hoffman recorded bill of sale 26 Nov. 1775 from Thomas Templin, for £7..15, one cow. Signed before Peter Burrel, and Andrew Erfer ? In German Script.

BD1:16-18. Jacob Warrenfeltz recorded deed 15 Jan. 1775 from Joseph Smith for £50 Pennsylvania, tract called *Joseph's Heritage* on a dry run on a road that leads from Fort Frederick to Fort Loudoun, 50 acres. Signed GS before Wm Baird, John Stull. Wife of Joseph Smith (not named) released dower.

BD1:19-21. William Molleson recorded mortgage 16 Dec. 1774 from Benjamin Notley Pearce, indebted to William Molleson of London, merchant, for £64..13..6, to Molleson's store in Georgetown, sells lot #28 in Georgetown, if sum paid by 1 June 1776, then sale is void. Signed before Robert Peter, Adam Stewart.

BD1:22-23. Andrew Maze recorded deed 14 Jan. 1775, from Allen Killough for £11..2, *Resurvey on part of Three Cuzins,* and the *Sixth Addition,* 50 acres.

BD1:24-25. Charles Beatty recorded deed 14 Jan. 1775, from Caleb Dorsey, son of John of Anne Arundel County, for £70, tract originally granted him as *Dorsey's Discovery,* in 1762. Signed before Elijah Robertson, Thomas Hammond.

BD1:25-27. Ludwick Hewett recorded deed 16 Jan. 1775 from Jacob Miller for £83, two tracts, on 6th line of *Stony Run,* 57 acres, and 36 acres. Anna Maria Miller released dower.

BD1:28-30 Melchior Beltshover of Elizabeth Town, recorded deed 14 Jan. 1775 from Jacob Rohrer for £51, on northwest side of Elizabeth Town, whereon Jacob Rhorer was living, opposite to six lots sold to Frederick Linthincum, called *Addition to Elizabethtown.* Christian Rhorer released dower rights.

BD1:31-32. Jacob Rise Jr. Recorded deed 14 Jan. 1775 from Jacob Rise Sr. For £400, tract *Jacob's Well,* wife not named, relinquished dower.

BD1:32-33. Wm Renneman recorded deed 14 Jan. 1775 from John Christ Renneman, of Manheim Twp., York County, Pennsylvania, son and heir of Christ Reineman late of Frederick County, deceased for £40, tract called *Hafer Seat.* Ursilla, wife of Christ Rineman released dower.

BD1:34-37. Mathias Sailer recorded deed 15 Jan. 1775 from Henry Funk for £50, part of *Renler's Delight,* part of *Resurvey on Locust Bottom.* Susannah Funk released dower.

BD1:38-40. John Linganfelter recorded deed 14 Jan. 1775 from Jacob Lease and Mary Dorothea his wife, and William Lease and Catharine his wife, £6, for lot #38 in Frederick Town, conveyed to John Linganfelter by Daniel Davis, deceased.

BD1:40-46. George Gallaspies recorded deed 14 Jan. 1775 from John Barnett for £1600, part of *Resurvey on the Three Friends,* 176 acres, and second part, 5 acres, and tract *Struggle.* Signed John Bonnett.

BD1:46-49. Jacob Martin recorded deed 4 Jan. 1774 [sic] from John Ingram and Elizabeth Clark, executors of Matthew Clark, for £1650 Pennsylvania, *Resurvey on Discontent,* 417 acres.

BD1:49-51. Jacob Burton recorded deed 14 Jan 1775 from Gerard Hopkins Junr. of Anne Arundel County, for 5 shillings, assigns 59 acres, adjacent to tract sold to Alexander Perry, called *None Left.*

BD1:51-55. Henry Crowl and Joseph Boiler, recorded deed 14 Jan. 1775 from John Beckleheimer, reed maker, for £525, part of *Resurvey on Good Neighborhood,* on Israel Creek, containing 227 acres, reserving for himself the right to bring hay of said Belehimer's meadow through Crowl and Boiler's meadow, provided he do not damage. Signed G.S. John Pecklehimer acknowledged deed, and Anna his wife released dower.

BD1:55-57. Jacob Kreps recorded deed 14 Jan. 1775 from Sebastian Mark for £182, tract *Polten's Seal,* on Antietam on third line of *Pile's Grove,* 27 3/4 acres. Magdalene, wife of Sebastian released dower.

BD1:57-59. Henry & Christian Newcomer recorded bond 14 Jan. 1775, from Michael Cyster for £200, to be paid, condition that as long as Cyster is in possession of land bought of James Patterson, lying near South Mountain, known as *Short Hill,* not to remove any timber on the within mentioned land. Signed German script.

BD1:59-62. John Barnett recorded deed 14 Jan. 1775 from John Ulrich [Little]. Whereas by indenture of bargain and sale made 28 August 1772, recorded I Liber T:302-303, assigned tract called *Struggle* being a resurvey on tract, *The Three Friends,* for 176 acres, for 5 shillings. Signed G.S., Johannes Ulrig, before John Stull, Wm Baird. Catherine Ulrich released dower right.

BD1:62-64. Henry Funk recorded deed 14 January 1775, from Mathew Saler for £150, *Rentche's Delight,* part of *Locust Bottom,* beginning at the 7th line of William Baker's part, containing 102 acres. Signed by mark. Modline Saler released dower.

BD1:65-67. Barton Duley recorded deed 14 Jan. 1775, from Doctor James Doull for £40, tract *Hunting Park,* beginning at 5th line of tract *James' Park,* for 50 acres; and another parcel called *Twenty Acre Island,* on island opposite to *Doull's Discovery*, in the Potomac River, and an additional 15 acres, 85 acres in all. Signed before Adam Stewart, Wm Deakins.

BD1:68. Jacob Smith recorded deed of gift 20 March 1775. I George Smith in consideration of the good will, love and affection for my son, give tract called *Make Shift,* containing 150 acres where he now lives. Signed in G.S. before Thos Price, Wm Beatty.

BD1:68-69. Samuel Phillips recorded deed 30 Jan. 1775, from John Cowman of Anne Arundel County, for £100, assigns tracts *Catch as Catch Can, He that Gets the Land is the Best Man*; on east side of Kitoctin Creek, containing 200 acres. Signed before Richard Harwood Jr., W. Watkins Jr. Sarah, wife of John Cowman released dower.

BD1:70-71. Tobias Rudicell recorded deed 14 Jan. 1775, from Raphael Taney of Saint Mary's County, for £6 assigns part of *Resurvey on Brother's Agreement,* beginning at line conveyed to Mark Alexander. Ellen Taney released dower.

BD1:71-73. John Melton of Saint Mary's County, recorded deed 14 Jan. 1775, from Richard Butler for £40 tract called *Mountain Lot,* near one of the head springs of Kittoctin Creek, 100 acres. Signed before Joseph Wood, Jos Ogle.

BD1:73-75. Jacob Baltzell recorded deed 25 Jan. 1775, made 21 Jan., from Hugh Larkin, son and heir of John Larkin late of Frederick County, for £42..16 sells tract called *Larkin's Lot,* originally granted John Larkins, 10 Aug. 1753, at foot of Kitoctin Mountain on the west side of a draught of Tuscarora, 45 acres. Signed before Thos Price, Wm Beatty. Sarah Larkin, wife, released dower.

BD1:75-76. James Downey recorded deed 25 Jan. 1775, from William Downey. Whereas on 12 July 1755, William made over to James, tract called *Walnut Point,* recorded in Liber E:784-785, and a mistake was made in the metes and bounds, this deed makes correction. Jane, wife of William Downey released dower.

BD1:76-78. David Moore recorded deed 14 Jan. 1775, from James Frasier for £1000, tracts called *John's Delight,* taken up by John Campbell for 50 acres, and *Partnership,* taken up by John Campbell and Lawrence Robinson, on north side of Talbot's Branch, on Linganore, containing 183 acres, made over to James Frasier by deed of gift. Margaret wife of James Frasier, released dower rights.

BD1:79-81. James Allen recorded deed from Thomas Edmonston and Mary his wife, Jeremiah Beall and Sabina his wife and Martha Beall, for £150, sterling, tract called *King Cole* containing 246 acres. Signed before Edward Burgess, David Lynn.

BD1:81-82. John Peter Boarer of Frederick town, and John George Boarer of Sharpsburgh, John William Boarer of the State of Virginia, and Anna Maria Boarer of Carolina, recorded deed 2 Feb 1775 from Conrad Grosh. Whereas Daniel Dulaney made deed to Conrad Grosh in trust, recorded in Liber P:545-546 for use of will of Abraham Bohrer, dated 18 October 1759, now deeds lot #101, now in possession of John Peter Bohrer. Sophia Grosh, wife of Conrad, released dower.

BD1:83-84. Thomas Cramphin Jr of Prince George's County, recorded mortgage 3 Feb. 1775, from Joseph Walker Burton for £85, two tracts, *Plummer's Hunting Lot,* near Sugar Loaf Mountain, 50 acres, and part of *None Left,* around that sold to Alexander Perry, containing 59 acres.

BD1:84-86. Andrew Boston recorded deed 6 Feb. 1775, from Joseph Wood Jr. For £5, tract called *Round About,* 147 acres. Ann wife of Joseph Wood Junr., released dower.

BD1:86-87. John Hanson recorded deed 8 Feb. 1775, from Basil Beall for £28..16, part of Thomas Taylor's *Resurvey on Hope,* adjacent to Henry Fortney's part, 85 acres. Mary, wife of Basil Beall released dower.

BD1:87-88. Andrew Rench recorded bill of sale 8 Feb. 1775. I Michael Schuster for £11..10..8, convey one bay mare, 3 years old, 13 hands high, signed German script before Otho H. Williams, John Stull. Bill of sale is to be collateral security; upon payment of sums, sale is void.

BD1:88-91. Jacob Miller recorded deed 9 Feb 1775, from Andrew Eavey for £520 five tracts of land, parts of *Huckleberry Hall,* to division line with Jacob Good, 52 1/8 acres; 2) *Outlet,* 80 perches east of Margaret Webb's land called *Darling Sale,* 50 acres; 3) tract called *Dry Land,* 50 acres; 4) *What You Please,* beginning at *Huckleberry Hall,* 12 3/4 acres; 5th & last, *Resurvey on Cold Weather,* and part of *Huckleberry Hall,* beginning at 19th line of a tract called *Warm Weather*, 2 1/4 acres. Barbara Evey released dower.

BD1:91-93. William Douglas recorded deed 0 Feb. 1775, from James Downey for £15, part of *Resurvey on Nicholases Contrivance,* 78 acres, adjacent to *Resurvey on Long Meadow Enlarged.* Isabella Downey released dower.

BD1:94-95. Francis Hoofman recorded deed 9 Feb. 1775, from Leonard Smith executor of Eleanor Medley, late of Frederick County, deceased, for £10, sells two lots, #3 and #33 in New Town, laid out by Leonard Smith, and yielding and paying rent to Elizabeth Sprigg Neale, wife of Bennett Neale during her life time and after her death to her children.

BD1:96-98. George Jacob Schley recorded deed 9 Feb 1775 from Thomas Schley of Frederick Town. In consideration of love and affection for his son, assigns lot in Frederick Town on east side of Market Street, adjacent to Casper Mantz's lot. Margaret Schley released dower.

BD1:98-100. Thomas Schley Jr., saddler, recorded deed 9 Feb 1775 from Thomas Schley, gentleman to his son, lot in Frederick Town on Market Street. Margaret Schley released dower

BD1:101-103. John Jacob Schley, house carpenter, recorded deed 9 Feb 1775 from Thomas Schley, gentleman, lot and house on corner of Market Street and First Street, in Frederick Town, Margaret Schley released dower

BD1:103-105. John Jacob Schley, house carpenter, recorded deed 9 Feb 1775 from Thomas Schley, gentleman, for 5 shillings, lot on West side of Market Street in Frederick Town.

BD1:105-107. Chrisopher Lowndes recorded deed 9 Feb. 1775, from Henry Warring of Prince George's County, for £150, lots #38 and #39 in Georgetown, first deducting that part already conveyed to Josiah Beall of Lot #39. Signed before Robert Peter, William Deakins, Junr.

BD1:107-109. Mary Richey recorded deed 9 Feb. 1775, from James Hooper for £15, lots #144 & 145 in *Addition to Georgetown.* Charlotte, wife of James Hooper released dower rights.

BD1:109-111. George Ransburgh recorded deed 9 Feb. 1775 from Leonard Smith, executor of Eleanor Medley, late of Frederick County, deceased. For £10, lot in New Town. yielding and paying rent to Elizabeth Sprigg Neale, wife of Bennett Neale during her life time and after her death to her children.

BD1:111-113. David Crawford of Prince George's County, recorded deed 9 Feb. 1775, from Thomas Johns for £25. Tract called *Bear Island,* lying below Great Falls in the Potomac, containing 9 acres. Sarah, wife of Thomas Johns released dower.

BD1:113-114. Stephen McCloskie recorded deed 9 Feb. 1775, from Jonathan Hager for £5, lot #82 in Elizabethtown.

BD1:114-116. William Downey recorded deed 9 Feb. 1775, from James Downey for £30, part of *Resurvey on Nicholas Contrivance,* adjacent to *Resurvey on Downey's Contrivance,* containing 285 acres. Isabella Downey, wife of James, released dower.

BD1:117-118. Thomas McGinnis recorded deed 9 Feb. 1775, from William Bayley Jr. For £75, 30 acres of *Round Bottom,* and 70 acres of *Rich Land,* together with dwelling houses, out houses, orchards, fences and all improvements. Signed before Wm Deakins, Jr., Adam Stewart. Susanna Fraser, wife of Wm Bayley, released dower rights.

BD1:118-120. John Smith, son of Leonard, recorded deed 9 Feb. 1775, from Leonard Smith executor of Eleanor Medley, late of Frederick County, deceased, for £10, sells two lots, #41 and #30 New

Town, laid out by Leonard Smith, and yielding and paying rent to Elizabeth Sprigg Neale, wife of Bennett Neale during her life time and after her death to her children.

BD1:120-122. Gabriel Thomas recorded deed 9 Nov. 1775 from Leonard Smith, executor of Eleanor Medley, late of Frederick County, deceased, for $5, sells lot #34 in New Town laid out by Leonard Smith on part of *Low Land*, and yielding and paying rent to Elizabeth Sprigg Neale, wife of Bennett Neale during her life time and after her death to her children.

BD1:122-124. Heronemas Hildenbrand recorded deed 9 Nov. 1775 from Leonard Smith, executor of Eleanor Medley, late of Frederick County, deceased, for $5, sells lot #34 in New Town laid out by Leonard Smith on part of *Low Land*, and yielding and paying rent to Elizabeth Sprigg Neale, wife of Bennett Neale during her life time and after her death to her children.

BD1:124-126. William House of Frederick Town, shoemaker, recorded deed 9 Feb. 1775, from Jacob Lewis and Dorothy his wife, and William Lewis & Catherine his wife, wife, co-heirs of Daniel Lewis, late of Frederick County, deceased; for £115 sells lot #39 in Frederick Town, part of the same lot belonging to John Jeremiah Myers in possession of Peter Huffman.

BD1:126-128. Andrew Kessler recorded deed 9 Feb. 1775 from Leonard Smith, executor of Eleanor Medley, late of Frederick County, deceased, sells lot #7 in New Town laid out by Leonard Smith, for £5, and yielding and paying rent to Elizabeth Sprigg Neale, wife of Bennett Neale during her life time and after her death to her children.

BD1:128-130. Felty Thomas recorded deed 9 Feb. 1775, from Leonard Smith executor of Eleanor Medley, late of Frederick County, deceased, for £5, sells the 36th lot in New Town on tract called *Low Land,* laid out by Leonard Smith, and yielding and paying rent to Elizabeth Sprigg Neale, wife of Bennett Neale during her life time and after her death to her children.

BD1:130-131. Abraham Leakins recorded deed 9 Feb. 1775, from Leonard Smith executor of Eleanor Medley, late of Frederick County, deceased, for £10, sells two lots in New Town, #2 and #39, laid out by Leonard Smith, and yielding and paying rent to Elizabeth Sprigg Neale, wife of Bennett Neale during her life time and after her death to her children.

BD1:131-133. William Elder Jr. Recorded deed 9 Feb. 1775 from Frederick Kemp for £5 confirms part of tract *Peace and Plenty,* containing 11 acres. Rachel Kemp released dower.

BD1:133-135. Bennett Heard recorded deed 9 Feb. 1775, from Leonard Smith executor of Eleanor Medley, late of Frederick County, deceased, for £5, sells lot #17 in New Town, laid out by Leonard Smith, and yielding and paying rent to Elizabeth Sprigg Neale, wife of Bennett Neale during her life time and after her death to her children.

BD1:135-137. Michael Walker recorded deed 9 Feb. 1775, from Leonard Smith executor of Eleanor Medley, late of Frederick County, deceased, for £5, sells lot #5 in New Town, laid out by Leonard Smith, and yielding and paying rent to Elizabeth Sprigg Neale, wife of Bennett Neale during her life time and after her death to her children.

BD1:137-138. Jacob Swink recorded deed 9 Feb 1775 from William Hill for 5 shillings, assigns lot #174 in Jerusalemtown. Elizabeth Hill released dower rights.

BD1:138-139. Joseph Leakins recorded deed 9 Feb 1775, made 16 Jan., from Leonard Smith, for £5, lot #4 in New Town, on the main street.

BD1:140-142. Melcor Tabler recorded deed 9 Feb. 1775, from Leonard Smith executor of Eleanor Medley, late of Frederick County, deceased, for £10, sells two lots in New Town, #6 and #35, laid out by Leonard Smith, and yielding and paying rent to Elizabeth Sprigg Neale, wife of Bennett Neale during her life time and after her death to her children.

BD1:142-143. James and William Cochran recorded deed 9 Feb. 1775, from Sarah Cochran of a tract of land called *Carrolsburgh,* widow and relict of William Cochran deceased, to his children and heirs for £50, 50 acres not previously sold by William Cochran. Signed by mark.

BD1:143-145. Richard Prather recorded deed 9 Feb. 1775 from Thomas Prather of Westmoreland County, Pennsylvania, for £250 tract called *Mades Fancy,* on east side of North Mountain, to Gilliland's Mill, containing 100 acres. Signed before Wm Baird, John Stull.

BD1:145-146. Philip Fishburn recorded deed 9 Feb 1775, made 13 Dec. 1774, from John Carter of Baltimore County, for £210 part of *Resurvey on Brother's Agreement,* 100 acres. Tamer, wife of said John released dower.

BD1:147-149. Henry Baker recorded deed 9 Feb 1775 from Conrad Kirkus for £350 part of *Resurvey on Charles Choice,* and part of tract called *Good Range,* beginning at a white oak near the main branch of Linganore, metes and bounds for 140 acres. Signed in German script.

BD1:149-150. William Stevens Jr recorded deed 9 Feb. 1775, from Jeremiah Covell for £100, tract *Wild Cat Hill,* for 100 acres. Ann, wife of Jeremiah Covell released dower.

BD1:151-152. William Murdoch of Prince George's County, recorded deed 9 Feb. 1775, from Walter Beall for £127, tract called *Snowden's Mill Land,* containing 3 3/4 acres. Susanna Beall released dower.

BD1:152-154. Philip Fishburn, merchant, recorded deed 9 Feb. 1775 from Raphael Neale of St. Mary's County, for £60 Pennsylvania, sells tract called *Brother's Agreement,* between Great Pipe Creek and Piney Creek. Elizabeth Neale released dower rights.

BD1:154-156. The Presbyterian Dutch Congregation recorded deed 9 Feb. 1775, from Jacob Bentz for love, good will and affection I have for the Dutch Reformed or Presbyterian Congregation of Frederick Town, assigns to John Brunner, George Bare, Valentine Swartz, Conrad Rode and Peter Greppel, elders or their successors, lot #64, and lot called the Presbyterian Burial ground, part of tract *Long Acre,* a part of *Tasker's Chance.* Margaret Bentz released dower.

BD1:156 Balsar Hess recorded deed 9 Feb. 1775, from Stephen McCloskie for £9, lot #94 in Elizabeth Town.

BD1:158-160. George Whannberger recorded deed 9 Feb. 1775 from Francis Deakins for £20, lot #129 in Adddition to Georgetown, on tract called *Knaves Disappointment.*

BD1:160-162. Christopher Edelen recorded deed 9 Feb. 1775, from Jacob Lease and Dorothy Lease his wife, and William Lease and Catherine Lease his wife, co-heirs of Daniel Davis, deceased, for £8..15 lot #19 in Frederick Town.

BD1:162-164. Henry Baker, saddler recommended deed 9 Feb 1775 from Lodowick Lemmon, tanner, for £50, tract *Resurvey on Nicholas's Chance,* for 51 acres. Elizabeth Lemmon released dower.

BD1:164-166. Eleanor Medley, widow, recorded deed 9 Feb 1775 from Melchor Tabler, made 15 Nov. 1774 for £293, tract called *Low Land,* on a branch called Prick Run of Kittoctin Creek, containing 98 acres; also part of *Children's Chance,* containing 3 acres. Catherine Tabler released dower.

BD1:166-168. Frederick Rohrer, tavern keeper, recorded deed 9 Feb. 1775 from Stephen McCloskie of Elizabeth Town, cordwainer for £9, lot #94 in Elizabeth Town.

BD1:169-170. Jonathan Harry, blacksmith, recorded deed 9 Feb. 1775 from Martin Harry Sr. of Elizabeth Town, tavern keeper, for 5 shillings, conveys to his son Jonathan, part of lot #2 in Elizabeth town where they now live. Anna Maria Harry releases dower.

BD1:171-174. John Bennett recorded deed 9 Feb. 1775 from George Gillespie Sr. For £1600, two tracts, *Gillespie's Bargain,* 474 acres and *Philadelphia,* a part of *Resurvey on Mountain of Wales,* containing 76 acres. Martha Gillespie released dower.

BD1:175-176. Richard Acton of Baltimore County, recorded lease 13 Feb. 1775, from Jonathan Rose for rents and considerations, for term of six years, part of *Boyle's Fancy,* said Rose to put a new roof on the kitchen, and maintain roofs. Said Acton may use pine wood for use of his smith's shop.

BD1:176-177. Samuel Warner Jr. Recorded bill of sale 13 Feb. 1775 from Samuel Warner Sr. For $100, assigns two Negroes, woman Rachel and boy named Boson, which Negro woman he hired to Mark William Harper some time past. Signed before Wm Luckett, Richard O'Doiell.

BD1:177-178. Jonathan Hager and Conrad Hogmire recorded deed 13 Feb. 1775, from Martin Harry of Elizabeth Town, for £327 Pennsylvania, tract *Grog,* 76 acres and lots #59 & #20. Ann Mary, wife of Martin Harry released dower rights.

BD1:179 Thomas Colwell executors [Mrs. Colwell, George Washington and John West] recorded power of attorney from John Semple 10 February 1775, to make deed to Msrs Adam Stewart, Thomas Montgomery and Cumberland Wilson for *Merryland,* containing 6300 acres, sold by Thomas Colwell, executor of John Colwell, deceased, by his bond 6 May 1765.

BD1:179 Basil Dorsey recorded bill of sale 18 Feb 1775, from Samuel Dorsey of Anne Arundel County, for £250, assigns eight Negroes, Saul, Taney, Cato, Flora, Cats, Dick, Simon and Jim, and also 30 head of black cattle. Signed before Ely Todd.

BD1:180-182. Denton Jacques, gentleman, recorded lease 21 Feb. 1775, from Lancelot Jacques of the City of Annapolis, gentleman, all that undivided moiety in the iron furnace called Fort Frederick Furnace, and the forge with improvements, Negro servants, and cattle, held jointly with Thomas Johnson, Junior, during their joint lives.

BD1:182 At the request of Jacob Henry will was recorded 25 Feb. 1775. I Jacob Henry, in perfect health of body and perfect mind and memory, ... bequeaths to Frederick Faw all my estate for him and his heirs and ordains him executor. Signed by mark 15 February 1775 before three witnesses, two in German script, and Wm Widmyer.

BD1:182-183. Richard Butler recorded release of dower 6 March 1775 from Thomas Brawner and Mary Brawner, his wife, heretofore widow and relict of Peter Butler, deceased, for £19 any right to land called *Turnstyle.* Signed before William Head, Lucy Head.

BD1:183-185. Leonard Backenbough recorded bill of sale 6 March 1775 from Valentine Everley for £7, two cows and five acres of wheat now sown. Sale void if sum paid with interest.

BD1:185-187. John Closser recorded lease 22 March 1775, from William Winchester for £12, lot #41 in town of Westminster, southeast of lot of Daniel Brown, containing 1/4 acres and part of *White's Level,* signed before Joseph Wells, Wm Blair.

BD1:187-189. Francis Deakins recorded deed 22 March 1775, from Bruce Townley for £410..15..7, for *Resurvey on Thoroughfare,* metes and bounds for 197 acres. Signed and acknowledged before David Lynn, Adam Stewart.

BD1:189-191. John Harwood recorded deed 22 March 1775 from Francis Deakins for £475, *The Resurvey on Thoroughfare,* metes and bounds for 197 acres.

BD1:191-193. James and Elizabeth Gatton recorded deed of confirmation 22 March 1775 from Silas Veatch, son and heir at law of John Veach. Whereas deed made 3 May 1759 and recorded in Liber F, Folio 723, to Elizabeth Gatton had incorrect metes and bounds, this deed corrects conveyance.

BD1:193-195. Joseph Sprigg recorded deed 22 March 1775, from James Downey for 5 shillings sterling, part of *Nicholas Contrivance,* east of tract called *Dorsey's Contrivance,* within the lines of Col. Henry Bouquet's *Resurvey called Long Meadow Enlarged,* 29 acres. Isabella, wife of James Downey, released dower.

BD1:195-196. Henry Hunter recorded release of dower 23 March 1775, from John Helm and Mary Ann, his wife, late relict and widow of the Rev. Samuel Hunter, for £200 quits dower claim on *Resurvey on Leonard's Good Luck, Darmstat, Pleasant Plain,* and *Doran's Choice.*

BD1:196-197. Peter Dick recorded deed 22 March 1775, from James Martin for lot #51 in Sharpsburg. Signed by mark.

BD1:198-199. Peter Shaver recorded bill of sale 2 March 1775 from Jacob Shugh, who is justly indebted for £7..5, and for 5 shillings he grants one red and white cow and one brown and white cow, which he bought of Casper Devilbiss and Henry Hawke. Nevertheless, provided he pay sums with interest sale is void.

BD1:199-200. Lawrence Creager recorded deed 22 March 1775 from James Wells of Prince George's County, for £150, one half of lot #4 on north side of Bridge in Georgetown, Signed before Isaac Gostling, Thomas Wiseham.

BD1:201-203. Thomas Dyson and others [Valentine Reintzel and Martin Hoofman] recorded mortgage 22 March 1775 from Jacob Upright of Georgetown, for £700 and £350 paid by 20th of this month, to pay balance with interest, sells lot #14 in Georgetown on Potomac River, and also tract called *Midgillygan,* a part of *Labyrinth*, containing 183 1/3 acres. Signed Jacob Eppracht, before Robert Peter, Adam Stewart.

BD1:203-204. Meverall Lock recorded deed 30 Sept. 1775, from Susannah Brady for £25, tract called *Brady's Lot,* 25 acres, and also part of tract called *Bailey's Rest,* bought of John Siscell, for 100 acres, recorded in records of St. Mary's County. Signed by mark before Archibald Boyd, Jacob Young.

BD1:204-206. Thomas Macklefish recorded land commission and depositions 22 March 1776, issued to Richard Carter, James Smith, Joseph Smith, and Charles Swearingen, to perpetuate the bounds of tract called *Chaney's Lott.* Commissioners met 6 Feb. 1775 and deposed Charles Chaney Sr., aged 74 years, at white oak on east side of Antietam Creek above Nicholas Warner's plantation that it was beginning tree of land laid out by said deponent for his brother Greenberry Chaney, by virtue of a 50 acre warrant which the said Greenberry purchased of a certain Thomas Powell. Deposition of William Flintham, aged 65 years, agreed about tree.

BD1:206-208. Benjamin Becraft Jr. And others recorded power of attorney from Robert Peter. Whereas Robert Peter, by deed of bargain and sale in 1773, conveyed land to Adam Austin, and has appointed him to convey said land to Benjamin Becraft Jr., Townley Bruce and Luke Marbury Wheeler.

BD1:208-211. Benjamin Becraft and others and Adam Austin recorded trust deed for tracts. Signed by all parties in above deed.

BD1:211-214. James Flemmng recorded deed 23 March 1775 from Philip Miller, on *Resurvey on Isaac's Range,* 150 acres.

BD1:214-216. William Deakins Junr. of Frederick County, recorded lease 25 March 1775, from Benjamin Dulaney Esq. of Fairfax County, Virginia, for yearly rents and covenants, assigns part of *Middle Plantation,* containing 592 acres near mouth of Seneca Creek, to pay £30 annually, and to build a substantial barn and two dwelling houses.

BD1:216. John McAllister and Jacob Good recorded receipt 27 March 1775. Received in Tawney Town, 14 Feb. 1775, from each of them in full for their proportion of bond given by them in company with Abraham Hayter and others for building the Monocacy Bridge. They are hereby discharged from said bond. £50. Jacob Myerer, witnessed by Saml Wilson, Jno Kleinhoff.

BD1:216-219. Peter Crapell of Frederick Town, recorded deed 25 March 1775 from Peter Balsel Jr. of Virginia, for £150 sells tract, *New Germany,* 100 acres. Catherine Balsell released dower.

BD1:219-221. Jacob Holtz recorded deed 25 March 1775 from John Stull for £450 Penn., for *Resurvey on Part of Chestnut Hill,* 192 acres. Signed by mark, Caty Stull released dower.

BD1:221-223. Conrad Recker, blacksmith, recorded deed 25 March 1775, from Leonard Smith executor of Eleanor Medley, late of Frederick County, deceased, for £5, sells lot in New Town, #30, laid out by Leonard Smith, and yielding and paying rent to Elizabeth Sprigg Neale, wife of Bennett Neale during her life time and after her death to her children

BD1:223-225. Yost Lesser recorded deed 20 March 1775, from Christian Kizer for £50, tract called *Quaker's Mistake,* containing 31 acres. Signed by mark. Mary, wife of Christian Kizer released dower.

BD1:225-228. [Ex'd & del'd John Jer Jacob, who married widow of grantee] Michael Cresap, son of Thomas, recorded deed 28 March 1775, from George Brent Esq. and Charity, his wife, for £500 tract called *Dispute,* formerly surveyed for Thomas Bladen Esq., on bank of Potomac, about 2 miles below Everett's Creek at Town of Old Indian Fields, 285 acres. Signed before Thos Waring, Ezekiel Cox.

BD1:228-230. David Moore recorded bill of sale 28 March 1775, from James Crawford for £42..14..6 twelve acres of wheat sown on tract called *Matins,* on a part of *Park Hall,* one mare and one mare colt; 2 sows, 3 shoats, 2 calves, a new plough, harnesses and so forth for two horses, 2 weeding hoes, one feather bed and bedding, two bedsteads, 2 iron pots, 1 doz. Pewter spoons, one table, one chest, one pair tongs and shovel; if sum paid with interest, by 15 July next, then bill of sale is void.

BD1:230-232. Peter Jesserang, blacksmith, recorded deed 28 March 1775, from Adam Everly for £22..10, part of *Resurvey on Chevy Chase,* adjacent to Leonard Everlaw's fence to 10th line of *Smithfield,* to the Great Road, 7 ½ acres. Signed in German script. Catherine Everley released dower.

BD1:232-234. Andrew Young recorded deed 28 March 1775 from Valentine Steckle for £80, and covenants and agreements, assigns lot #127 in Frederick Town, to pay rents to Daniel Dulaney. Signed in German script. Sevilia Steckle released dower rights.

BD1:234-236. Abraham King of Germany Township, York County, Pennsylvania recorded deed 28 March 1775 from Michael Danner, Jr., carpenter, for £98, tract called *White Oak Woods,* beginning near a small draught of Piney Creek, containing 46 acres. Signed by mark before Thos Price, Joseph Wells. Esther, wife of Michael Danner, released dower rights.

BD1:237-239. Eve Winter, spinster, recorded deed 28 March 1775, from William Winchester for £3, and performance of covenants and agreements, assigns lot #10 in Westminster, on east side of Main Street, bounded by lot now in possession of John Chamberlain, on 1st line of *White's Level*, containing 1/4 acre.

BD1:239-241. Henry Fullwider recorded deed 28 March 1775, from Conrad Crone, for 20 shillings Pennsylvania, assigns his right to lot #9 in Middletown. Ann Margaret Crone released dower.

BD1:241-243. Samuel Schertz recorded deed 28 March 1775, from Anthony Hardman, for £80, tract called *Bare Ridge,* beginning at head of spring running into Hunting Creek, about 2 miles southwest of Henry Rowdes's containing 60 acres. Signed before Thos Price, Wm Beatty. Margaretha, wife of Anthony Hardman, released dower.

BD1:243-245. George East recorded deed 28 March 1775, from John Stone for £50 part of tract called *Smith's Mistake Rectified,* containing 23 7/8 acres. Elizabeth Stone, wife of John, released dower.

BD1:245-248. Jacob Balsell recorded deed 28 March 1775, from Peter Balsell Jr., of Virginia, for £50, tract called *Mountain Lot,* at foot of the South or Kittoctin Mountain on east side thereof, for 25 acres. Signed by mark. Catherine Balsell, wife of Peter, released dower rights.

BD1:248-250. Anthony Deardorff recorded deed 28 March 1775, from David Weaver of York County, Pennsylvania, for £30 Maryland money, sells tract *Friends Good Will,* containing 27 acres. Signed German script. Alienation fine paid Wm M. Beall.

BD1:250-252. Thomas Noland recorded deed 28 March 1775 from Philip Noland Jr. of Loudoun County, Virginia, for £100, assigns all that tract called *Partnership* on east side of the main road leading from the Mouth of Monocacy to Frederick Town. Molly Noland, wife of Philip, released dower.

BD1:253-255. [Exam'd & del'd to heirs of A. King, 28 April 1809]. Abraham King recorded deed 30 March 1775, from Christian Kizer for £100 Pennsylvania, part of tract called *Quaker's Mistake,* to a corner of *Little Good,* containing 136 1/4 acres. Signed by mark. Mary, wife of Christian Kizer released dower.

BD1:255-257. Christian Erb and Charles Angle, executors of Peter Erb Jr., recorded deed 28 March 1775, from Michael Quinn, for £35, part of tract called *Ohio,* beginning at John Jones's land, containing 50 acres. Signed by mark before Joseph Wells, W. Winchester. Mary wife of Michael Quinn released dower.

BD1:257-260. Thomas Humphreys, tanner and currier, recorded deed 28 March 1775 from Michael Cresap, son of Thomas, for 5 shillings, assigns one and one-half lots in town of Skipton, containing 3/4 acres. Signed before T. Waring, Enoch Innis. Mary Cresap released dower.

BD1:260-262. Peter Studey recorded deed 28 March 1775 from Peter Sheffer for £34..3..9 Pennsylvania, sells parcel called *Sampson,* 6 3/4 acres. Signed in German script before Thos Price, Wm Beatty. Louisa Shaffer released dower.

BD1:262-264. Casper Beckenbaugh recorded deed 28 March 1775, from John Stone for £53, two tracts, four acres of *Foxe's Hole,* and 22 acres of *Smith's Mistake Rectified,* contiguous to each other. Elizabeth Stone released dower rights.

BD1:264-268. Jacob Barton, cordwainer, recorded deed 28 March 1775 from John Robinson, of Elizabethtown, saddler, for £80, assigns lot granted to him 16 Jan. 1773 by Jacob Hose for ½ of lot #81, where he now lives. Signed before John Stull, Wm Baird. Elizabeth Robinson released dower.

BD1:268-270. George Brent recorded deed 28 March 1775 from Michael Cresap for £500, tract called *The Big Spring,* at point of ridge in Devils Hole Gap, about 30 yards from large spring that empties into Murley's Branch of Old Town Creek, containing 42 acres. Mary Cresap released dower.

BD1:271-273. Christopher Myers recorded deed 28 March 1775, from John Chrisman for £60, lot in Westminster, #17 on northeast side of Main Street, part of *White's Level,* northwest of lot occupied by John Bittle, containing 1/4 acre.

BD1:273-275. Jacob Holtz recorded deed 28 March 1775, from Francis Jacob and Benedict Holtz for £160..10, Pennsylvania, part of *Resurvey on Stony Hill,* and *Shoemaker's Choice,* adjacent to *Holtz Choice,* a part of *Partnership,* to *Resurvey on Chestnut Hill,* containing 54 acres. Signed in German script, Frantz Jacob, Benedict Holtz. Elizabeth Jacob and Susanna Holtz, wives of Francis and Benedict released dower rights.

BD1:276-277. Jacob Gromet with Henry Medart, both of Frederick Town, recorded agreement 23 Nov. 1775. Jacob Gromet acting for Samuel Mansfield, to lease house and lot adjacent to the Lutheran Church yard for term of 6 or 7 years, made 1 April 1775. Henry Mettart to rebuild said improvements in tenantable repair.

BD1:277-278. John Swartz of Baltimore County recorded deed 20 March 1775 from Christopher Miller for £60 tract called *Philips' Delight,* on Bentley's branch, a draught of Great Pipe Creek. Signed in German script. Catharine, wife of Christopher Miller released dower.

BD1:279-280. Jacob Keller recorded deed 20 March 1775, from Christian Kizer for £50, tract called *Quaker's Mistake,* next to tract called *Beauty Spot,* 52 ½ acres. Signed by mark. Mary Kizer released dower.

BD1:281-282. Thomas Taylor recorded deed 20 March 1775, from Leonard Smith for £5, executor of Eleanor Medley, late of Frederick County, deceased, sells lot in New Town, #10, laid out by Leonard Smith, and yielding and paying rent to Elizabeth Sprigg Neale, wife of Bennett Neale during her life time and after her death to her children

BD1:282-284. John Christman recorded deed 20 March 1775, from Charles Clance of Westminster, taylor, for £6, lot in Westminster, formerly called *New London*, 1/4 acre. Mary Clance released dower.

BD1:284-286. Jacob Young and Otho Holland Williams recorded deed 20 March 1775, from Peter Jesserang, blacksmith, for £18, lot in Middletown, adjacent to alley of dwelling house of Valentine Summer, 6t ft by 365 ft. Eve Jesserong released dower.

BD1:286-288. Leonard Storum recorded deed 28 March 1774, from Henry Baltzell for £290, part of *Resurvey on Tom's Gift,* containing 150 acres, subject nevertheless to a mortgage for £75. Both parties signed in German Script. Margaretha, wife of Henry Balsell, released dower.

BD1:288-290. Thomas Ford recorded deed 28 March 1775 from Thomas Johnson Junr., Lancelot Jacques and Denton Jacques, all of the City of Annapolis, Anne Arundel County, for £100 parcel called *Rocky Neck*, Anne Johnson released dower rights.

BD1:291-292. George Hoover, weaver, recorded deed 28 March 1775, from Andrew Young, huckster, one moiety of lot #127 in Frederick Town, to hold during his natural life and that of his wife Catharine Hoover, for ever.

BD1:292-293. Peter Ham recorded deed 20 March 1775, from William Chapline for £7..15, lot #8 in Sharpsburgh. No dower release.

BD1:293-294. John Schoolfield recorded deed 28 March 1775, from James Wells of Prince George's County, for £150, the east half of lot #4 in Georgetown on the north side of the Bridge street.

BD1:295-296. John Watters recorded deed 28 March 1775, from William Ballenger for £22 sterling, *Elisha's Chance,* on small branch south of Bush Creek. Signed before Wm Beatty, Thos Price. Cassandra Ballenger released dower. Alienation fine paid Wm M Beall.

BD1:296-298. William Ballenger recorded deed 28 March 1775, from John Watters, son of John, for £25 sterling, all his interest in tract called *Turkey Flight,* on fork of a branch, commonly called the Long Branch of Bush Creek, containing 25 acres, land originally granted to John Prather on 13 Nov. 1752, and by writ of attachment in 1774, then to John Watters. Jane Watters released dower.

BD1:298-300. Thomas Fisher of York County, Pennsylvania, recorded deed 28 March 1775, from Patrick Hinds for £224. Part of tract *Hibernia,* containing 112 acres. Mary, wife of Patrick Hynds released dower.

BD1:301-302. Joseph Reynolds recorded deed 28 March 1775 from William Reynolds of the City of Annapolis for 5 shillings, grants to his son, tract called *Ward's Spring,* formerly in Prince George's County, now in Frederick County, containing 29 acres by patent. Signed.

BD1:302-304. Martin Keplinger recorded deed 22 June 1775, from Peter Hargate for £367..5, two tracts, *Non Such,* on Tobias's branch of Kitoctin Creek, 100 acres; and *Philadelphia,* adjacent to tract *Great Desire,* containing 40 acres. Signed in German Script. Catherine Hargate released dower.

BD1:305-306. Samuel Thomas recorded deed 28 March 1775 from Andrew Hyme for £111, grants tract originally granted to James Barrance on 30 October 1769, beginning at tract called *Flag Pond,* granted to Jacob Duckett, containing 74 acres of land. Signed German Script. Mary Himes released dower rights.

BD1:306-309. Philip Ablon recorded deed 18 March 1775, from Christian Miller for £260, tract called *Christian's Chance,* a part of *Hard Grumbling,* 163 acres. Signed by mark. Cathrine, wife of Christian released dower.

BD1:309-312. Lawrence O'Neale recorded mortgage 1 Sept. 1775, from Thomas Dyson for £500, tract called *Last Kiff,* containing 150 acres, and five Negro wenches: Dublin, Kate, Cintily, Juda and Nell and their increase; the true intent is if Thomas Dyson, pays sum with interest by 1 March next, sale is void. Signed by both parties.

BD1:312-314. Conrad Leghlider recorded deed 28 March 1775, from Charles Carroll of Annapolis, for £81, sells tract called *First Dividend,* containing 81 acres.

BD1:314-315. William Ballenger recorded deed 28 March 1775, from Samuel Plummer for £13..10, all his interest in three tracts, *Rocky Hill, Lost Breeches,* and *Fox Harbour,* on Bush Creek, containing 9 ½ acres. Mary wife of Samuel Plummer, released dower.

BD1:315-316. James White of Prince George's County, recorded deed 28 March 1775 from James Flemming of Frederick County, part of *Hobson's Choice,* on branch called Captain John's, described in a deed from Doctor James Doull to Zachariah White, and containing 7 ½ acres. Elizabeth, wife of James Flemming released dower.

BD1:317-318. John Mountz recorded deed 28 March 1775, from Thaddeus Beall for £253, lot #11 in Georgetown on Potomac River, adjacent to High Street. Amelia, wife of Thaddeus released dower.

BD1:319-320. Henry Crise recorded deed 28 March 1775, from Charles Carroll of Annapolis, for £20, part of *Sixth Dividend,* adjacent to 7th line of Daniel Pittinger's part, containing 87 acres.

BD1:320-323. John Everett recorded deed 28 March 1775, from John McCorkle for £110..11, a part of *Goose Quarter,* 153 acres. Elizabeth, wife of John McCorkle released dower.

BD1:323-325. John Everett recorded deed 28 March 1775, from William Pidgeon and Rachel, his wife for £3, tracts on west side of Monocacy Creek, near temporary line, part of two tracts, *Edward's Lot,* and *Hobson's Choice,* on a draft of Cattail Branch. Containing 60 acres. Signed & acknowledged.

BD1:325-327. Abraham Plummer recorded deed 28 March 1775 from Joseph Plummer for £50, 58 acres on north side of Bennet's Creek, called *Small Hopes.* Sarah Plummer released dower rights.

BD1:327-329. Jacob Hoffman recorded deed 28 March 1775, from Joseph Reynolds, joiner, of Frederick County, for £100 tract called *Jacob's Purchase,* a part of tracts *Surely Got,* and *Addition to Ward's Spring,* on main road west ward from Antietam's Bridge. Signed before Sam'l Beall Jr., and John Stull. Lucy Reynolds released dower.

BD1:329-331. John McKorkle recorded deed 28 March 1775, from John Everett for £153..12, part of *Goose Quarter,* 102 acres. Jane Everett released dower.

BD1:332-333. George Smith recorded deed 28 March 1775, from Levy Cohan, both of Sharpsburg, for £16, grants lot #35 for George Smith now lives.

BD1:333-335. John Beckwith recorded deed 20 March 1775. Made 9 March 1775 between William Williams Senr. For 15 shillings, tract called *Hobson's Choice,* beginning at 40 perches at 4th line of *Conclusion,* metes and bounds given for 97 ½ acres of land. Signed William Williams. Verlinda Williams, wife of William released dower rights.

BD1:335-337. Christian and Samuel Bralier recorded deed 28 March 1775, from Christopher Burckhart for £50, part of *Buckhart's lot,* 60 acres. Signed German script. Cathrine, wife of Burkhart released dower rights.

BD1:337-340. Christian Sailor recorded deed 28 March 1775, from John Smouse for £250, tract on Little Pipe Creek, called *Come by Chance,* for use as a grist mill. 50 acres. Signed German script before Joseph Wood, Rebecca Wood. Dorothy, wife of John Smouse, released dower right.

BD1:340-342. William Otto recorded deed 28 March 1775, from Raphael Neale of Saint Mary's County, for £97..10 Pennsylvania, part of tract called *Bedford,* beginning at 1st line of land conveyed by Normand Bruce and Edward Digges, metes and bounds for 150 acres. Elizabeth Neale released dower rights.

BD1:342-345. Henry Coonce recorded deed 28 March 1775 from Raphael Neale of Saint Mary's County, for £97..10, part of *Bedford,* on Great Pipe Creek, metes and bounds for 150 acres. Elizabeth Neale released dower.

BD1:345-346. James White of Prince George's County, recorded deed 28 March 1775 from James Flemming for £12 sterling, two lots in Addition to Georgetown, originally conveyed to Zachariah White. Elizabeth Fleming released dower rights.

BD1:346-349. Philip Sower, blacksmith, recorded deed 28 March 1775, from John Smouse, for £170 assigns his interest in tract, *Come by Chance,* on south side of Little Pipe Creek on Beaver Dam Branch, to 6th line of Christian Sailor's part, containing 87 acres. Dorothy Smouse released dower rights.

BD1:349-351. William Pidgeon recorded deed 28 March 1775, from John Everett for 20 shillings, part of two tracts, *Hobson's Choice,* and *Edwards Lot*, adjacent to *Frenchman's Choice*, containing 19 acres. John Everett signed before Wm Blair, Jos Wood.

BD1:351-353. John Myers recorded deed 28 March 1755 from Solomon Miller for £150 all his interest in tract, *Brother's Generosity,* on Sams Creek, adjacent to *Poorman's Loss.* Signed before Daniel Richard, Henry Hartsock. Sarah wife of Solomon released dower.

BD1:353-355. William Baker recorded deed 28 March 1775 from Archibald Edmonston for part of *Resurvey on Batchellor's Forest* for £28, beginning at end of 13th line of *Bradford's Rest,* to part conveyed by Alexander Beall to Robert Beall son of James, and Archibald Edmonston to Nicholas Baker. 16 acres. Signed before David Lynn, Edward Burgess.

BD1:356-357. Conrad Heyberger, potter, recorded deed 28 March 1775, from William Browne of Berkeley County, Virginia, tanner, assigns lot #11 in Sharpsburgh. Elizabeth Browne released dower.

BD1:357-359. Peter Whetzell recorded deed 28 March 1775, from John Harkness for £30, tract called *Exchange,* beginning at tract called *Retirement,* containing 17 ½ acres.

BD1:359-360. John Malone of Marsh Hundred, recorded bill of sale 28 March 1775, from William Kendle of Conecocheague, for £24, sells one grey mare, one black mare, one black colt of said mare about 6 months old and also two red cows. If sum paid in 12 months, sale is void.

BD1:360-361. Daniel Moore recorded deed 30 March 1775, from Samuel Kelly for £150, tract *Kelly's Purchase,* a part of *Hunting the Hare,* containing 50 acres. Ann Kelly released dower.

BD1:362-363. Thomas French, sheriff of Frederick County, recorded sale 31 March 1775 from George Beckwith for £45..11 delivers one sorrel horse, 8 yrs old; one sorrel mare 7 years old; one black mare 12 years old; 5 head of cows, four 2-year old cattle, 15 hogs and 7 head of sheep.

BD1:363-365. William Patterson recorded lease 31 March 1775, from James Chapline, for yearly rents, leases *Resurvey on Hills, Dales and Vineyard,* now in possession of James Chapline, 150 acres, from 1st Feb. Last for term of 19 years to pay £6 yearly rent to James Chapline.

BD1:365-366. Mary Owen recorded deed of gift 31 March 1775, from Ruth Owen for natural love and affection, assigns one female Negro child, Nora.

BD1:366-369. Leonard Roderick recorded deed of confirmation, 31 March 1775, from George Fraser Hawkins of Prince George's County, surviving executor of Thomas Stone Hawkins, for deeds made 10 May 1771 for consideration therein, recorded in Liber O;323, and there were errors in the description, gives correct metes and bounds for tract *Grandfather's Gift,* containing 155 acres, on west side of the Blue Ridge Mountains, 1/4 mile from the Potomac River, at the north end of tract called *Merryland,* adjacent to parts conveyed to John Nicholls by George Frazer Hawkins, and to Frederick Craft.

BD1:369-370. Catherine Loveless recorded deed of gift 31 March 1775, from Catherine Ferguson, widow, for natural love and affection for her granddaughter, assigns one Negro wench, Easter, about 20 years old. Signed by mark before David Lynn, John Lacklen.

BD1:370-373. Thomas French recorded deed 1 April 1775, from George Poe for £100, tract called *The Forrest,* originally granted to Osborn Sprigg for 300 acres; metes and bounds given for 100 acres; if sum paid by 1 September next, sale is void. Signed before Bartholomew Booth, Archibald Boyd. George Poe recorded release of the aforesaid mortgage, 17 Feb. 1776, from Thomas French with receipt for £105..5 in full satisfaction.

BD1:373-376. Jacob Cartenhouer recorded deed 1 April 1775, from David Ross of Prince George's County for £85, part of *Abstone's Forest,* beginning at 1st line of tract conveyed to Thomas Wale by Joseph Chapline, containing 62 acres. Ariana Ross released dower rights.

BD1:376-379. Adam Neff recorded deed 2 April 1775, from Christian Kizer for £100, part of *Pick All,* called *Quaker's Mistake,* near division line between John Neff and Jacob Keller, near a stone quarry, containing 124 acres. Signed before Wm Luckett, Thos Price. Mary, wife of Christian Kizer released dower rights.

BD1:379-380. William Flick recorded deed 3 April 1775, from Peter Melott for £2..10, conveys an out lot in town of Sharpsburgh, containing 20 perches by 40 perches, paying rents to Joseph Chapline of 5 shillings annually. Sarah, wife of Peter released dower rights.

BD1:381-382. Charlotte Mantz, spinster, and heir at law of Peter Mantz, late of Frederick County, deceased, recorded deed 3 April 1775, from Daniel Dulaney. Agrees to lot adjacent to lot known as the Potters Lot, Lot # 266 & 267, which Henry Link assigned his right to Peter Mantz, deed made for 5 shillings.

BD1:382-384. Joseph Fierarer recorded deed 4 April 1775, from Jacob Shoop for lot #108 in Elizabethtown, adjacent to Michael Tamer's lot. Margaret Shoop released dower.

BD1:384-386. Charles Beatty recorded deed 6 April 1775, from William Deakins Jr. for £10, lot in tract called *Frogland,* #9, 386 ft. from stone #1, in beginning of Second Addition to Georgetown, provided Charles Beatty is not to improve lot to the detriment of the navigation of the river.

BD1:386-388. William Deakins Jr. Recorded deed 6 April 1775, from Charles Beatty for £31..5, lot #8 in *Frogland,* adjacent to *Second Addition to Georgetown,* provided that he not improve the lot to detriment of navigation of the river.

BD1:388-390. Francis Deakins recorded deed 6 April 1775, from William Deakins Junr., for £5, sells all his interest, one moiety or half share of three tract, *Well Fare,* 7 acres formerly patented by Zachariah White; part of *Resurvey on Buckfield,* and also *Good Cheer,* signed before Robert Peter, Adam Stewart. Jane wife of said William Deakins released dower.

BD1:390-392. John Cookerly recorded deed 7 April 1775, from Charles Carroll for £200, part of *Bear Den,* containing 500 acres.

BD1:392-394. Conrad Grosh recorded deed 7 April 1775 from Samuel Armitt. Whereas a certain Robert DeButts, late of Frederick County, the father of Abigail Armit, in his life time, sold unto Conrad Grosh a certain lot #14 in Frederick Town,, and said Robert DeButts died, leaving two daughters, namely _____[left blank] Barnard and Abigail Armitt, co-heirs. Now this indenture for the further sum of 1 shillings, paid Samuel Armitt and Abigail his wife, made deed.

BD1:394-400. George Graff and Mary his wife, recorded deed 8 Apr 1775 from Abraham Farree of Strassburgh Township, Lancaster County, and Elizabeth his wife. Whereas Isaac Elting late of Frederick County, deceased, was in his life time possessed in fee of the following five tracts of land: *Seneca Ford*, 160 acres of land, *Mill Road,* containing 240 acres; *Isaac Elting,* containing 112 acres; *Cornelius's Chance,* containing 100 acres; *Fortune,* containing 118 acres, and in his last will and testament, 13 March 1756, devised that if all his children should die before they came to age 21 years, in that case, his estate to be divided in 3 parts equally, that part of his real estate given his wife during her natural life, and 1/3 part to his sister Elizabeth Ferree who is the party of the first part hereof, and the remaining two thirds unto the children of his sister Yacominte Thompson, deceased, namely William Thompson, Caroline Thompson, John Thompson, and Ann McDonald wife of Angus McDonald, and whereas the heirs have agreed among themselves, have divided land and recorded in Liber O:266-267. Now this indenture, for consideration of the natural love they bear to their son in law George Graff and daughter Mary Graff, they assign all the herein described tracts of land, being a mill seat commonly distinguished by the name of *Seneca Ford* on Seneca Creek, adjacent to *Middle Plantation,* metes and bounds given.160 acres and 5 other tracts described. Signed in the presence of Israel Ferree, Mary Stalcap. Signed before Justices of the Peace, Everett Gruber, of the Court of Common Please, County of Lancaster, J. Edward Shippen, Clerk.

BD1:400-403. Henry and Christian Newcomer recorded deed 8 April 1775, from Michael Cyster for £3000 money of Pennsylvania, 712 acres, part of *Resurvey on Stull's Forrest,* to Morningstar's part of said resurvey, 106 perches to Daniel McKay's part, laid out for 167 acres; and also another part of the said Resurvey, beginning at tract called *Shoe Spring,* to end of tract called *Pleasant Hill,* to the beginning of Morningstar's part of said resurvey, to James White's part, containing 441 acres; also one other tract called *Ovid,* adjacent to Resurvey, containing 104 acres. Signed before John Stull, Wm Baird. Mary, wife of Michael Cyster released dower.

BD1:404-405. Benedict Holtz recorded deed 10 April 1775, from Benjamin Howard of Anne Arundel County, for £3 a tract beginning at end of *Mary's Delight,* containing 2 1/4 acres of land.

BD1:405-407. Nicholas Shaver recorded deed 10 April 1775, from Daniel Dulaney, Esq., Barister at Law, surviving executor of Daniel Dulaney Esq. Whereas in his life time on 3 July 1747, he surveyed and laid out tract called *Long Hill,* for 100 acres, and he bargained and agreed with a certain William Thompson, for value received did on 23rd March 1761, assigns all his interest unto Henry Snavely, and the said Henry Snavely on 12 May 1774 assigned his interest in the contract unto Nicholas Shaver.

BD1:408-410. Abraham Leakin recorded deed of confirmation, 10 April 1775, made 8 April, from James Hook. Whereas about 20 August 1771, the aforesaid James Hook sold 100 acres, part of a tract called *Resurvey on John and Sarah,* upon a late inspection of the bounds of said lands there appears to have been errors committed in the aforesaid deed, this corrects survey. Signed by James Hook, no dower release.

BD1:410-413. Henry Ransburgh recorded deed of gift 10 April 1775, from Stephen Ransburgh, for the natural love and affection he hath and beareth unto the said Henry and ten shillings, part of tract called *Mortality,* containing 200 acres, except for privilege unto John Storm for carrying his mill race through the said land, to have the said 200 acres. Signed by both parties. Ursula, wife of Stephen released dower rights.

BD1: 414-416. Ludwick Cammara recorded deed 10 April 1775, from Daniel Dulaney Esq., surviving executor of Daniel Dulaney deceased. Whereas in his lifetime, 17 July 1745, surveyed a tract called *Buck Spring,* for 100 acres, and he bargained with aforesaid Ludwick Cammara, for the sale, in full consideration of £35. Signed Dan'l Dulaney. Alienation fine paid Wm M Beall.

BD1:416-418. Jacob Harmon, millright, recorded lease 11 April 1775, from John Beall, for rents services and covenants, leases tract upon Great Bennett Creek, which was demised to him by Joseph Beall for a term yet unexpired, 100 acres more or less to pay £100 for each year on 24th March until, 1779 and then beginning 24 March 1780 to pay £50 a year until expiration of term lease, after which yearly rent of one peppercorn if same should be demanded.

BD1:418-420. Basil Magruder recorded deed 14 April 1775, from Archibald Orme for £223, part of *Resurvey on Rich Meadows,* containing 270 ½ acres. Elizabeth Orme released dower rights.

BD1:420-423. John Flora recorded deed 14 April 1775, from Frederick Leatherman for £28..15, sells parts of tracts, *Owl Hollow,* 27 acres, and *Farewell Owle,* containing 25 acres, on road leading to Christian Leathermans. Catharine, wife of Frederick Leatherman released dower.

BD1:423-425. Peter Zeller recorded deed 14 April 1775, from Adam Ox for £52, for tract called *Trifle,* beginning at tract *Miller's Chance,* containing 21 1/4 acres. Elizabeth Ox released dower rights. Alienation fine paid Wm Murdoch Beall.

BD1:425-427 William Baker recorded deed 14 April 1775, from John Baker, in consideration of brotherly love and affection and 5 shillings, conveys tracts *Tobacco Bed,* on south side of Rock Creek, original beginning of patent to Nicholas Baker for 19 acres; also *Baker's Rich Meadow,* granted John Baker for 55 acres, and tract *Addition to Hazard,* on east side of Rock Creek, 150 yards from bridge, in an old field, granted the said John Baker for 44 acres. Signed before David Lynn, Edward Burgess. Judith, wife of John Baker released dower.

BD1:427-430. Jacob Steiner recorded deed 14 April 1775 from Thomas Schley for £200, sells messuage or dwelling house and part of lot #54 in Frederick Town on north side of first street, also parts of lots #129 and #130 on west side of Market Street. Margaret Thomas Schley released dower.

BD1:430-432. William Deakins Junr recorded deed 15 April 1775, from Doctr Sam'l WAG [William Abbott Guy] Cornish. Whereas on 5 May 1769, he did mortgage unto John and Thomas Hartley, merchants in Whitehaven, lot #2 in Georgetown for debt of £99..4, which he failed to pay, so merchants did on 10 July last set up to highest bidder at public sale. Deed sold for £130. By Doctor Samuel Cornish.

BD1:433 Paul Zentzinger of Lancaster County, Pennsylvania, recorded mortgage on 15 April 1775, from Thomas Pollhouse of Frederick Town for £60, assigns lots in Frederick Town, lots #234 and #3, which formerly belonged to Joseph Hardman, and other lots mentioned. If sum paid, sale is void.

BD1:436-437. Jacob Boyer recorded deed 15 April 1775, from William Burneston, executor of Joseph Burneston. Whereas Joseph Burneston did in his lifetime, bargain for part of three lots in Frederick Town and died before the deed was made, for £22 sells lots #156, 157 and 158, on main road that leads from Frederick Town to Georgetown. Ann Burneston, widow of Joseph, released dower rights.

BD1:438-439. Jacob Good recorded deed 17 April 1775 from Conrad Boner, taylor for £15, lot near Taneytown, #14, containing 10 acres. Signed before Wm Beatty, Arch Boyd.

BD1:439-440. Michael Ott recorded deed 20 April 1775, from John Stull for £7..10 lot on tract called *Whiskey,* also *Addition to Elizabethtown,* lot #4, 82 ft by 240 ft., paying on 12 March annually, rent of 4 shillings to John Stull or his heirs. Mary Stull released dower rights.

BD1:440-442. William Conrad recorded deed 20 April 1775 from John Stull, for £7..10 lot on tract called *Whiskey,* also *Addition to Elizabethtown,* lot #5, 82 ft by 240 ft., paying on 12 March annually, rent of 4 shillings to John Stull or his heirs. Mary Stull released dower rights.

BD1:442-443. William Molleson, merchant of London, recorded bill of sale 20 April 1775, from Richard Collins for £45..5..10, one steer, three cows, one yearling, two calves, 13 head of sheep, 15 head of hogs, and all my household stuff, and everything I am now possessed of, also two feather beds. Signed by mark before Will Deakins Junr., Peter Kurtz.

BD1:443-445. William Molleson, merchant of London, recorded bill of sale 20 April 1775, from William Parker, physician, for £500 assigns one bay horse, Burton; one black horse, Butcher; other horses called Roan, Bay, Jolly, blackbird, Sorrell; one wagon and harness for 4 horses; Negroes: wench Kate, girl Rachel, boy Sam, child Amelia; 16 head of cattle, 6 head of sheep, 66 head of hogs; 5 feather beds and furniture, 9 mahogany chairs, two arm chairs, one mahogany dining table, mahogany tea table; all my plows, harnesses and plantation utensils and seven white servants named: John Row, John Warring, Patrick Riley, Charles O'Bryan, and Philip Keen. Provided always that if he shall satisfy and pay sums with interest within three years, sale to be of no effect.

BD1:445-446. George and Andrew Boner recorded sale 21 April 1774 from Conrad Boner of Taneytown, for £50..16..3, sells all the household goods in annexed schedule, now in my dwelling house in Taneytown. Detailed inventory of over 50 items each valued, begins with clock at £9..0..0, chest of drawers 4..0..0; listing furniture, housewares, coffee and tea pots, coffee mill, tableware, a cow, candlesticks, blankets, sheets, down to two chaff beds at 0..4..0. Acknowledged before William Beatty.

BD1:446-448. Henry Earlingbough recorded deed 20 April 1775, from Martin Lyon and Peter John, executors of the will of John Heldebrand, for £80 sells tract *Chestnut Spring,* on dry branch of Antietam, containing 50 acres. Signed before John Stull, William Baird.

BD1:448-450. Philip Englar recorded deed from Solomon Miller, Nathan Haines and William Farquhar, for £50 tract called *The Unity,* on Muddy Run that falls into Little Pipe Creek, containing 25 acres excepting a small piece of land called the graveyard, about 2 perches by 2 perches. Signed before Joseph Wells, Mordecai Roberts. Acknowledged before Upton Sheridine, Joseph Wells. Alienation fine of 1 shilling paid by Peter [sic] Engler, to Wm Murdock Beall.

BD1:450 Joseph Doll recorded deed 24 April 1775, from John Brooner, house carpenter, for £100, lot #102 in Fredericktown, adjacent to lot of Peter Bohrer. Signed in German script, Johannes Bruner, before Thomas Price, Arch Boyd. Mary Brooner, released dower rights.

BD1:452-453. John Worthington of Ann Arundel County, recorded deed 24April 1775, from Thomas Beatty for £40, *Solomon's Flower,* on south side of Bennett Creek, containing 50 acres. Signed before Thos Price, Wm Beatty. Catherine Beatty released dower rights.

BD1:453-455. John Pilmore, schoolmaster, recorded deed 24 April 1775 from John Stull for £5..1, lot on tract *Whiskey,* also *Addition to Elizabethtown,* lot #2, 82 ft by 240 ft., paying on 12 March annually, rent of 4 shillings, 6 pence to John Stull or his heirs. Mary Stull released dower rights.

BD1:455-457. Felix Souther recorded deed 24 April 1775, from Henry Miller for £75 Pennsylvania, lot #72 in Elizabeth Town, kept by Jonathan Hager. Signed before Wm Baird, John Stull. Catrine Miller released dower rights.

BD1:457-458. John Hummell recorded deed 25 April 1775, from Valentine Stickle for £50, lot #110 in Frederick Town, on Market St. Sybilla, wife of Valentine released dower.

BD1:458-460. Christian Rhodes of Frederick Town, recorded deed 25 April 1775 from Samuel Flemming for £35, part of lot #169, adjoining lot belonging to George Whitshair, 24 ½ ft by 60 ft., and other lots, to comply with covenants in a deed from Daniel Dulaney to a certain Joseph Hardman, deceased. Signed by Samuel Flemming, and Christian Rhodes by mark CR.

BD1:460-462. Valentine Adams recorded 27 April 1775 from William Ogle. Whereas Joseph Ogle, late of Frederick County, by his will recorded in the Prerogative Court, bequeath to his children Sarah, Eleanor, Joseph, Benjamin, Thomas, William, James and George Ogle, and a double share to his wife Sarah, had by deed of partition assigned to William, *Black Walnut Bottom,* 155 acres for £450.

BD1:462-463. Jacob Funk recorded deed 28 April 1775, from Christian Rhorer, for £20, for part of *Addition to Good Luck,* containing 119 acres.

BD1:463 Henry Koonce recorded deed 29 April 1775 from John Marquart, stocking weaver, for £30 Penn., lot #177 in Additional lots of Frederick Town. Signed German Script.

BD1:465-467. George Burkett, innholder, recorded deed w May 1775 from Basil Dorsey for £200 tract *Still Work,* 45 acres, and another tract, *Dorsey's Search,* beginning at *Turner's Forrest,* tract *Burkhart's Forrest,* 50 ½ acres.

BD1:467-469. Conrad Kreighbaum recorded deed 3 May 1775, from Michael Dudderow Jr. For £400, tract called *Peace,* a resurvey on *Swinburg,* and *New Germany, Resurvey on Stoney Hill,* and *Shoemaker's Choice,* 124 acres. Elizabeth Dutrow released dower rights.

BD1:469-470. Jacob Michael recorded mortgage 4 May 1775 from John Marquart of Frederick Town for £20, lots #170 and #178 in Additional Lots of Frederick Town.

BD1:470-472. Anna Maria Beckenbaugh recorded deed 4 May 1775, from Thomas Schley for £117, lots #129 & 130 on west side of Market Street, in front with Peter Engle's line, to Gilbert's part. Margreth Schley released dower rights.

BD1:472-473. Benjamin Whitman recorded deed of confirmation, 5 May 1775, from William Digges of Prince George's County, for 5 shillings, correcting deed recorded in Liber H:453-454, for 120 acres of *Resurvey on Diggs Lot.*

BD1:473-474. Herbert Hiner recorded deed 5 May 1775, from Wilfred Neale, Elizabeth Neale, Eleanor Diggs executor of John Digges, heirs at law of Edward Digges, late of Saint Mary's county, for £50 assigns tract *Bedford,* containing 156 acres. Signed before William Hanson, Dan St. Jenifer, Phil R. Fendall, clerk of Charles County Court.

BD1:474-476. [Marginal note, del'd Peter Orndorf, 28 May 1782] Henry Smith recorded deed 5 May 1775, from Wilfred Neale, Elizabeth Neale, Eleanor Diggs executor of John Digges, heirs at law of Edward Digges, late of Saint Mary's county, for £50 assigns tract a part of *Brother's Agreement,* at beginning of David Maxwell's. 320 acres. Signed before William Hanson, Dan St. Jenifer, Phil R. Fendall, clerk of Charles County Court.

BD1:476-478. Raphael Brooke recorded deed 6 May 1775, from Jacob Good of Tawney Town, for £5, lot #17 in Tawney Town on the main road. Elender, wife of Jacob Good released dower.

BD1:478-480. Daniel Bussard recorded deed 6 May 1775 from Henry Crowle for £100, resurvey made on *Hard Quarters,* and part of *Williams Neglect,* on draught of Little Pipe Creek, which said tracts were conveyed by Mounts Justice to Christian Light, 14 Oct. 1770, and condemned to the use of Henry Crowle by attachment of Frederick County Court. Tract on 6th line of *Hammond's Strife,* 29 acres. Signed before Upton Sheridine and Eleanor Sheridine. Margaret wife of Henry Crowle released dower right.

BD1:480-484. Thomas Sim Lee of Prince George's County recorded deed 6 May 1775 from Adam Steuart of Frederick County and Thomas Montgomerie and Cumberland Willson of Prince William County, Virginia, for £1807..16..7, several lots [2, 3, 10, 11] in tract of *Merryland.*

BD1:485-487. Philip Bier recorded deed 7 May 1775 from Thomas Schley for £200, assigns messuage and dwelling house on west side of lot #55, on north side of the first street in Frederick Town, adjacent to lot #56. Also parts of lots 129 & 130 on Market St. Margaret Schley released dower.

BD1:487-489. Peter Tofler recorded deed 7 May 1775 from Thomas Schley, lots #129 & 130. Margaret Schley released dower rights.

BD1:489-491 Christian Shyrock, shoemaker, from Samuel Snowden, John Snowden and Thomas Snowden, of Prince Georges and Anne Arundel Counties, iron masters, for valuable consideration made and satisfied by a certain Nathaniel Wickham, and for 5 shillings, part of *Lisbon,* 200 acres. Signed and acknowledged before Basil Burgess, H. Ridgely, justices of the peace, John Brice, clerk.

BD1:491-493. Alexander Ogle, miller, from Samuel Snowden John Snowden and Thomas Snowden, of Prince Georges and Anne Arundel Counties, iron masters, for valuable consideration made and satisfied by a certain Nathaniel Wickham, and for 5 shillings, part of *Lisbon,* and part of *Good Luck,* containing 150 acres more or less. Signed and acknowledged before Basil Burgess, H. Ridgely, justices of the peace, John Brice, clerk.

BD1:493-496. Henry Broadbeck recorded deed 8 May 1775 from John Everlaw for £330, part of tract called *The Bad Wife,* on first line of *The Good Wife,* on draught of Abraham's Creek, to third line of Conrad Crown's part, containing 92 acres, also *Resurvey on Wymer's Change,* to beginning tree of

Jacob Bowle's part, 26 acres, together 118 acres. Signed German script, Johannes Everlaw. Catherine Everlaw released dower rights.

BD1:496-498. William Sabatier recorded deed 8 May 1775 from Charles Martin for £48..13, tract called *Alexandria,* containing 30 acres more or less. Signed in G.S., Karl Martin, before Thos Price, Edward Burgess. Mary, wife of Charles Martin released dower.

BD1:498-499. Philip Fishburn recorded deed 8 May 1775 from Wilfred Neale, Elizabeth Neale, Eleanor Diggs, executors and John Diggs heir at law of Edward Diggs, late of Saint Mary's County and province of Maryland, deceased. For £5 sterling, part of tract called *Bedford,* containing 91 acres. Signed Wilfred Neale, Elizabeth Neale, Eleanor Digges, John Digges.

BD1:500-501. Jacob Ockerman, miller, recorded deed 8 May 1775, from Jacob Koontz for £400 tract called *Blacksmith's Mill,* on Piney Run, a draught of Linganore, beginning at tract called *Duke's Woods,* containing 35 acres with improvement. Motline, wife of Jacob Koontz released dower.

BD1:502-503. Conrad Hogmire recorded deed 11 May 1775, from Hance Waggoner for £20, tract called *Sink Hole,* adjacent to Sink Hole Spring, 50 acres. Signed German script.

BD1:503-506. Jacob Huffer recorded deed 11 May 1775 from Jacob Bowman for £1000, the five following tracts: *Malborough Field*, 100 3/4 acres; *Resurvey on Baker's Lookout,* 3 ½ acres; tract called *Egypt,* 84 acres; *New Store,* 64 acres, and *Walnutt Bottom,* 3 3/4 acres. Metes and bounds given, for 256 acres in whole, with all houses, buildings, and improvements, gardens and orchards. Signed in German script. Barbara Bowman released dower rights.

BD1:506-509. John Sturm recorded deed 12 May 1775, made 8 May, from Michael Tanner for £150 part of *Resurvey on Owings Choice,* beginning at south line of *Miller's Chance,* 51 acres. Also part of *Miller's Chance,* at 2nd line of *Piney Grove.* Eva, wife of Michael Tanner released dower.

BD1:509-512. John Glassford & Co. of Glasgow, Scotland, merchants, recorded deed 12 May 1775, from Joseph Belt of Georgetown, for £850, lot #51 in Georgetown, where Jos Belt dwelleth, backs to Water Street. Esther Belt, wife of Joseph released dower.

BD1:512-514. Michael Crist recorded deed 13 May 1775 from John Leather for £160, tract on side of small head of a path that leads from Leonard Everly's to Peter Balsel's, 50 acres. Signed before William Beatty, Archibald Boyd. Anna Maria wife of John Leather released dower.

BD1:514-516. John Kleinhoff recorded deed 13 May 1775, from Conrad Boner for £150, lot #7 in Tawney Town, on main road from Frederick Town to York Town.

BD1:516-518. William Good recorded deed 13 May 1775, made 3 March, from Moses Chapline heir at law of his brother, Joseph Chapline, deceased, for £108, tract called *Old Purchase,* part of *Resurvey on Mount Pleasant,* on second line of tract called *Mountain.*

BD1:518-520. Francis Fair recorded deed 14 May 1775, from Frederick Starts deed made 5 May for £11..7, lot #124 in Jerusalemtown. Sybilla, wife of Frederick Starts released dower.

BD1:520-522. James Fraser recorded release 15 May 1775. Whereas John Campbell Senr. of Ann Arundel County, by deed of conveyance recorded 11 November 1772 [Liber P:448 & 449] conveyed 180 acres of *Partnership,* and 59 acres of *Johns Delight,* after his decease, now for love and affection he has for John Fraser, and 5 shillings, releases same to him. Signed mark before H. Ridgely, John Burgess.

BD1:522-525. Jacob Barr recorded deed 16 May 1775, made 13 May, from Paul Roads. For £125, Pennsylvania, part of *Dry Spring,* granted to Jacob French in 1752 and conveyed to Paul Roads in 1754, beginning at division line between said Barr and Jacob Tuttle. 50 acres. Signed German script. Barbara Roads released dower.

BD1:525-529. Jacob Tuttle recorded deed 16 May 1775 from Paul Roads, made 13 May, part of two parcels, one called *Dry Spring,* containing 50 acres; and the second, part of *Rich Barrens,* originally patented Paul Roads in 1759. Signed in German script. Barbara Roads released dower right.

BD1:529-531. John Hanson recorded deed 16 May 1775 from Basil Beall for £77, *Resurvey on Limestone Park,* 38 ½ acres. Mary wife of Basil Beall released dower.

BD1:531-533. Jacob Thomas recorded deed 16 May 1775 from Andrew Capeheart for £84 Pennsylvania, parcel called *Not at Home,* on north side of Totem's Run, near widow Morney's. 50 acres. Signed by mark. Nancy, wife of Andrew released dower.

BD1:533-535. Casper Swink recorded deed 18 May 1775 from Christian Kyple for £42..1..9, *Resurvey on part of Burkett's Lot,* 22 3/4 acres. Wife not named, released dower.

BD1:535-537. John Cary and Christopher Edelen recorded deed of trust, 18 May 1755 from Moses Chapline, for 5 shillings, assigns for use of his creditors, *Resurvey on Mount Pleasant,* 471 acres, except for 77 acres called *Old Purchase,* deeded to William Good on 3 March 1775; and tract called *Josias Belt,* 50 acres. Signed before Arch Boyd, Thos Price.

BD1:537-539. Griffin Willet recorded deed19 May 1775, from James Roberts for £68, *Resurvey on Groe's Adventure,* 56 acres. Mary wife of James Roberts released dower.

BD1:539-541. John Garver recorded deed 22 May 1775. Whereas on 3 June 1767, Jacob Danner sold tracts called *Groom's Good Luck,* part of *Spring Plains,* recorded in Liber L:515-516, this is to make correction to metes and bounds. Elizabeth Danner released dower.

BD1:541-543. Lodowick Solomon Miller recorded deed 26 May 1775 from John Shoeman for £53 Pennsylvania, assigns house and lot #27 in Elizabethtown. Signed German Script. Barbara released dower rights.

BD1:543-546. Peter Newcomer, blacksmith, recorded deed 26 May 1775 from John Shockey for £335 for part of *Third Resurvey on Sarah's Delight,* in two parts, 102 acres and 30 acres, patented by Christopher Shockey, also tract *Brookes Blunder,* 9 acres. Susanna Shockey wife of John released dower rights.

BD1:546-548. John Neff recorded deed 27 May 1775 from Christian Kizer for £50 two parts of a tract called *Quakers Mistake,* 50 acres and 5 acres. Signed by mark. Mary wife of Christian released dower rights.

BD1:549-550. John Showman recorded deed 29 May 1775 from Thomas Smith for £25 sells tract *Hickory Lane,* 20 acres. Elizabeth wife of Thomas Smith released dower.

BD1:550-552. John Showman recorded deed 29 May 1775 from George Sturrum, for £650, *Marshall's Plains,* 200 acres. Barbara, wife of George released dower rights.

BD1:553-554. Peter Slusser recorded deed 29 May 1775 from Michael Thumb for £160 Pennsylvania, sells *Stony Ridge,* 73 3/4 acres. Catherine wife of Michael Thumb released dower.

BD1:555-560. John Garrett recorded deed 29 May 1775 from Adam Steuart of Georgetown, Frederick County and Thomas Montgomerie and Cumberland Willson of Prince William County, Virginia, for £1000, several lots #13, 171 acres; #14, 256 acres; #15 150 acres, and #22, 135 acres, in tract called *Merryland*, metes and bounds given, parts adjoin *Paines Delight.*

BD1:560-562. Jacob Klem recorded deed 31 May 1775, from Basil Beall, for 5 shillings, part of *Resurvey on Anchor and Hope,* 80 acres. Mary Beall released dower rights.

BD1:562-568. Christian Lance recorded deed 24 May 1775, from John Rife, late of Lancaster County, Pennsylvania, mason, assigns four tracts: part of *Skipton Craven,* 177acres; part of *Quarry,* a resurvey on part of *Resurvey on Well Taught,* patented to George Jacob Poe, 179 acres; and tract called *Wive's Choice,* surveyed by Jacob Liter Senr., and willed by him to John Rife, for 144 acres; the fourth part is tract originally patented to Michael Miller, called *Miller's Fancy,* beginning at an oak, standing between John Wilson's and Michael Miller's plantation, 36 acres. Signed in German Script. Receipt for £2350 Pennsylvania. Ann Rife, wife of John, released dower rights.

BD1:568-570. Wendle Steurm recorded deed 1 June 1775 from Harman Joist, for £215, lot #3, in Middletown, to pay Conrad Crown 7 shillings, 6 pence rent annually. Mary Joist, wife of Herman released dower rights.

BD1:570-572. Nicholas Saum recorded deed 3 June 1775, from Christian Eversole for £6 Pennsylvania, assigns lot #39 in Sharpsburg. Wife [blank space] released dower rights.

BD1:572-573. Daniel Butcher recorded deed 6 June 1775 from George Bond Jr. for £112, part of tract called *Resurvey on Meschacks Garden,* beginning at boundary of *Old Fox Deceived,* for 45 acres. Signed before Wm Baird, J. Stull. Mary Bond released dower rights.

BD1:573-574. Jonathan Hager recorded bill of sale 7 June 1775, from Adam Addelman for £72..11..6, sells 22 acres of wheat, 8 acres of rye, now growing, 7 cows, 8 young black cattle, four horses and a young colt. Signed by mark before John Stull.

BD1:575-576. Samuel Willson recorded deed 7 June 1775, from Augustus Sharrar for £27, lot #24 in Taney Town on Main Road that leads from Frederick Town to York Town. Signed in G.s. before Thomas Price, and John Sturm (by mark). Madalena, wife of Augustus Sharrar, released dower.

BD1:576-578. Daniel Bussard recorded deed 8 June 1775 from John Orr for £9..15 all his interest in tracts *Hard Quarters,* and *Williams Neglect* on Little Pipe Creek, 107 3/4 acres conveyed by Mounts Justice to Christian Light, and 4 3/4 acres. Signed and acknowledged by John Orr.

BD1:578-580. John Smith recorded bill of sale 8 June 1775, from Frederick Hammon for £10, sells yellow bay mare, with colt, one brindle cow, one heifer, one black bull, and one steer; nevertheless if sum paid with interest, sale is void.

BD1:580-582. Peter Witsell recorded deed 12 June 1775, from Christian Kingrey for £200 sells five tracts of land, *Resurvey on Well Thought* [sic], 23 acres; second part of the aforesaid *Resurvey on Well Taught,* beginning at *Perry's Retirement,* 9 acres; 3rd part containing 19 acres; 4th part, a part of *Perry's Retirement,* 4 ½ acres, and 5th, 26 acres, the whole containing 81 ½ acres. Signed in German Script. Wife of said Kingrey [name left blank] examined apart and released dower.

BD1:583-584. John Derr recorded deed 12 June 1775, from Adam Whitenour for £75 sells tract, *All I Can Get,* containing 33 acres, signed by mark before Archibald Boyd, Thos Price. Barbara Whitenour released dower rights.

BD1:584-586. John Norris recorded deed 12 June 1775, from Simon Meredith of Frederick County, for £470 all his interest in tracts on Sams Creek, a draught of Little Pipe Creek, viz., *Walnut Bottom, and part of Resurvey on Walnut Bottom,* beginning at two bound white oaks, containing 100 acres; and also part of *Dillon's Contrivance,* and part of *First Addition,* containing 4 acres of land. Cathrine, wife of Simon Meredith released dower rights.

BD1:587-589. Simon Meredith recorded deed 12 June 1775 from Nathaniel Norris and John Norris. Whereas John Phillip late of Frederick County, did by his will dated 28 June 1769 leave all his land to be sold by his sons-in-law, Nathaniel Norris and John Norris. For £470 they sell *Walnut Bottom,* and *Resurvey on Walnut Bottom,* 100 acres; to part of *Dillon's Contrivance,* and *First Addition,* containing 3 acres; and part of *Second Addition,* containing 4 acres. Signed by Nathl Norris, John Norris. Elizabeth Justice, late the widow of the said John Phillips, deceased, released dower rights.

BD1:589-593. Charles Beatty recorded deed 13 June 1775, from George Frazer Hawkins of Prince George's County. Whereas Stephen West, of Prince George's County, by deed of bargain and sale recorded in Liber N folio 234, did convey to said Beatty and Hawkins, parts of tract known as *Knave's Disappointment,* for 100 acres and a second part of 136 acres; for £1000 conveys all his interest on the said lot. Susanna Trueman Hawkins released dower rights.

BD1:593-595. Benjamin Mussellman recorded deed 14 June 1775, from Henry Funk and Susannah, his wife, for £16 part of tract called *Locust Bottom,* laid out for 36 acres. Signed before Wm Baird, John Stull.

BD1:595-597. Jacob Cassell recorded deed 15 June 1775, from Martin Winter for £25, sells part of *Stocksdale's Hills,* laid out for 21 ½ acres of land. Signed German Script. Mary, wife of Martin Winter, released dower rights.

BD1:597-599. Jacob Cassell recorded deed 15 June 1775, from Martin Winter for £65, Pennsylvania, part of *Stocksdale's Hills,* and part of *Good Fellowship Resurvey,* containing 18 ½ acres. Mary Winter released dower rights.

BD1:599-601. John Everly recorded deed 15 June 1775, from Martin Winter for £388, tracts, part of *Stocksdale's Hills,* and *The Resurvey of Good Fellowship,* to the division line with Francis Logsdon's land, to 7th line of a tract called *Father's Care,* metes and bounds given for 105 acres. Signed in German script. Mary wife of Martin Winter released dower rights.

BD1:601 Michael Arter, carpenter, recorded deed 15 June 1775, from Edward Lamb for £10, part of *Resurvey on Good Fellowship,* to end of 6th line of a tract called *Father's Care,* laid out for 4 acres. Signed by Edward Lamb before Jos Wood and Martin Winter (in German script). Receipt and acknowledgment by Edward Lamb before Jos Wood, Thos Price. Alienation fine paid Wm M Beall.

BD1:603-604. William Lamb recorded deed 15 June 1775, from Edward Lamb, part of tract called *Resurvey on Lambs Choice,* and part of a tract of land *The Resurvey on Locust Neck,* known to be the second vacancy, adjacent to Henry Hauptman's land, containing 196 acres more or less.

BD1:604-606. Martin Winter recorded deed 15 June 1775, from Edward Lamb for £8 Pennsylvania, part of a tract of land called *Resurvey on Good Fellowship,* to the given line of a part of land sold Andrew Shriver, then to tract sold Thomas Logsdon, to 7th line of tract *Stocksdells Hills,* now laid out for 8 acres. Signed and acknowledged.

BD1:606-608. Frederick Rise recorded deed 16 June 1775, from Conrad Hogmire for £20 tract called *Sink Hole Spring,* containing 50 acres. Signed before J. Stull, Ezekiel Cox. Magdalena, wife of Conrad Hogmire released dower rights.

BD1:608-610. John Snowden Hook recorded deed 17 June 1775, from James Hook Jr. for £35 part of *Resurvey on John and Sarah*, near Kitoctin Mountains. 34 acres. Mary, wife of James Hook Jr released dower rights before Arch'd Boyd and Thomas Price.

BD1:610-612. Christian Kemp recorded deed June 19, 1775, from Peter Hargate for £30 part of tract called *Philadelphia,* along a line of the *Resurvey on Great Desire,* containing 17 acres. Signed in German script. Katherine wife of Peter Hargate released dower.

BD1:612-614. Nathaniel Large recorded deed 19 June 1775, from Robert Bennet for £50, assigns tract called *Narrow Bottom,* granted Robert Bennett in 1766, containing 25 acres. Signed before John Stull, Ezekiel Cox. Comfrett Bennett released dower rights. Alienation fine paid Wm M Beall.

BD1:614-615. Williams Wiggins recorded deed 19 June 1775, from Joseph Flint for £40, tract called *Grassy Cabin,* 50 acres. Charity Flint released dower rights.

BD1:615-616. George Witmire recorded deed 19 June 1775, from John Swank for £20 part of tract of land called *Neglect,* beginning at a tract taken up by Matthew Clark called *Discontent,* laid out for 10 acres of land. The wife of John Shank, (not named) was examined apart and released dower.

BD1:616-618. George Witmire recorded deed 19 June 1775, from George Adam Keedy for £120 tract called *Lypsuck*[6]*,* lying at first line of tract called *Discontent,* adjacent to John Hanson's land, containing 43 acres. Signed before J. Stull, Wm Baird. Barbara, wife to said Keedy released dower rights.

BD1:618 Leonard Kitzmiller recorded deed 20 June 1775, from Jacob Stoner, Philip Englar and Andrew Young. Whereas Jacob Molendore, late of Frederick County, deceased, died seized in fee of a tract of land called *Shear Spring,* containing 170 acres, and by his will appointed executors above to sell his estate. Sold for £450.

---

[6]*Lypsuck Lying,* was patented by George Adam Kedey, for 50 acres, 18 March 1764, according to Coldham's series, *Settlers of Maryland.*

BD1:620-622. John Whaley recorded deed 20 June 1775, from Michael Cresap for £100, lot in town of Skipton, on which the said Whaley now lives. Mary Cresap released dower rights.

BD1:622-625. John Rench recorded deed 20 June 1775, from Jacob Brombaugh Sr., for £80, lot known by name, *Resurvey on Brombaugh's Lot,* Mary Brombaugh released dower rights.

BD1:625-627. Jacob Kestler recorded deed 20 June 1775, from Charles Angle, Christopher Erb and Judith Erb, legal executors of the last will and testament of Peter Erb, deceased, for sum of £200 sells tract on a draft of Great Pipe Creek, called Silver Run, tract of land called *High Germany,* containing 110 acres.

BD1:627-628. Michael Sister recorded deed 20 June 1775, from George Sharar for 5 shillings, lot #166 in Jerusalemtown. Rossina, wife of George Sharar released dower.

BD1:628-629. John Wyatt recorded deed 20 June 1775, from Martin Study and Daniel Stiverson, for 10 shillings, part of *High Germany,* containing 30 acres more or less.

BD1:629-631. John Mathous recorded deed 20 June 1775, from John Wyatt for £300 Pennsylvania, sells and assigns tract called *High Germany,* containing 120 acres more or less. Signed by mark before Wm Blair, Wm Beatty.

BD1:631-634. Henry Leatherman recorded deed 20 June 1775, from Peter Balsel, for £800 part of parcel of land called *Content,* adjacent to *Tennach,* and *New Germany,* containing 393 acres. Signed by mark before Thos Price, Jacob Young.

BD1:634-636. John Grabill recorded deed 20 June 1775, from Jacob Danner for £1704, 222 ½ acres of tract called *Spring Plains,* and 53 acres of tract called *Henry's Ridge,* Elizabeth Danner released dower rights.

BD1:636-638. Peter Rubble recorded deed 20 June 1775, from Normand Bruce, for £17..6 confirms unto him part of tract called *Mount Sinai,* beginning at a bounded white oak the beginning tree of a tract called *Billy's Good Will,* granted unto Edward Grimes, containing 27 3/4 acres.

BD1:638-640. George Merkle recorded deed 20 June 1775, from Christian Everhart, for £250 Pennsylvania, part of tract called *Good Will,* containing 141 acres. Signed in German script. Savilla Eberhard released dower rights.

BD1:640-641. John Coor recorded lie bill 20 June 1775. To all people, whom it may concern, be it known that I, William Powell, cooper of Frederick County, hath at sundry times for six or seven years past, to Edward Lamb, Henry Stevenson, Thomas Durbin, Conrad Sissle and Pearce Lamb and to Diverse others let fall from my mouth the most [heaneas Pergerd - sic - heinous perjured] words which are as follows, declaring that a certain Moses Cose, son of John Cose, who departed this life about 16 or 17 years ago, at the age of 8 or 9 years, that he the said Moses Cose in time of sickness and on his death bed, did order his father John Cose to give unto me the said William Powell the sum of twenty shillings, and also requesting his father and mother that when ever his sister Saria becomes of age, to give her to me in marriage and further declaring that I have often seen the Gost of him the said Moses since his death and spoke with it concerning the above which I now having as true sense of this my great and miserable crimes, do freely acknowledge to be entirely false, and that I of my own self propagated the matter through spite and malice with out any reason, hoping to be forgiven of God, and the world for this my abominable sin and I do promise never to vilify or aspers the character of John Cose or any of his family from the date hereof. In witness I have hereunto set my hand and seal this fifteenth day of June 1775, William Powell. In presence of us, Pearce Lamb, Thos Durbin, Conrad Sesell (GS) Thomas Maguire, James Maguire, others.

BD1:641-642. Ludwick Young recorded deed 20 June 1775, from Samuel Bachtel and his wife, Ann, for £9 assigns tract *Bachtel's Delight,*

BD1:642-644. James Marshall recorded deed 21 June 1775, from David Kennedy of York County, Pennsylvania, for £150 all that tract included in a deed from Charles Carroll Esq. To Amos Maginley, who conveyed part of the tract to Richard Baird, and unto the above named David Kennedy, being recorded in Frederick county land Records, beginning on north bank of Middle Creek, in corner of William Rusk's land (formerly), containing 55 acres. Mary, wife of David Kennedy released dower.

BD1:644-646. John Booser recorded deed 21 June 1775, from Samuel Beall Junr., for £110 part of *The White Oak Levels,* laid out for 278 acres. Eleanor, his wife released dower rights.

BD1:646-648. Valentine Linganfelter recorded deed 21 June 1775 from Peter Tyshee, for £40, part of tract, *Resurvey on Mistaken Friend,* adjacent to Philip Rodenpiller's land, containing 35 acres. Signed in German script. Wife (name omitted) of said Tyshee, released dower rights.

BD1:648-650. Alexander McAllister recorded deed 21 June 1775, from Adam Hope and Margaret Hughes of York County, Pennsylvania, executors of the estate of John Patterson, deceased. For £467 sells part of *Exchange,* which John Briel esq., made over to Anthony Sell, and by him conveyed to the said John Patterson. Metes and bounds given for 150 acres.

BD1:650-652. Michael Sturm recorded deed 21 June 1775, from Peter Balsell for £800, part of tract called *Content,* adjacent to tract *Tennock,* 162 ½ acres. Signed by mark.

BD1:652-654. Martin Study recorded deed 21 June 1775, from Daniel Stevenson, tract called *High Germany,* 101 acres. Mary Elizabeth Stevenson released dower.

BD1:654-655. Henry Koontz recorded deed 21 June 1775, from Charles Angel, Christopher Erb and Judith Erb, executors of the estate of Peter Erb, deceased, for £46, tract *Dyer's Mill Forest,* adjacent to *Davis's Luck,* containing 50 acres.

BD1:655-657. Daniel Stevenson recorded deed 21 June 1775, from Martin Study for £39, three parcels, parts of *High Germany,* the first part conveyed to Study by Daniel Carroll, for 33 acres; also 92 acres of part conveyed to Stevenson and Study by Carroll, the third part is 25 acres. Signed by mark. Ann Margaret Study released dower.

BD1:657-658. Martin Study recorded agreement 21 June 1775. Daniel Stevenson agrees to allow use of a tail race through his land for the mill.

BD1:658-660. William Toms recorded deed 21 June 1774, from Valentine Summers for £5, *High Germany,* adjacent to *John Tom's Folly,* and *Palentine.*

BD1:660-662. Michael Kigga recorded deed 21 June 1775 from George Brent and Charity his wife. Whereas Thomas Cresap, late of Frederick County, was seized of a tract at the mouth of

Conecocheague, and having no issue but one surviving daughter, Charity, she now sells *Enochson's Delight,* containing 80 acres.

BD1:662-664. Nathaniel Patterson recorded deed 21 June 1775 from William Pidgeon, for £70..10 Pennsylvania, part of *Resurvey on Edward's Lot, and Hobson's Choice* on line of *Frenchman's Purchase.* 19 acres, 1 rood. Rachel Pidgeon released dower.

BD1:664-666. Samuel Toms recorded deed 21 June 1775, from Valentine Summers for £80, part of *Resurvey on Christian's Good Will,* 40 acres.

BD1:666-668. Valentine Summer recorded deed 21 June 1775, from Deedrick Henig Housar, taylor, for £6, sells lot #21 in Middletown. Signed German script, Anna Henig Howser released dower.

BD1:668-669. James M. Lingan recorded deed 21 June 1775 from Charles Beatty of Frederick County and George Fraser Hawkins of Prince George's County. For £6 sterling, they sell lot #4 in Addition to Georgetown, part of tract called *Knave's Disappointment,* to pay annual rents. Signed C. Beatty, G. Fraser Hawkins before Adam Stewart, William Deakins, Jr. Receipt. Martha wife of Charles Beatty and Susanna Truman, wife of George Fraser Hawkins, examined and released dower rights. Alienation fine of one farthing sterling paid Wm Murdock Beall.

BD1:669-671. Valentine Nicodemus recorded deed 21 June 1775 from David Ross, Richard Henderson of Prince George's County and Samuel Beall Jr., partners in Frederick Forge, for $250 (agreed to and paid to David Meek, their manager at the forge) they assign tract *Fellowship,* beginning at *Nelson's Folly,* 140 acres. Ariana Ross and Sarah Henderson released dower and Eleanor Beall relinquished her dower rights.

BD1:671-673. Richard Craddick recorded lease 21 June 1775 from Henry Clagett, tract called *Clagett's Folly,* except for the mill seat, containing 150 acres, adjacent to *Offutt's Pasture.* Rents specified in tobacco, and dependent on number of laborers, not including Craddicks wife, and male children under 21 and female children under 16 years. Craddick is to build a suitable dwelling cabin, a tobacco house and plant an apple orchard during term of lease.

BD1:674 John Poole recorded assignment of lease 21 June 1775, from Isaac Johnson for £70, assigns property and improvements for the remaining term of lease.

BD1:674-676. Nicholas Smith recorded lease from Samuel Bennett Chew for rents and consideration herein, assigns 100 acres, lot #21 on Chew's Farm, for 21 years, to a build a frame house and plant apple orchard.

BD1:676-677. George Sturrum recorded deed 21 June 1775 from Richard Burrell for £75, tract called *End of Strife,* adjacent to *Resurvey on Content* and *Higginbotham's Loss*, 60 acres. Signed by mark. Susanna Burrell relinquish right of dower.

BD1:678 Jacob Danner recorded deed 22 June 1775, from David Moore. Whereas a certain John Campbell of Anne Arundel County, by deed dated 11 Nov. 1772, recorded in Liber P;448-449, sold to James Frazer, 180 acres originally granted in 1743 to Campbell and Lawrence Robinson, by name of *Partnership,* and an additional tract containing 59 acres called *John's Delight,* for £1200, sells tracts, metes and bounds given for 234 acres in whole.

BD1:680-681. John Toms recorded deed 22 June 1775 from Lawrence O'Neale for £17..10, sells 17 ½ acres. Henrietta, wife of Lawrence O'Neale released dower.

BD1:681-683. Jacob Good recorded deed 22 June 1775, from Charles Clance for £72, lot #22 in Taneytown, and four other lots, near the main road from Frederick Town to York town. The wife, not named, examined apart and released dower rights.

BD1:683-684. Gilbert Watson recorded deed 22 June 1775, from Wilfred Neale, Elizabeth Neale, Eleanor Digges and John Digges, heirs at law of Edward Digges, late of Saint Mary's County, for £5 sells part of *Resurvey on Brother's Agreement,* 175 acres.

BD1:684-685. Daniel Miller recorded bill of sale 22 June 1775, from George Wolfe, taylor, for £6..8 one table, chair, spinning wheel, bench, chest with drawers, tea kettle, bed bedstead and furniture, cradle and other items listed, mortgaged.

BD1:685-687. Archibald Orme recorded deed 23 June 1775, from Thomas Johns for 10 shillings, tract called *Piney Grove,* at end of third line of tract *Evan's Choice,* granted to Evan Jones and now in the possession of Joshua Harbin, containing 263 acres; adjacent to *Orme's Meadow,* containing 19 acres. Sarah Johns released dower rights

BD1:687-689. George Tienn recorded deed 23 June 1775 from Henry Shriock of Elizabeth Town, sells lot #97, next to half lot of John Oster and lot of John Unseld. The wife of Henry Shriock, not named released dower rights.

BD1:689-690. William Howard recorded deed 29 June 1775 from John Hughes, for £150, tract called *Indian Field,* on draught of Buck Lodge, containing 50 acres; and 2nd tract called *John's Lot,* and third tract called *Addition,* containing 20 acres. Sarah Hughes released dower rights.

BD1:691-692. Charles Marteney recorded deed 29 June 1775, from Christian Everhart, for £250, tract called *Little Left,* beginning at *Watson's Welfare,* containing 100 acres. Signed in German script before Thos Price, Archibald Boyd. Sevilla, wife of Christian Everheart released dower rights.

BD1:692. Henry Reed recorded deed 4 July 1775 from John Cookerly for £100, tract *Resurvey on Bare Den,* 42 acres. Signed in German script before Upton Sheridine, Wm Beatty. Margaret, wife of John Cookerly released dower rights.

BD1:693 Thomas Contee and Leonard Hollyday recorded bill of sale 4 July 1775, from Thomas Warring for £80 mortgages one Negro man, Edward, woman Eleanor and girl Jane, horses, cattle, and other items, if sum paid by July next, sale is void.

BD1:694-695. Arthur Nelson recorded deed 4 July 1775, from Elias Delashmutt for £25, tract called *No Name,* on south side of Kittoctin, 33 acres. Witnesses: Archibald Boyd, John Nelson.

BD1:695-697. John Wood recorded deed 6 July 1775, from John Maginnis, part of tract called *Hickman's Discovery,* containing 85 acres. Margaret, wife of John Magginis released dower.

BD1:697-698. Conrad Mangins, recorded deed 10 July 1775, from Henry Leatherman, for £25, tract containing 28 acres, and also part of *Resurvey on Friendship Dropt,* containing 9 acres, 30 perches. Signed in German script before Thos Price, P. Waring. Wife examined apart and released dower.

BD1:699. William Howard recorded bond 10 July 1775 from Ignatius Hagan, bond for £100, h agrees to convey tract called *Indian Fields.*

BD1:699-700. Mary Jacobs recorded bill of sale 17 July 1775 from John Becraft for £20, one cow and calf, a yearling and heifer. Signed by mark.

BD1:700-701. William Barrick recorded deed 17 July 1775 from Henry Reed for £400, tract called *Link,* beginning at tract *Bare Den,* containing 158 acres; and also *Resurvey on Bare Denn,* 42 acres. Jane wife of Henry Reed released dower.

BD1:701-702. John Duncan recorded power of attorney from Daniel Culp and Ester his wife, legally seized of lot #8 in Sharpsburgh, empower John Duncan to sell same. Signed in Martinsburg, Berkeley County, Virginia.

BD1:702-703. Christopher Shockey recorded bond from Philip Stansburgh. Bond to let Cow Run, a draught of Catoctin, run in its natural course after he has use of it two days per week.

BD1:703. Christopher Shockey recorded bond from Valentine Shockey of Cumberland County, Pennsylvania

BD1:703-704. Negro Scott recorded manumission 24 July 1775 from Joseph Talbot.

BD1:704-705. Samuel Hardy's heirs recorded deed 29 July 1775 from John Nobbs. Tract called *Hard To Get,* 8 ½ acres. Receipt from Fielder Hardy, executrix of Samuel Hardy. Elizabeth, wife of John Nobbs released dower rights.

BD1:705-706. John Summers recorded bill of sale 31 July 1775 from Joseph Hagan for £63 sells one Negro girl, Terry. Signed by mark before Peter Hoey, Bennet Hagan.

BD1:706-707. Abraham Lingenfelter recorded deed 13 May 1774 from Joseph Chapline, for £1, lot #60 in Sharpsburgh Town.

BD1:707-708. Abraham Lingenfelter recorded deed 13 May 1774 from Joseph Chapline, for one shilling, lot #8 in Sharpsburgh Town.

BD1:708-709. Abraham Lingenfelter recorded deed 13 May 1774 from Joseph Chapline, for £2..10, lot #79 in Sharpsburgh Town.

END OF VOLUME BD1

Frederick County Deeds, Liber BD2

BD2:1-2. George Scott recorded deed 9 Aug. 1775 from John Carey of Fredericktown, for 5 shillings, one undivided moiety or half share of 151 acres tract, *Landstoll,* Signed before Jacob Young, Archibald Boyd. Mary Carey, wife of John released dower.

BD2:2-4. John Crissman recorded deed 9 August 1775 from John Betts, joiner, of Baltimore County, for £6, lot #10 in Town of New London, on tract, *Timber Ridge.* Signed before James Clarke, John Moore.

BD2:4-6. John Beall recorded deed 9 Aug 1775 from Charles Beatty and George Fraser Hawkins. For £6, lot #184 in *Addition to Georgetown,* on tract called *Knave's Disappointment.* Martha wife of Charles Beatty and Susan Freeman wife of George Fraser Hawkins released dower rights.

BD2:6-7. Thomas Swearingen recorded deed 10 August 1775 from Alexander Beall for £20, tract called *Trouble Enough,* containing 103 acres. Elizabeth Beall released dower.

BD2:7-9. Jacob Merryfield recorded deed 14 August 1775 from Peter Krowle. For £300, *Much Grumbling,* 21 acres, also tract *Stephen's Hope,* 141 acres. Signed German Script. Carolina, wife of Peter released dower.

BD2:9-11. Edward Inmann recorded lease 15 August 1775, from Mary Hall, executrix of Benjamin Hall Junr., deceased, late of Frederick County, for 21 years, tract called *Hall's Chance,* containing 74 acres, he to pay annual rent of £8 and to build a dwelling house 20 ft. by 30 ft. Signed by both parties.

BD2:11-12. Henry Coonce recorded deed 15 August 1775 from Rudolph Brubach, in exchange for one tract, part of *High Germany,* containing 2 1/4 acres. Signed in German script. Margaret released dower rights.

BD2:13-14 Rudolph Brubach recorded deed 15 August 1775, from Henry Coonce, in exchange for one tract, part of *High Germany,* containing 2 1/4 acres. Signed in German script. Fronica Koontz released dower rights.

BD2:14-16. John Lawrence recorded deed 15 August 1775, from Robert Wood for £112..10, tract called *Pleasant Forrest.* 132 acres. Catharine Wood, wife of Robert released dower.

BD2:16-18. Samuel Boggess recorded deed from Solomon and Mary Turner for £100 tract called *Crouches Chance* on Bush Creek, for 25 acres, and the *Resurvey* laid out for 92 acres. Signed before Upton Sheridine, Lewis Mobberly. Acknowledgment before Upton Sheridine, Wm Beatty.

BD2:18-25. John Lackland recorded land commission and deposition, issued to Andrew Heugh, Zadok Magruder, Thomas Cramphin and David Lynn on part of tract *Prevention.* Advertisement posted at Rock Creek Church, Rock Creek Chapel, The Paint Chapel and at Georgetown. Met at the place where the beginning tree of *Joseph's Park* formerly stood, deemed to be a tree of *Prevention,* 9 March 1773. John Hardie, aged 44 years deposed that 14 years ago, he was with his uncle John

Allison, who was a renter of John Lackland, and disputes arouse among the tenants regarding the bounds, and this deponent along with Jeremiah Lackland were chain carriers after William Dent, surveyor on tract. Jeremiah Lackland, age 45 years, deposed that beginning tree was near the south east corner of the plantation where Samuel Prather dwells, belonging to a child of the late Jacob Barnes. John Hardie further deposeth regarding a heap of white stones lying in the corner of a fence near where he lately lived near to James Higgins' plantation, and further deposeth that he and his father, John Hardie lived for 30 years on said land as tenants to the late Capt. James Edmonston. Signed by mark. On 16 Nov. 1773, met at John Lackland's quarter, at the house the late John Allison Sr. Lately lived, on John Lackland's plantation, and ran courses with Thomas Belt, who ran four different lines. On 17 May 1774, met at John Lackland's quarter. John Jones Sr., aged upwards 70 years deposed that he has lived in the neighborhood about 43 years, and he understood from the late John Allison Senr. That Capt. Alexander Beall laid off the land where he lived, John Hardie and Francis Abstone when they became tenants to Capt. James Edmonston. Signed by mark. On 14 Nov. 1774, met at the house of Samuel Prather and took the deposition of Weaver Barnes, aged 73 years or thereabouts, who deposed that 14 or 15 years ago he came to this place to purchase part of *John Richard's Lane,* a part of *Prevention,* which had been attached by the late James Perry and William Williams, and the aforesaid white oak tree was the beginning tree of tract he was shown. William Deakins, aged 55 or thereabouts, said about 14 years ago, he came to area to purchase a tract of land of John Richard's which he then lived on, and was shown the said white oak. On Tuesday, 25 July 1775, met one Colonel Samuel Beall, aged 60 years, to best of his memory, 27 years ago last spring, at instance of William Beall, he left his house in order to run out a piece of land he had sold to John Richards, out of tract of land called *Hermitage,* claimed by Thomas Butler, and tree he now touches was beginning tree of *Addition,* Philip Lee's land, and a tree of *Prevention.* He further states that about 19 years ago, Isaac Brooke showed him the beginning of *The Addition,* then Hancock Lee's land. James Moore, aged 56 years, deposed that 10-12 years ago, Luke Windsor showed deponent this tree and said it was the beginning of *Addition,* Hancock Lee's land.

BD2:25-26. Peter Engle recorded bill of sale 17 Aug. 1775 from Jacob Youler for £3..18, one cow.

BD2:27-28. Francis Deakins recorded deed 10 August 1775, from Michael Cresap for £5, lot #1 in Skipton, containing ½ acre. Signed before Thos Cresap, Th. Weller.

BD2:28-31. George Scott recorded deed 10 Aug. 1775, from Benjamin Burdette for £100. Whereas Alexander Grant on 18 Oct. 1770 sold to Benjamin Burdette, two parcels granted to him, one on 20 Dec. 1749, for 30 acres by the name of *Alexander and John,* and the other granted 22 October 1761, for 50 acres called *John's Delight,* standing near Gunners Branch a draught of Seneca. Charity, wife of Benjamin Burdette released dower.

BD2:31-33. Peter Beshear recorded deed 19 Aug. 1775, from Valentine Stickle, lot #131 in Frederick Town. Sybilla Stickle released dower.

BD2:33-34. Edward Lingan Boteler recorded bill of sale 20 August 1775, from John Demorak for 5 head of cattle and 7 yearling calves for £35. Signed by mark before Abraham Lemaster, Rachel Lemaster.

BD2:34-37. Philemon Plummer recorded deed 21 August 1775, from Thomas Snowden, John Snowden and Samuel Snowden of Prince George's and Ann Arundel Counties, ironmasters, for £63 sells three parts of *Addition to Brooke Grove,* containing 159 ½ acres; 6 3/4 acres on Hawlings River, and third part, 6 1/8 acres adjacent to *Bradley's Choice,* plus another part for 47 ½ acres. Signed before Basil Burgess, H. Ridgely.

BD2:37-39. George Brengle recorded deed 23 Aug. 1775 from Adam Beckenbaugh for £5, sells lot #128 in Fredericktown. Signed in German script.

BD2:39-40 Peter Albough, recorded assignment, an agreement of co-heirs on a lease between Peter Albough and the representatives of Zachariah Albough deceased, died intestate possessed of 25 acres of land leased on Monocacy Manor. For 5 shillings, assign all our right in lease of *Addition to Story's Chance,* for the unexpired term of said lease, made 19 September 1774, William Albough, James Albough, John Arnold, Zachariah Albough, Reinhart Voltz and Philip Danner. Receipts from James Albough, William Albough and Reinhart Voltz for their shares of lease.

BD2:40-41. Solomon Turner recorded bill of sale 26 August 1775, from Wm James Turner for £30, four head of cattle, three sheep and 13 hogs, together with beds, pots, pewter, household furniture provided if sum paid by 26 August 1776, sale is void.

BD2:41-42. Samuel Beall recorded release 26 August 1775 from William Chapline, James Chapline, and Joseph Chapline, executors of the will of Joseph Chapline, deceased, for 5 shillings, release and quit claim to tract, *Little I Thought It,* containing 190 acres.

BD2:43-44. Abraham Faw recorded bill of sale 27 August 1775, from Jacob Shue for £50 one black mare, 2 red and white cows, red and white heifer, two calves, two feather beds and furniture; other housewares listed.

BD2:44-46. John Hanson Jr. recorded bill of sale 1 Sept. 1775, from Samuel Irwin for £150, sells all the books in the schedule hereunto attached being in his house in Frederick Town, next door to John Goff, barber. Sale is void if sum is paid. John Hanson is put in full possession by delivering to him one book, called Jus Parliamentarium, in the name of all the said books. Signed by both parties. The appended list was recorded: Items listed:

Attorneys Pocket Book 2 vol.	Law of Arrests
Attorneys Practice on K. B. 2 vol.	Treatise of Distresses
Attorneys Practice in C.P. 2 vol.	Law of Executors
Barons Abridgement 5 vol.	Law of Awards
Bingamon's Conveyance	Law of Moiety
Burns Justice 4 vol.	Hales History of the Law
Coke on Littleston	Wills
Common Law Common Placed	Law of Errors
Complete Attorney and Solicitor	Harrisons Chancery Practice 2 vols.
Commission on Bills	Swinburn on Wills
Every Mans Lawyer	Heaths Maxims
Fitzharborts Natura Bisvinim	Suffering or the Law of Nature
Law of Trusts	Demals Civil Law 2 vols.
Law of Ejectments	H. Gratius de Jure ...
Law of Devises	Jacobs Law Dictionary
Law of Evidence	Woode Institute

Law of Executions	Hawkins Pleas of Crown
Practice Court of Chancery	Jus Parliamentarium
Gilberts Replavin	Lilly's Entries
Treatise of Tenants	Woods Conveyancing 3 vols.
Gilberts Common Pleas	Lea Parliamentoria
Treatise of Rents	Cokes Reports 7 vols.
Cokes Reports	Nemans Reports 2 vols.
Stranger Reports 2 vols	Williams Reports 3 vols.
Atkins Reports 3 vols	Raymonds Reports 3 vols.
Burrows Reports 3 vols.	Dyers Reports
Wilsons Reports	Hobarts Reports
Vaughans Reports	Crokes Reports 3 vols.
Ventrie Reports	Leveney's Report, part 192
Salkeld's Reports 172 parts	Carillence Reports
Plowden's Reports	

Statues at Large from Magna Carta to 10 Geo III, 10 vol.

BD2:46-47. Ludwick Byerly and Jacob Harbough recorded bill of sale from Philapena Marner, in consideration of their serving as her sureties as administrator of the estate of Lawrence Benson, assigns one copper still with all tubs and things belonging thereto, 11 head of horned cattle, 3 horses, 13 sheep, 11 hogs, 4 feather and chaff beds, 3 iron pots, 1 plow, 1 iron harrow, 2 chested; provided she makes settlement of the estate in good time, bill of sale is void.

BD2:47-49. William Booth, gentleman, recorded deed 6 Sept. 1775, from Lewis Smith, farmer, for £26 assigns tract called *Chestnut Thickett,* on south side of the Bleu Mountain, near the lower main road, 21 acres. Signed before Jacob Young, Bartm Booth. Margaret Smith, wife of Lewis Smith released dower.

BD2:49-53. The Rev. Bartholomew Booth recorded deed 6 Sep 1775 from Fielder Gantt of Frederick County and Edward Gantt of Calvert County, of the first part; and William Deakins Junr., Thomas Johns and Adam Stewart of the second part. Refers to prior deed for parts of *Swede's March,* and two parts of *Fielderea Manor,* part adjacent to *Hawkin's Plain,* 96 ½ acres. Deed corrects errors in prior deed's metes and bounds. Signed by all parties.

BD2:53-56. Bartholomew Booth recorded trust deed 6 Sept. 1775 from Adam Stewart, William Deakins and Thomas Johns recorded trust deed from Adam Stewart; refers to deed made to Caleb Dorsey in 1766.

BD2:56-59. Bartholomew Booth recorded release 6 Sep 1775 from Caleb Dorsey of Anne Arundel County and Fielder Gantt. Release includes mention of Negroes, and issue of female Negroes.

BD2:59-60. Gilbert Hickman, son of Joshua Hickman. recorded bill of sale 6 Sept. 1775, from Aeneas Campbell, a mulatto slave named Bell and her increase. Signed before Archibald Boyd.

BD2:61-64. Hugh Riley recorded land commission and depositions, 6 Sept. 1775, to Thomas Cramphin Jr., Simon Nicholls, Nathaniel Magruder, son of Alexander, and George Beall, on part of

Dann, on Rock Creek. On 6 Dec. 1774, Charles Jones of Rock Creek, 65 years old or thereabouts, deposed about two trees on south side of Penson's Spring Branch of Rock Creek, about 180 years from the main branch on the west side, deposed that about 50 years ago, William Penson requested him and several others to see the beginning of aforesaid tract, when John Flint and Caleb Litton attested to the beginning tree. Tuesday 14 Feb. 1775, at house of Hugh Riley, on *Dann,* deposition of Samuel Beall, aged 59 years, at oak described by Charles Jones deposition, in 1743, he came to this tree in company of Francis Warring and Thomas Cleland to lay off parcel which was a certain William Penson's when they told him that tree was the beginning of Penson's land which he bought of Clement Brooke. A few years after the death of William Penson, he was riding past tree with William Beall who told him it was the beginning tree of William Penson's land, then in possession of Mrs. Riley. Thomas Pritchett, aged 64 years, deposed that about 40 years ago in company with William Penson, Caleb Litton, John Flint and Charles Jones, and John Pritchett his father, made oath before Captain Alexander Magruder, then a magistrate, that the aforesaid bounded red oak was the beginning of Penson's land. Stone planted saying: H Riley 1775, on this date, being the beginning tree of *Dann.*

BD2:65-66. Joseph Belt recorded release of mortgage 7 Sept. 1775, from John Glassford & Co. Of Glasgow, Scotland, merchants, for 5 shillings, lot #50 in Georgetown, and slaves, etc. recorded in deed records in Frederick County, 1 October 1762, slaves Suck, Saul, James, Peter, Sue and Joanis. Signed by Henry Riddall, attorney for John Glassford & Co., before Jas Beall, Luke Marbury.

BD2:66-69. Henry Stevenson Jr. recorded deed 13 Sept. 1775, from Henry Stevenson Sr. of Baltimore County, for £5, 16 acres of *Resurvey on the Dairy,* beginning at part of *Kelly's Delight.*

BD2:69-70. Thomas Chatwell, collier, recorded deed 13 Sep 1775 from Andrew Ifer for £30, part of tract *Foland,* signed by mark. Christina Ifer released dower.

BD2:70-76. Thomas Johnson Jr., attorney at law, recorded mortgage 14 Sept 1775, from Denton Jacques, late of the City of Annapolis, now of Frederick County. Whereas it was contracted and agreed that Johnson would make over his share of the iron furnace and forge commonly called Fort Frederick Iron Furnace, this mortgage for £11,500 is agreed to, to pay £1500 1 July 1776, and annually, until paid with interest.

BD2:77-78. Henry Child recorded bill of sale 15 Sept. 1775, from Laurence O'Neale for £121, Negro woman Frann, Negro men, Harry and Charles.

BD2:78-79. Adam Knouff recorded bill of sale 15 Sept. 1775, from Jacob Turscheimer, for £23, sells 3 cows, 2 red heifers, 8 sheep, bay horse, 10 to 11 years old. Signed German script.

BD2:79-81. Henry Newcomer recorded deed of gift 20 Sept. 1775, from Ann Garber for 10 shillings sterling, assigns all her right to a bond given to her by Michael Garber for £250, Pennsylvania, and also legacy bequeathed to her by her father John Garber, deceased, to be paid at decease of Elizabeth Garber, wife of John Garber. Signed before John Stull, Elie Williams.

BD2:81-84. George Swingley recorded deed 26 Sept. 1775, from Michael Kirkpatrick for £100, tracts *John's Lott,* and part of *Dickenson's Pleasure,* on east side of Antietam Creek, containing 18 acres. Sarah, wife of Michael Kirkpatrick released dower.

BD2:84-87. George Scott recorded deed 26 Sept. 1775, from Andrew Scott, attorney at law, for £378..3..10, assigns several tracts: *Walnut Bottom,* 750 acres; *Dumfries* 200 acres; *Castle Hill*, 50 acres; *Cocklefield*, 350 acres; *Williams Advice*, 150 acres; *Deer Park*, 400 acres; *Frenche's Defeat*, 425 acres; *Defiance*, 445 acres; *Land of Promise*, 1339 acres taken up and surveyed for Andrew Scott, Walter Hanson, Jennifer and John Swan; and the following Negroes: Phillis, Suck, Charles, Tom, Harry, Moll, Rose, Lee, Frank, Poll, Grace, Ned, Jane, Jacob, Frederick, Cupid and Peter; part of the estate of George Scott, late of Prince George's County, deceased, father of Andrew Scott, and sundry books and articles on attached schedule. Whereas Andrew Scott put list of fees in hands of Thomas French, Esq., sheriff of Frederick County in the present year; and also three different lists put in the hands of Lawrence O'Neale in 1772, 1773 and 1774. Signed Andrew Scott, George Scott. Attached list of books in Andrew Scott's library: Burrows Reports two vols., Lou Raymonds Reports, 2 vols.; Jere Williams Reports, 2 vols., Keebles Reports, three volumes, Stranges Reports, 2 vols; Saklelds Reports one vol.; Cookes Reports, one vol. Bacons Abridgment, 5 vols.; Lily's Ditto, 2 vols.; Rolles Dt. Two volumes; Cartheur Reports one vol.; Hobarts Reports one vol; Croke Reports 2 vols; Justinian Ins. One vol.; Coke's Institutes 2 vol.; Woods Institutes one vol.; Ludwick's Reports 2 vol.; Cokes Entries one vol. Clifts Entries one vol.; Blackstone's Commentaries, 4 vol.; Blackstones, Appendix one vol.; Blackstones Law Tracts, 2 vol.; Statues Abridged, 8 vol.; Wingates Statutes, 1 vol. Wrights Tenures, one vol.; Attorney's Practice 2 vol.; Attorney's Practice Kings Bench, 2 vols.; Gilberts Evidence, one vol.; Law of Ejectment, one vol. Styles Practical Register, one vol.; Shepherds Discourses, one vol. Swinburn on Wills one vol. A valuable book; Hornes Pleader one vol.; Browns Modua Intrandp. One vol. Every Mans Own Lawyer, one vol.; Attorneys Companion one vol.; Pleas of the Crown, one vol.; Doctrine of Dominions 1 vol.; Maritime Laws, 1 vol.; Complete Attorney, one vol.; Modern Conveyancing, one vol.; Doctor and Student, one vol.; Student's Guide, one vol.; Nelson's Justinian, one vol.; Impartial Lawyer, one vol.; Trials from law, one vol.; Conveyances 2 vols.; Precedents for Pleading 7 vols.; Jacobs Law Dictionary one vol.; Law French Dictionary, Hawkins Abridgement of Cohen Institute; Bunlanague on Public Law; B. Johnson Plowden's Reports one vol.; S. Irwin has same book; Baron's Laws of Maryland 1 volume. Signed by Andrew Scott. Witness Jacob Young, Arch Boyd.

BD2:88-89. Samuel Flemming recorded deed 2 Oct. 1775 from Jacob Trout for £185, *Rich Bottom,* 75 acres. Signed before Thos Price, Archibald Boyd.

BD2:90-91. [Del'd Upton Beall, 17 May 1799] Brooke Beall recorded deed 2 Oct 1775, from Thomas Johns for 10 shillings, part of *Piney Grove,* beginning at tract called *Piney Level,* taken up by James Wallace, for 286 acres. Sarah Johns released dower.

BD2:92-93. John Thomas recorded deed 2 Oct. 1775, made 8 Sep 1775 from Leonard Smith for £21..17, part of tract called *Victory,* at 7th line of *Poplar Thickett,* for 12 ½ acres. John Thomas is to keep a lane upon wide enough for a wagon to go through from the tract *Content.* Elizabeth Smith released dower rights.

BD2:93-95. James Stimson recorded deed 2 Oct. 1775 from Nicholas Seybert for £5..15, assigns part of *Pleasant Fields,* formerly resurveyed by Samuel Reyley for 5 3/4 acres.

BD2:95-97. James Stimson recorded deed 2 Oct. 1775 from Nicholas Seybert for one shilling sterling, part of tract called *Pleasant Plains,* for 9 acres.

BD2:97-99. Peter Wampler recorded deed 2 Oct. 1775, from David Moore, shop keeper for £160, all his interest in a tract called *Pork Hall,* on south draught of Little Pipe Creek for 45 acres. Signed before Wm Beatty, Archibald Boyd.

BD2:100-101. Andrew Arnold recorded deed 2 Oct. 1775, from Gilbert Middleton of the City of Annapolis. Whereas Horatio Samuel Middleton, late of Annapolis, died possessed of *Pools Delight Enlarged,* to be sold by Ann Middletown, who has also departed this life; and whereas Joseph Middleton, William Middleton, Ellen Atkins and the said Gilbert Middleton for himself as well as on behalf of Elizabeth Middleton to whom he is guardian, since the death of Ann Middleton by their petition in chancery for sum of £414. Sell 287 acres. Signed Gilbert Middleton before Dan of St. Thos Jennifer, W. Coale.

BD2:101-103. Sarah Plummer recorded deed 2 Oct. 1775, from William Ballinger for £80 part of *Turkey Flight,* on north side of Bush Creek, for 25 acres, originally granted John Prather 23 Nov 1752, and by virtue of attachment obtained against said Prather 17 June 1755, then condemned for the use of a certain Christopher Lowndes and conveyed by Lowndes to a certain John Waters, son of John, and then to William Ballinger. Signed before Jacob Young, Archibald Boyd. Cassandra Ballinger released dower rights.

BD2:103-105. Casper Beckbough recorded deed 2 Oct. 1775, from Henry Vollenmyder, glassier, for £35 Pennsylvania, all his interest in lot in Middletown. Signed G.S., Barbara Vollenmyder, released dower.

BD2:106-108. Joseph Hobbs recorded deed 2 Oct. 1775, from Dickerson Simpkins for £36, tract called *Alder Spring,* into a branch of Linganore, 49 acres. Signed by mark before Wm Beatty, Henry Barnes. Mary Simpkins released dower.

BD2:108-110. John Nicholls recorded deed 2 Oct. 1775 from John Garrett for £61, lot #22 on *Resurvey on Merryland,* 50 ½ acres. Signed by mark before Bartholomew Booth, Jacob Young.

BD2:110-111. Nicholas White recorded deed 2 Oct 1775 from Michael Holler of Frederick Town, lot #179 in Additional Lots of Frederick, as in deed from Jacob Brand. Dorothy Holler released dower.

BD2:112-114. Daniel Loehr, taylor, recorded deed 2 Oct. 1775, from Valentine Stickle of Fredericktown, lot #131, as in deed recorded in Liber J:442-443, adjoins Peter Bohrer's lot. Signed by both parties. Sybella Stickle released dower rights.

BD2:115-117. George Murdoch recorded deed 2 Oct. 1775, from Lawrence O'Neale, sheriff. Whereas Thomas Taylor, obtained against Fielder Gaunt and James Hunter for £952..6..8, tract called *Cut Knee,* by patent, 315 acres.

BD2:117-118. John Holmes recorded bond 3 Oct. 1775, from Michael Bence of Prince George's County, taylor, for £200 assigns tract where the said Michael Bence formerly lived adjacent to *Roger's Race Ground,* known by the name of *Snowden's Manor Enlarged,* containing 100 acres by courses specified in deed from Richard Snowden, deceased to Michael Bence, and also his wife's release of dower.

BD2:118-120. Richard Gartrell recorded deed 3 Oct. 1775, from Thomas Moore for £299.10, part of *Snowden's Manor Enlarged,* for 100 acres. Signed before David Lynn, Edward Burgess. Sarah, wife of Thomas Moore released dower.

BD2:120-121. James Hudgson recorded deed of gift 9 Oct. 1775, from Eleanor Morris for love and affection towards my son, James Hudgson, one bond from George Arehart for £10, and one bond on John Stull for £8 and £2 on book account from George Arehart, one white cow, one black and white cow, two white steer calves, one feather bed with curtains and other furniture, one other bed, and all my household stuff. Signed by mark before George Erhart, William Johnson.

BD2:121 Francis Thomas recorded assignment of lease 11 Oct. 1775, from Charles Beckwith for £100, as executor of George Beckwith, deceased, transfer lease. Signed 10 October 1775. [Memo: lease assigned stands recorded in Liber G:folio 64].

BD2:122-123. Rev'd John Lewis of St. Mary's County, recorded deed 15 Oct. 1775, from Thomas Drury of St. Mary's County for £60, tract called *Conclusion,* containing one acre. Signed by mark.

BD2:123-124. Elihu Hickman, son of Margrate Campbell, recorded deed of confirmation 21 Oct. 1775, from Aeneas Campbell and his wife, Margrate Campbell, in consideration of natural love and affection, confirm and 5 shillings, confirms prior deeds for all their interest in a tract of land, and the goods and chattels given.

BD2:125-126. William Luckett recorded deed 21 Oct 1775, made 22 May, from James Rimmer for £165, tract called *Chance,* containing 145 acres. Signed by mark.

BD2:126-128. Joseph Burkhart recorded deed 24 Oct. 1775, from John Birkett, for £45 all his interest in tract *Black oak Stripe,* beginning at 3d line of *Winfield's Delight,* granted John Ross, containing 31 acres. Signed in German script. Mollena, wife of John Burkhart released dower.

BD2:128-129. Christian Stouder recorded assignment of lease 24 Oct. 1775, from John Brown for £8..10 indemnifies him for rents due next November on lease for five years from Jacob Shuh to John Collins and said Brown. Signed by mark before Robert Wood.

BD2:129-130. Jeremiah Orme recorded deed 25 Oct. 1775, from Nathaniel Beall for £28, part of tract called *Easie Purchase.* Signed before David Lynn, Edward Burgess.

BD2:130-131. Christian Welty recorded deed 30 Oct. 1775, from Thomas Ringold of Chestertown, Maryland, merchant, for £96, 24 acres adjoining tract called *St. John's,* agreeable to a plat by Thomas Brookes.

BD2:131-133. Robert McNull recorded lease 2 Nov. 1775, from Joseph Chapline, made 8 May 1775 between Robert McNaught for rents and covenants herein, Joseph Chapline assigns tenement called *Joe's Lot,* containing 100 acres, for him to let for 21 years, to build a dwelling house 24 ft by 26 ft with a brick or stone chimney, and also a barn, 50 ft. by 24 ft, including a threshing floor 16 ft. by 24 ft. and to pay quit rents due on the land. Signed by both parties.

BD2:133-135. Alexander McNull recorded lease 2 Nov. 1775, from Joseph Chapline lets to Alexander McNaught for yearly rents and covenants, part of tract called *Joe's Lot,* containing 117 acres, with improvements, for 15 years, to pay yearly £15 Pennsylvania rents, and to maintain tenement, if wood on lot not sufficient may cut timber on the adjacent land belonging to Chapline.

BD2:135-137. Samuel Jones of Prince George's County, recorded deed 4 Nov. 1775, from Snowden Sargent for £520, part of *Resurvey on Dorsetshire,* containing 300 acres. Mary, wife of Snowden Sargent released dower.

BD2:137-139. Peter Engle Jr., recorded mortgage 8 Nov. 1775, from Margaret Klein, spouse of George Klein, deceased, and George Klein for £63..3, tract called *What You Will,* containing 100 acres.

BD2:139-141. Thomas Belt recorded deed 11 Nov. 1775, from Joseph Sprigg for £500 sterling, part of *Long Meadow Enlarged,* adjacent to Mr. Thomas Sprigg's part of said tract, containing 420 acres. Hannah Sprigg, wife of Joseph Sprigg released dower.

BD2:141-144. William Murdoch Beall recorded deed 13 Nov. 1775, from James Marshall, part of *Gantt's Garden,* adjacent to Daniel Jacob's part, containing 260 acres. Signed before T. Bowles, Archibald Boyd. Alienation fine paid Dan'l of St. Thos Jennifer.

BD2:144-146. Barton Philpott recorded deed 13 Nov. 1775, from Thomas Gantt Jr., of Prince George's County, for £120, part of two tracts, *Hawkin's Merry Peep a Day,* and *Merryland,* beginning at *Payne's Delight,* to *Coxon's Rest.* Signed before Jeremiah Belt 3d, Jno Cooke. Susannah, wife of Thomas Gantt released dower.

BD2:146-149. Jacob Hains recorded deed 13 Nov. 1775, from Allen Pearson of Liverpool, Lancaster County, Great Brittain, who constituted Henry Thompson of Baltimore County to act as his attorney, who did appoint Samuel Owings to serve as Attorney. For £165, sells tract called *Fells Retirement,* signed before Hercules Courtenay and James Clarke, J.P.'s for Baltimore County.

BD2:149-153. Hannah Raitt, formerly Hammond, of Frederick County, and Ann Hammond and Ruth Hammond of Anne Arundel County, recorded deed of partition 15 May 1776. Whereas their father Nathan Hammond, of Anne Arundel County, deceased, devised to them a tract called *Friendship,* containing 475 acres, following is the metes and bounds description of the division of the tract. Signed by all three parties before Jacob Young, George Scott.

BD2:154-155. Thomas Bayne recorded deed 15 Nov. 1775, from John Bayne for 5 shillings, assigns tract called *None Such,* containing 75 acres. Signed before Jacob Young, Archibald Boyd.

BD2:156-157. David Smith recorded deed 13 Nov. 1775, from Samuel Krebill for £50, tract called *White's Delight,* a part of *Resurvey on Old Fox Deceived,* beginning at wagon road that leads from John Stulls to Peter White's, where Hugh Terrence did live, containing 144 acres. Signed Samuel Crebil. Hannah wife of Samuel released dower.

BD2:157-159. Francis Deakins recorded deed 13 Nov. 1775, from Daniel Veatch for £37..12..6, tract called *Doe Neck,* adjacent to *Meredith's Hunting Quarter,* 20 ½ acres. Deed made to better secure debt. Signed before David Lynn, Edward Burgess.

BD2:159-161. Peter Smeltzer recorded deed 13 Nov. 1775, from Jacob Miller for £217 Pennsylvania, part of tract called *Wooden Platter,* on east side of Kittoctin Creek, containing 108 ½ acres. Susanna, wife of Jacob Miller, released dower.

BD2:162-163. Benjamin Gassaway recorded deed 13 Nov. 1775, from Joseph Hobbs for £50, all his right to tract called *Alder Spring,* on south side of bottom that descends into Linganore. 49 ½ acres. Anne Hobbs, wife of Joseph, released dower.

BD2:164-165. Ludwick Rothrock recorded deed 13 Nov. 1775, from John Garrett for £47..5, lot #22 on *Resurvey on Merryland,* 25 acres. Signed by mark before Bartholomew Booth, Jacob Young. AF paid Wm M. Beall.

BD2:165-167. Samuel Prather recorded deed 13 Nov. 1775, from John Garrett for £210..17..6, lot #15, on *Resurvey on Merryland,* 153 acres with improvements. Signed by mark before Bartholomew Booth, Jacob Young. AF paid Wm M. Beall.

BD2:167-169. John Carlock recorded deed 13 Nov. 1775, from Edward Perryn, John Perryn and Joseph Perryn, executors of John Perrins for £25 Penn. tract called *Perryns Venture,* beginning at Mill branch, containing 50 acres. Signed before John Stull, Sam'l Beall Junr.

BD2:169-171. William Cornell recorded deed 13 Nov. 1775, from Richard VanDike for £200, part of *Maiden's Point,* containing 100 acres. Signed before Jacob Wimmer, Richard Cornell. Eleanor Van Dike, wife of Richard released dower.

BD2:171-173. James McAllister recorded deed 13 Nov. 1775, from John Garrett for £300, part of *Resurvey on Merryland,* on the main road, containing 92 acres with improvements. Signed by mark before Bartholomew Booth, Jacob Young. AF paid Wm M. Beall.

BD2:174-176. Ann Arnold Key recorded deed of gift 13 Nov. 1775, from John Ross Key of Frederick County, to his mother, the widow of Francis Key, parcel called *Epping Forrest,* on 11th line of land lease to John Allison, containing 400 acres.

BD2:176-179. Henry Hunter recorded power of attorney and deed 13 Nov. 1775, from John Whitset of Orange County, North Carolina, for good consideration paid by Samuel Hunter, now deceased, in his lifetime, and also by his son Henry Hunter, heretofore, appoints Basil Beall his lawful attorney to make deed. Deed recorded for £100 for tract on east side of Ballinger's Creek.

BD2:180-181. Joseph Hobbs recorded deed 13 Nov. 1775, from Benjamin Gassaway for £155, tract called *Nothing Venture, Nothing Gett,* on east side of Monocacy Creek near *Joseph's Friendship,* containing 100 acres. Ruth Gassaway released dower.

BD2:181-184. Christian Lance recorded deed 13 Nov. 1775, from Jacob Lighter for £5 *Resurvey on Well Taught,* adjacent to *Skipton Craven,* on Antietam Creek. 2 ½ acres. Signed in G.S., Jacob Leidert. Euliana Lighter released dower rights.

BD2:184-186. Joseph Flint recorded deed from Edward Perryn, John Perryn and Joseph Perryn, executors of John Perrins Sr., for £130 tract called *Perrin's Fancy,* on south side of Little Tonoloway Creek, 3 miles from mouth of said creek, containing 95 acres. Signed by all three before Sam'l Beall, John Stull.

BD2:186-188. John Powell Jr. recorded deed from Edward Perryn, John Perryn and Joseph Perryn, executors of John Perrins Sr., deceased, assigns to John Powell, tract called *Killam's Advantage,* containing 50 acres. Ann Perrin, wife of Edward Perrin, released dower rights.

BD2:189-192. Bernard Hershberger recorded deed 13 Nov. 1775, from Leonard Smith and Bennett Neale and Elizabeth Sprigg Neale his wife. Whereas Daniel Johnson Lane of Prince William County, Virginia, did on 9 Nov. 1741, made a deed to Isaac Wells, recorded in Prince George's county, for tract called *Low Land,* and by his will, devised to his son John Wells, this tract, and tract called *Children's Chance,* in same plantation, and John Wells then died intestate without issue, leaving his brother Samuel Wells his heir at law, and Samuel Wells and Isaac Edward Wells by indenture of bargain and sale in 1763, assigned 5 acres to Joseph Ray, who has since died intestate, and his son Thomas Ray, was lawful heir, and he sold tract to Melchior Tabler in 1764, and he in 1774, sold 98 acres *Children Chance* and 3 acres of *Low Land* to Eleanor Medley, and she is now deceased. By her will she appointed Leonard Smith, executor, with Bennett Neale and Elizabeth Sprigg Neale, directed that said land should be sold. Now for £195 sells the two tracts above, near a branch of Kitoctin Creek, called Prick Run.

BD2:193-195. Henry Piper recorded deed 13 Nov. 1775, from Elizabeth Walker and Renalder Walker her son, parts of two tracts containing 164 ½ acres, *Virgin's Delight,* and *Resurvey on Virgin's Delight,* adjacent to Philip Trine's part. Signed before Archibald Boyd, Thomas Lamar.

BD2:195-198. William Molleson of London, England, merchant, recorded mortgage from Mordecai Gist, consisting of four bonds of obligation, one for £200 and three in the amount of £1269 each with penalties, to pay 5% interest. Secured with several tracts, *Gist's Ambition,* 627 acres; *Gist's Friendship,* 80 acres patented by Thomas Gist in 1752 supposed to be in Baltimore County, but now in Frederick County; and tract *Gist's Deer Park,* 169 1/4 acres.

BD2:198. John Brunner recorded certificate 30 Nov. 1775, from John Delasmith. Whereas I sold *Swede's Folly,* he now swears to show bounded tree to John Hoffman.

BD2:199-201. John Kelly recorded deed 15 July 1776, from John Wayman for £512..15 tracts *Rich and Level,* on side of Snowden's Rivers, and two parts of *Gaither's Forest,* adjacent to first tract, on Gaither's Branch, containing 67 acres and 23 acres. Signed before John Burgess, H. Ridgely, J.P.s of Anne Arundel County. Anna Wayman released dower rights.

BD2:201-202. Henry Snavely recorded bill of sale 16 Nov. 1775, from Jacob Snyder of Frederick County, Colony of Virginia, for £5 assigns one red cow about 6 years old and one calf.

BD2:202-203. Thomas Cramphin of Prince George's county, recorded mortgage 23 Nov. 1775, from Samuel Hanson, for £32, tract called *Red Oak Level,* on east side of Sugar Loaf Mountain, on branch which falls into Bennett's Creek, 31 acres. Signed by mark before David Lynn, Alexander Clagett, Edward Burgess.

BD2:204-205. Michael Suter recorded lease from Joseph Beall, son of Ninian Beall, for 100 acres of *Choice Improved,* covenants to raise an apple orchard of 150 trees. Signed by Joseph Beall, Michael Suter by mark, before Archibald Boyd.

BD2:205-206. Michael Waggoner recorded deed 23 Nov. 1775, from Thomas Farris of Cumberland Valley, Bedford County, Pennsylvania, for £1150 sells *Resurvey on Harris' Delight,* containing 273 acres. Margaret, wife of Thomas Farris, released dower, before Thos Price, Jacob Young.

BD2:207-208. Thomas Sprigg recorded deed 23 Nov. 1775, from Joseph Sprigg for £1200 sterling, tract called *Long Meadow Enlarged,* adjacent to *Downey's Contrivance,* taken up by William Downey, and *Nicholas's Contrivance,* containing 1000 acres. Hannah Sprigg released dower.

BD2:209-210. Levi Davis recorded lease 10 May 1776, from Thomas Darnall, in consideration of rents and covenants, lets 50 acres of tract, *The Hope,* he is to plant an apple orchard of 50 trees within four years.

BD2:210-212. Robert Hunt recorded deed 6 June 1776, from Joseph Plummer for £45, 30 acres, part of the *Land of Promise,* at north end of hill, being 1st course of Samuel Water's land, to 4th line of Thomas Grave's land. Sarah, wife of Joseph Plummer released dower rights.

BD2: 212-213. Thomas Contee of Prince George's county, recorded mortgage 22 Jan. 1776 from Edward Gantt of Calvert County and Fielder Gantt of Frederick County, iron master. Whereas be became security for a bond at Fielder Gantt's request, this deed is to indemnify him to hold four Negroes, Bob, Miah, Cupid and Cockeranacrow. If sum of bond, for £200 paid within time limits, mortgage is void.

BD2:213-215. Samuel Duvall recorded deed 23 Jan 1776 from William Duvall for £150, *Addition to Grimmit's Prospect,* on Bennet's Creek containing 551 acres. Signed by mark. Priscilla Duvall released dower rights.

BD2:215-216. Catharine Booker and others recorded bond 30 August 1776, from John Booker to Catharine Booker, Jacob Booker, Eleanor Booker, Frederick Booker and Charlotte Booker, heirs and representatives of Nicholas Booker, deceased, for £300 to be paid to them in full. Whereas Nicholas Booker by his will appointed his wife Eleanor Booker and Valentine Rape his executors, and did empower them to sell part of a tract of land called *Truro* containing 275 acres and to distribute the proceeds to his children to wit, John Booker, Catharine Booker, Jacob Booker, Eleanor Booker, Frederick Booker and Charlotte Booker, but the said land not being as yet exposed to sale, disputes have arisen among the heirs, that John Booker as heir at law should receive the full amount. The above bond from him, is that he shall not demand more than each of the remainder of the heirs and representatives.

BD2:216-218. William Murdoch Beall recorded deed 24 May 1776, from James Brookover. Whereas 19 March 1767, Jacob Brookover by deed of mortgage made over 114 acres of *Fat Oxen* and his wife Mary Brookover released dower rights, recorded in Liber K:1108-1111, for £200 deeds over tract beginning at 18 acres of tract set off for Edward Willson,

BD2:218-222. William Murdoch Beall and Elisha Beall recorded deed of partition 24 August 1776, tracts, *The Two Brothers,* patented for 371 acres and *Resurvey on Fall Oxen,* 253 acres, which were granted to them jointly by their father, Nathaniel Beall, and *Resurvey on Willsons Lot,* 9 ½ acres, formerly deeded to William Murdoch Beall by Rebecca and Edward Willson, and a survey of vacancy, *Resurvey on Two Brothers*, adding 106 acres, and one other tract, *Little Did I think It,* also *Be Content, Tho Your Lot be Small,* 19 acres. Tract, *I Don't Care What,* 51 1/4 acres; *Tobacco Hook,*

71 acres; Hit or Miss, Luck's All, 82 acres, and *The Addition,* 6 3/4 acres. Being desirous to divide the lands, they present metes and bounds of their division.

BD2:223-224. Valentine Reintzell recorded deed 23 Nov. 1775, from Jacob Epprecht, both of Georgetown, Frederick County, for 5 shillings. Whereas the said Valentine Reintzel, together with Thomas Dyson and Martin Hoffman, for a certain sum of money, specified in a mortgage given by the said Jacob Eppracht, in trust, agrees to sell now to discharge the debt. Signed before Edward Burgess, David Lynn.

BD2:224-226. Michael Fackler of Elizabeth Town, tavern keeper, recorded mortgage 22 Nov. 1775, from Henry Shyriock of Elizabeth Town, for £210 assigns a certain stone house and office on lot #110 whereon the said Henry Shryock lives. Catherine Shyrock released dower.

BD2:227-228. John Emmigh of York County, Pennsylvania, recorded deed 3 October 1776, from Humphrey Cunningham, part of *Resurvey on Brother's Agreement,* beginning at a stump of Spanish Oak, in a swamp in a line of George Leacoby's land, and near a corner of Patrick Watson's land, containing 151 acres. Signed before George Scott, Wm Beatty. Roah, wife of Cunningham released dower.

BD2:228-229. John Mobberly recorded deed 17 Oct. 1776, from James Crouch, made 30 July for £400, part of *Pleasant Valley,* containing 335 acres, excepting 100 acres of said land, and covenants with him, to make good deed and pay all costs and charges within seven years. Signed before Jacob Young, Upton Sheridine.

BD2:230. James Young recorded deed 23 Oct. 1776, from James Crough for 5 shillings, 40 acres of *Pleasant Valley,* signed before same witnesses.

BD2:231. John Kessler recorded deed 4 Sept. 1776, from John Pelly Jr. For £18, two lots #177 & 178 lying in Addition to Frederick Town, between Jacob Michaels and Michael Hildebrand. Signed before Jacob Young, George Scott.

BD2:232-233. Abraham Faw recorded deed 23 Dec. 1775, from Eleanor Charlton of Frederick Town, executrix of Arthur Charlton, late of Frederick County, deceased, for £50 one half of three lots in Frederick Town, bounded on south side of aforesaid three lots sold to W. James Smith, and on north side by tract sold Francis Mantz, originally lots #159, 160 & 161. Signed by both parties.

BD2:233-235. Abraham Faw recorded deed 26 June 1776, from Jacob Shuh, miller, made 13 May, for £300 125 acres of *PawPaw Bottom.* Barbara wife of Jacob Shuh released dower.

BD2:235-236. Jacob Shuh recorded release of mortgage 8 Nov. 1776 from John Rensburgh. Release signed by both parties. Whereas I became bound for £121 to Mr. Peter Bruner and Mary Peckerbach on account of Jacob Shuh, on 15 Dec. 1773, as security to mortgage for 125 acres of *PawPaw Bottom,* as recorded in Liber U:335-358.

BD2:236-237. William Murdoch Beall recorded deed 5 Aug. 1776, from Edward Willson for 5 shillings, *Abners Choice.* Signed by mark, 3 Aug. 1776. Alienation fine paid to Daniel of St. Thomas Jennifer, Esq.

BD2:238-240. Matthias Graff of the Borough of Lancaster, Lancaster County, Pennsylvania, recorded mortgage deed, 31 Oct. 1776, from Thomas Beatty, now possessed of 208 acre tract called *Rocky Creek* on west side of Monocacy, from deed from John Beatty and Cornelius Brink of Ulster County, New York, and Peter Huff and Susannah his wife, George Beatty and Abraham Huff and Jean his wife for 518 ½ acres, made 15 June 1759 and recorded in Liber F:151, and also one other deed from Henry Cock and William Beatty, executors of Ezra Beatty, deceased; Ezekial Beatty and Elijah Beatty, all of Frederick County for 116 acres; recorded in Liber V:546 for £500; assigns all except for 50 acres conveyed to Baltis Fout, 40 acres to Christian Pringle and 50 acres to Catharine Beatty, wife of Thomas. Signed by Thomas Beatty.

BD2:241-242. Andrew Keller recorded deed 25 Dec. 1776,from Charles Beatty of Frederick Town, for 5 shillings, tract originally granted him 19 April 1775, called *Loss Gained.* Martha Beatty released dower rights.

BD2:242-243. Mathew Galt Junr recorded bill of sale 19 March 1776, from Matthew Galt Senr. for natural love and affection he has for his son, assigns all goods and chattel, farm equipment, books, one black mare, and son is to provide sufficient meat and drink, washing and mending of linens, and enough firewood for his use during his natural life.

BD2:243-244. Jacob Methard recorded deed 6 June 1776, from Valentine Reb for £150, for ½ part of lot #104 in Frederick Town where Toby Butler now lives. Clara, wife of Valentine Reb released dower.

BD2:244-245. Thomas Gassaway Jr. and Philip Maroney recorded deed 9 April 1776, from Adam Hardman, wheelwright, sells 100 acres *Turkey Foot Bottom.* Signed in German Script.

BD2:245-247. Thomas Samuel Poole (or Pole) recorded deed 3 August 1776, from David Shriver for £40, sells lot #27 in Westminster, containing 1/4 acre.

BD2:247-248. Jacob Warnfelt recorded deed 26 June 1776, from Jacob Balzer (Paulsel), taylor for £39, tract called *Bad Enough,* 30 acres, together with tract *May's Folly,* beginning at spring in the Shandore Mountain, containing 18 acres. Signed Jacob Baltzel. Ann Maria, wife of Jacob released dower.

BD2:248-249. David Lynn recorded deed 21 March 1776 from Archibald Edmonston, part of *Resurvey on Batchelor's Forest.* For £11, conveys two acres, part adjacent to that conveyed by Alexander Beall, Robert Beall and Archibald Edmonston Jr. to aforesaid David Lynn.

BD2:249-251. Jacob Lewis recorded deed 30 August 1776, from Thomas Fletcher. Whereas Thomas Price of Frederick Town, by deed sold to Thomas Fletchall lot #163 recorded in Liber N:559-560, for £7 same lot assigned.

BD2:251-254. Samuel Fleming recorded deed 31 Dec. 1776, from Joseph Sim of Prince George's County, for £615..15, tract called *Friendship,* granted to William Murdock and Mr. Henry Addison, 20 Sept. 1749, for 410 acres.

BD2:254-255. George Gobble recorded bill of sale 20 March 1776 from Casper Zear for £83..11, 35 acres of wheat and rye in the ground, on plantation leased to the said Casper Zeim, from Jno Glosser and Caleb Nicol, called part of *Five Sisters,* a two year old bay filly, a brown cow, and other livestock, farming equipment, including a windmill.

255-256. Half of 255 is blank as is page 256.

BD2:257. George Custer, blacksmith, recorded deed 18 Sept. 1776, from George DeMent for £45, sells lot #8 in Jerusalemtown. Sarah wife of George DeMent released dower rights.

BD2:258-259. Philip Harding recorded deed 10 Oct. 1776, from John Mobberly for £400 tract called *James Park,* beginning at Ben's Branch, a draught of Linganore, in 25th line of *Darby Delight,* running to tract called *Mount Pleasant,* taken up by James Crouch. 55 ½ acres. Signed by mark. Cloe, wife of John Mobberly released dower.

BD2:259-261. Philip Harding recorded deed 10 Oct. 1776, from John Mobberly and Cloe his wife, tract called *Mount Pleasant* and the Resurvey thereon, 122 acres.

BD2:261. Andrew Beall recorded bill of sale 15 Feb. 1776, from Beckett Nicholls for £24..18, one black horse, one sorrel mare, one cow and calf. Signed before Edward Burgess.

BD2:262-263. Martin Keplinger recorded deed 4 April 1776, from Henry Hunter for £17..10, part of tract called *Castle Henry, Resurvey on Leonard's Good Luck,* adjacent to 33rd course of Basil Beall's part of *Castle Henry,* 247 acres. Ann Hunter released dower.

BD2:264-265. Nicholas Fringer of Baltimore County, recorded deed 16 July 1777, from John Cloper of Winchester Town, Frederick County, inn keeper for £100 and performances and covenants herein, assigns lot in town on the south side of the Main Street, #40, adjacent to lots of Daniel Bower, 1/4 acre. Catharine, wife of John Cloper released dower.

BD2:265-266. Thomas Jones recorded deed 20 January 1777, from Michael Sawyer, Michael Duttrow and Geo Zimmerman Sr., for £40, assigns *Resurvey on Limestone Rock,* 21 ½ acres, and another tract, part of *Deer Spring,* together containing 41 ½ acres. The wife of Michael Sawyer, [name blank] and Dorcas Baltis and Katharina Zimmerman, wives, all examined and released dower rights.

BD2:266-268. Catharine Fortney recorded deed 26 June 1776,from Basil Beall for £44, part of *Resurvey on Limestone Rock,* adjacent to *Make Shift.* Mary Beall released dower rights.

BD2:268-269. Christian Easterday recorded deed 5 August 1776, from Andrew Kessler for £8, lot #7 in town laid out by Leonard Smith, executor of Eleanor Medley, deceased, containing ½ acre. Rents to be paid to Elizabeth Sprigg Neale, wife of Bennett Neale, during her lifetime, and then to her heirs.

BD2:269 Jacob Geiger and Anthony Stokes recorded agreement 9 April 1776, regarding one half shares of well, Jacob Geiger to pay £11. Both signed.

BD2:269-271. Jacob Linn recorded deed 4 April 1776 from Lazarus Fundenbergh, for £10, sells all his right to tract, *Carmack's Advise,* a part of *Resurvey on Good Neighborhood,* on north side of Israel's Creek, on third line of tract, *Long Meadow.* Phebe, wife of Lazarus Fundenberg released dower.

BD2:271-272. John Roberts recorded deed 10 Sept. 1776, from Charles Carroll for £39..19..3, part of *Sapline Valley,* on south side of Little Pipe Creek, containing 53 acres. Alienation fine paid to George Scott.

BD2:272-273. Phillip Hammond recorded deed 30 January 1777, from Joseph Chapline and James Chapline, parts of *Resurvey on Hills, Dales and Vineyard,* at 6th line of *Doran's Neglect,* 25 acres; 2nd tract, a part of *Burrell's Chance,* 1 ½ acres; also tract beginning at *Ward's Spring,* 4 ½ acres.

BD2:273-275. Phillip Hammond recorded deed 6 May 1775, from Joseph Reynolds for £52..10, part of *Ward's Spring,* and also the *Addition to Ward's Spring,* on banks of Antietam; 8 1/4 acres. Lucy Reynolds released dower.

BD2:275-276. Christian Welty recorded deed 23 December 1775, from Samuel Volgamot for £57, part of tract called *Hallum's Lookout,* containing 12 ½ acres. Signed in German script. Barbara, wife of Samuel released dower rights.

BD2:276-277. Jacob Welty recorded deed 23 December 1775, from Samuel Volgamot for £129, part of tract called *Hallum's Lookout,* containing 42 ½ acres. Signed in German script. Barbara, wife of Samuel released dower rights.

BD2:277-278. Henry Stoffell recorded deed 19 Aug. 1776 from Jacob Peter Tyshee (Dysher), part of tract *Tuskorouroh,* containing by estimation 100 acres, and one other tract. Franny Dysher released dower.

BD2:278-279. Jacob Capple (or Eaple) recorded deed 20 August 1776, from Andreas Filler, for tract called *Andrews Venture,* part of *Resurvey on Weaver's Loom,* 90 acres. Signed in G.S. Mary, wife of Andrew released dower.

BD2:279-280. John Hanson recorded deed 15 May 1776 from Daniel Dulaney. Whereas an agreement was made conveying to John Holm, who passed his bond in 1772 to John Hanson, Dulaney deeds tract *Epinah* for 120 acres.

BD2:280-282. William Waters recorded deed 22 July 1776, from Jeremiah and Margaret Mullikin of Anne Arundel County, for £192, all that tract Samuel Waters Sr., gave to his daughter Margaret Mullikin, part of *Water's Purchase,* formerly called *Charles and Benjamin,* containing 96 acres.

BD2:283. Nathan Maynard recorded bill of sale from Jonathan Jones for £9..13, obligation as surety on debt due from Jones to David Moore, secured with a chest of joyners and carpenters tools.

BD2:284 Andrew Hawn recorded deed 22 July 1776, from Magdalena Pepple for £30, tract called *The Meadow Enlarged,* on 6th line of *Sapling Hill,* containing 30 acres.

BD2:286-287. John Donovan recorded deed from William Russell and George Fraser Hawkins, lots in Williamstown, being part of a tract called *Calledoren* the said 6 lots contain 3 acres. Signed before Geo Brent, Jacob Young.

BD2:288-289. Nicholas Hobbs recorded deed 1 August 1776, from Philip Davis who is possessed with rights of his wife Rebecca, in tract called *Tryal,* 114 acres for term of eight years, as appears in will of Joseph Wright, deceased, late husband of Rebecca, assigns all interest in tract, in trust for use of Rebecca Davis. Signed by mark before Wm Beatty, Samuel Irwin.

BD2:289-291. Casper Shurfigg recorded deed 15 August 1776, from Upton Scott of Annapolis, physician, for £130..10 assigns part of *Runnymeade,* adjacent to part sold previously to John Casler, containing 58 acres. Elizabeth, wife of Upton Scott released dower rights.

BD2:291-294. Phineas Dawson of York county, Pennsylvania, recorded release 5 August 1776, from William Elder. Whereas he previously sold 15 acres of *Resurvey on Walnut Bottom*, this corrects deed, for further consideration of £10 Pennsylvania, and released mortgage.

BD2:294-296. John Willson recorded deed 5 August 1776, from Phineas Davison of York County, Pennsylvania, for £110, part of *Resurvey on Black Walnut Bottom,* 15 acres and part of tract called *Chance.* Patience, wife of Phineas Dawson released dower.

BD2:297-301. Jacob and John Michael recorded deed 5 August 1776, from Wm Schooley of Virginia, and Ann, his wife, widow and relict of Daniel Matthews, late of Frederick county. In 1760 they conveyed to Michael Hillman, 188 acres of *George's Discovery,* and said Hickleman conveyed same to Conrad Shaw in November 1766, and he sold the same to William Michael, who by his will devised same to his two sons, Jacob and John Michael; and whereon the original deed from Ann was erroneous in describing the land, the deed correct and confirms the description of the *Resurvey on George's Discovery,* beginning at *Poplar's Thickett,* originally granted to T. Beall and Doctor Cragg.

BD2:301-303. Humphrey Cunningham recorded 5 August 1776, from Raphael Tawney and William Diggs, made 27 July 1773, for £38, part of *Resurvey on Brother's Agreement,* metes and bounds for 51 acres. Honor wife of Raphael Tawney and Catherine wife of William Digges released dower.

BD2:304-305. Edward Willson recorded deed 5 August 1776, from Elisha Beall for 5 shillings, tract *The Two Brothers,* which lies between *Abner's Choice,* and *Resurvey on Willsons Lott.* Alienation fine guessed at 25 acres, by order of court, paid to George Scott.

BD2:305-307. John Casler recorded deed 5 August 1776, from Upton Scott of Annapolis, for £108 part of tract called *Runnymeade,* containing 48 acres. Signed before Hugh Scott, Phillip B. Key. Elizabeth Scott released dower.

BD2:307-309. Clement Hollyday recorded deed 6 August 1776, from Thomas Gantt Junr. of Prince George's County, for £500 sells part of *Hawkins Merry Peep a Day,* beginning at *Coxen's Rest,* on the Potomac River, adjacent to part sold to Barton Philpot, containing 201 acres. Susanna, wife of Thomas Gantt Jr released dower rights.

BD2:310-312. John Ashbrunner recorded deed 7 August 1776, from Magdalena Pepple. [Marginal note: Exam'd & del'd enclosed to Thomas Langton of Baltimore, co-partner of the grantee who is dead, by Mr. William Davy. The post on 22 April 1783.] for £600, part of *The Meadow,* 243 ½ acres, expecting the privilege of water to Abraham Rowland's mill race. Signed before Wm Blair, Joseph Wells. Alienation fine paid to George Scott.

BD2:313-315. Magdalena Pepple recorded deed 7 August 1776, from Andrew Hawn for £30 part of *Hawn's Meadows,* containing 24 ½ acres. Signed in German Script. Wife of Andrew Hawn, Eve Hawn released dower rights.

BD2:315-318. John Martin Derr recorded deed 9 August 1776, from Christian Cassell for £5 sells parts of *Miller's Chance,* on 2nd line of *Cooper's Point,* metes and bounds for 134 ½ acres. Christena Cassell released dower rights. [Marginal note that deed del'd to Christian Cassell, in 1784].

BD2:318-320. [Marginal note that deed was del'd to Christian Cassell, in 1784]. Peter Cassell recorded deed 9 August 1776, from Christian Cassell for £5, parts of *Miller's Chance, Cassell's Desire,* and *Cooper's Point,* containing 134 ½ acres. Signed by Christian Cassell, Christena Cassell, his wife released dower rights.

BD2:320-322. Nicholas Dell of Westminster, recorded deed 20 August 1776, from Simon Baum of Baltimore County, for £80, sells lots #1 and #2, in Westminster, adjacent to lot owned by John McHarge, and tract *White's Level,* and lot #26, adjacent to lots of Enoch Davis, deceased, Thomas Samuel Pole and William Winchester. Signed before W. Winchester and Abraham Davis. Catherine Baum released dower.

BD2:322-325. Nicholas Dell of Westminster, recorded deed 20 August 1776, from Simon Baum of Baltimore County, for £30, part of tract *Friendship Completed,* containing 9 acres. Signed before W. Winchester and Abraham Davis. Catherine Baum released dower.

BD2:325-328. Stephen Miller recorded deed 20 August 1776, from John Braselton Junior for £80, all his right to tract called *Stringer's Neglect,* standing on Beaver Dam Branch of Little Pipe Creek, containing 47 acres. Sarah wife of John Braselton released dower rights.

BD2:328-331. Jacob Getzendanner recorded deed 20 August 1776, from Martin Keplinger for £74, part of *Castle Henry.* Elizabeth Keplinger (Ceplinger) released dower rights.

BD2:331-336. John Brunner recorded land Commission on *Sweeds Folly*, 21 August 1776. Mssrs James Marshall, William Lucketts Jr., Francis Cost and Joseph Hill appointed commissioners. Francis Cost, aged about 36 years deposed that 14 or 15 years ago, William Thomas deceased, came to his still house and told him he was going through the woods ... James Hook, aged about 58 years, deposed that 10 or 12 years ago, Elias Delasmutt Senr showed him the beginning tree of *Sweed's Folly,* Arthur Nelson, aged about 51 years deposed. Joseph Hill, aged about 54 years deposed that 14 years ago he was called upon by Notley Thomas to carry the chain, to set aside a dispute between said Notley Thomas and Elias Delasmutt. Andrew Michael aged about 46 years, deposed that 3 months before he was called by Jacob Hoffman to tree. John Thomas, aged about 24 years, called as a witness to Andrew Michael. Katherine Thomas, aged about 43 years said her husband bought the land for John Brewner from John Delasmutt. John Ramdery, aged about 25 years, carried the chains. Edward Tanzey, aged about 41 years, deposed that 7 years ago, William Thomas Senr deceased told him he was present when land was surveyed for old John Browner.

BD2:336-338, William Ricketts recorded deed 21 August 1776 from Benjamin Ricketts for £100, tract deeded to Benjamin Ricketts from Richard Snowden, 9 Nov. 1743, part of *Snowden's Addition,* being then in Prince George's County, beginning at southernmost corner of Wm Thomas's land to Dr. Charles Carroll's land, then to the land Snowden gave his daughter Elizabeth Thomas. Signed by mark. [no dower release]

BD2:338-340. Michael Gollar (Kollar) recorded deed 24 Dec. 1776, from Conrad Reycher for £250, part of *Mathew's Good Will.* Signed in German Script, before George Scott, Jacob Young. Elizabeth, wife of Conrad released dower.

BD2:341-343. Philip Jacob Sheffer recorded deed 21 August 1776, from Adam Knouff (Neff) for £50, part of *Resurvey on Martiataney,* metes and bounds for 50 aces. Signed by mark.

BD2:344-345. Enoch Fry records bond 21 August 1776, from Philip Ambrose for £300, the condition is that he will make a good deed for part of *Arnold's Delight,* beginning at Jacob Ambroses's part, for 100 acres.

BD2:345-348. Gabriel Swineheart Jr. recorded deed 24 August 1776, from Adam Knouff (Neff) for £50, part of *Resurvey on Marlitaney,* containing 55 acres. Signed by mark.

BD2:348-350. Gabriel Swineheart Sr. recorded deed 24 August 1776, from Adam Knouff (Neff) for £20, for part of *Resurvey on Marlitaney,* containing 20 acres. Signed by mark.

BD2:350-353. John Neff recorded deed 24 August 1776, from Adam Knaff (Neff) for £50, part of *Resurvey on Marlitaney,* containing 50 acres. Signed by mark.

BD2:353-357. Wadsworth Willson recorded land commission and depositions 31 August 1776, to remember the metes and bounds on *Progress.* To Mssrs Capt. William Lucketts, Francis Deakins, Edward Jones and Hezekiah Veatch appointed commissioners. Nathan Veatch, 51 years old deposed that 40 years ago, he was with James and John Veatch, and Nathan Masters and John Veatch showed his brother, James, the bound tree near the bank of the Potomac. Thomas Wilson, aged about 56 years deposed that 40 years ago, he, John Veatch and Nathan Masters were going down the Potomac, turkey hunting, and the bound oak was pointed out. Thomas Veatch, about 40 years old, deposed that tree stands on the east bank of the Potomac River at upper end of Island called *Master's Island*, three or four miles below the mouth of the Monocacy.

BD2:357-360. John Stone recorded deed 21 August 1776, from John Carey for tract originally granted to him in 1773 by the name of *Foxes Hole,* on the west side of Kittoctin Mountain, near the wagon road from Stull's Mill, containing 100 acres. Mary, wife of John Carey released dower.

BD2:360-362. Thomas Bissett Sr. recorded deed 22 August 1776, from Joseph Chapline, acting with power of attorney from Van Swearingen of West Augusta County, Virginia, in consideration of £20 paid by Bissett to John Duncan on account of Van Swearingens, assigns to him lot #34 in Sharpsburg.

BD2:362-364. Thomas Bissett Sr. Recorded deed 22 August 1776, from Joseph Chapline for £10, lot #58 in Sharpsburg. He is to pay the annual rents of 10 shillings.

BD2:364-367. Joseph Wood Jr recorded deed 22 Aug 1776 from Henry Barton for £60, one full moiety or half part of lot #86 in Fredericktown, formerly conveyed to Jacob Barton by Daniel Dulaney in 1751 and granted to Henry by his will, subject to his wife's dower rights. Mary, wife of Henry released dower rights. For 5 shillings, Henrietta Barton, widow of Jacob Barton, released her claim to dower before Wm Beatty, George Scott.

BD2:367-369. William Toms recorded deed 22 August 1776, from Ullerick Blickerstaff, for £60, assigns tract called *Good for Naught,* on one of the draughts called String Run, of Kittoctin Creek, metes and bounds given for 70 acres. Receipt and acknowledgments.

BD2:369-372. James Suter recorded deed 23 August 1776, from Zachariah Thompson and Sarah, his wife, taylor, for £8, part of *Resurvey on Saint Mary's,* containing 5 ½ acres. Signed before Robert Peter, David Lynn.

BD2:372 William Beckwith, recorded land commission on *Beckwith's Hope* 24 August 1776. Witnesses to appear at George Roberson's mill, on the 24th April next. Deposition of Mrs. Susanna Boyd, aged about 58 years, says 6 or 7 years ago, she was showed by her husband, John Boyd, a white oak on the side of a hill, a small branch, running into Rock Creek, called Little Rock Creek, bounded with 16 notches. June 8, 1776, deposition of John Swearingen, aged about 83 years, some time past, Thomas Thompson said the tree was the bounded tree of William Beckwith's land, on a knoll on west side of a creek commonly known by the name of a fork of Rock Creek, or Little Rock Creek, near Swearingen's mill. Deposition of Van Swearingen, aged about 29 years, son of John Swearingen.

BD2:376-378. Major Thomas Price of Frederick County, recorded deed 28 August 1776, from Benjamin Mackall 4th of Calvert County, for £100 tract called *Tuscarora,* containing 100 acres. Rebecca Mackall, his wife released dower rights.

BD2:378-380. Bernard Hershberger recorded deed 16 September 1776, from Bennett Heard for £5, lot #17 in the New Town, to pay Elizabeth Sprigg Neale, wife to Bennett Neale, during her lifetime, and after her death unto the children of Elizabeth Sprigg Neale, annual rents. Signed before George Scott, Wm Beatty.

BD2:380-384. John Castle recorded deed 18 September 1776, from James Flemming for £131, sells part of tract originally granted Thomas Johnson, by the name of *Resurvey on Stoney Level,* and conveyed by him to said Fleming, part of said 172 acres. Metes and bounds given by Troutman's 50 acres, containing 122 acres. Signed before C. Beatty and Martha Beatty. At the same time, the wife of said James Flemming appeared (but not named) and released dower rights.

BD2:384-387. Tempest Tucker recorded deed 14 Oct 1776 from Martin Dagen, for £270 part of tract called *Resurvey on White Oak Grove,* Elizabeth Dagen, wife of Martin released dower.

BD2:387-391. Rudolph Elting recorded release 20 September 1776, from Noah Elting of the New Paltz, in Ulster county, New York, for £5, tract called *Frozen Levels,* containing about 200 acres and the 2nd lot, *Abraham's Lot,* containing about 300 acres. Also a tract, *New Esopas,* containing about 200 acres; the fourth parcel, being part of a tract called *Concord,* containing about 263 acres; 5th piece, tract called *The Forest,* containing 140 acres; 6th, also a part of *Concord,* containing 100 acres, as expressed in a certain indenture from Petrus Eltinge of the precinct of the Wallkill in the county of Ulster, province of New York, of one part and the widow Mary Elmendorph of Kingstown, in the county and Province aforesaid, bearing date 15 August 1767, and the said Noach Elting, appointed Charles Beatty, James Beatty and Abraham Haff or the survivors thereof, with power of attorney.

BD2:391-397. Rudolph Elting of Marble Town, Ulster County, recorded release 20 September 1776, from Mary Elmendorf of Kingston in Ulster County, New York, widow, for £400 current money of New York, transfers into possession and to his heirs, four equal indentures, of all these six certain tracts, situated at Potomack in the Colony of Maryland, tracts same as in above release, with metes and bounds given.

BD2:397-401. [Marginal note, delivered to Mr. Rudolph Eltinge, 26 June 1784] Rudolph Elting recorded lease 20 September 1776, from Mary Elmendorf of Kingston, Ulster County, New York, for 5 shillings current money, for receipt has bargained and sold four several separate tracts or pieces of land in the colony of Maryland, *Frozen Levels, Abraham's Lot, Forest,* and part of *Concord.*

BD2:401-403. Sarah Bradford recorded deed 2 October 1776, from John Reynolds, for one shilling, lot #14 in Sharpsburg. Signed by mark before Saml Beall Senr., John Stull.

BD2:403-406. Ninian Beall, James Beall and Zephaniah Beall, sons of James Beall, recorded deed 14 October 1776, from Elizabeth Beall for 5 shillings, all of the following tracts, part of *Boiling Spring,* on the north branch of Tuscarorah Creek, containing 40 acres, and the other, part of *Mistaken Rival,* adjacent to 4th line of *Boiling Spring,* Signed by mark before Jacob Young, George Scott. George Scott received alienation fine of 3 shillings.

BD2:406-408. Benjamin Mackall recorded deed 14 October 1776, from Brooke Beall, for £75, tract called *New England Toddy,* containing 100 acres. Signed before David Lynn, Robert Peter. Margaret Beall, wife of Brooke Beall released dower.

BD2:408-410a. Casper Wizner recorded deed 14 October 1776, from Samuel Owings of Baltimore County, for £5, part of tract called *Ohio,* adjacent to tract called *Spealmann's Discovery,* containing 50 acres of land. Deborah, wife of Samuel Owings released dower rights.

BD2:410a-414. Nicholas Dill recorded deed 14 October 1776, from Samuel Owings of Baltimore County, for £28..4 assigns part of tract called *Ohio,* metes and bounds given, adjacent to *Resurvey on High Germany,* Deborah Owings released dower. [page 411 blank, 2 pages 410 in book.]

BD2:414-417. Michael Keebler recorded deed 14 October 1776, from Samuel Owings of Baltimore County, for £78, part of *Ohio,* beginning at the 11th line, containing 148 acres, and a second part, beginning at 5th line of *Resurvey on Peter's Lot,* containing 12 acres. Signed before John Moale, Bale Randall, J.P.s of Baltimore County. Deborah Owings released dower rights.

BD2:417-420. Michael Miller recorded deed 14 October 1776, from Samuel Owings of Baltimore County, for £12, part of tract called *Owings Corner,* containing 12 acres. Signed before John Moale, Bale Randall, J.P.s of Baltimore County. Deborah Owings released dower rights.

BD2:420-423. Paul Rinacre recorded deed 14 October 1776, from Samuel Owings of Baltimore County, for £3..15 sterling, part of tract called *Ohio,* beginning at 1st line of a tract called *Leonard's Lot,* containing 75 acres of land. Signed before John Moale, Bale Randall, J.P.s of Baltimore County. Deborah Owings released dower rights.

BD2:423-426. [Ex'd & del'd Ralph Crabb by adm. Grantee, filed 12th January 1790] Henry Shope recorded deed 14 October 1776, from Samuel Owings of Baltimore County, for £27 part of tract *Ohio,* beginning at north east side of a swamp, containing 54 acres. Signed before John Moale, Bale Randall, J.P.s of Baltimore County. Deborah Owings released dower rights.

BD2:426-429. [Ex'd & del'd George Michal Tar on 10th May 1784] George Michael Tar [Derr] recorded deed 14 Oct. 1776, from Samuel Owings of Baltimore County, for £7..10, part of tract, *Ohio,* adjacent to tract called *Fair Hill,* containing 15 acres. Signed before John Moale, Bale Randall, J.P.s of Baltimore County. Deborah Owings released dower rights.

BD2:429-432. [Examined and delivered Jacob Read, per order March first 1799.] George Ege recorded deed 14 October 1776, from Samuel Owings of Baltimore County, for £50, part of tract, *Ohio,* containing 100 acres of land. Signed before John Moale, Bale Randall, J.P.s of Baltimore County. Deborah Owings released dower rights.

BD2:432-435. Frederick Solloday recorded deed 18 October 1776, from Thomas Cowan of Frederick County, Colony of Virginia, for £350 Pennsylvania, assigns tract called *Captain John's Bottom,* beginning at a bounded white oak on Potomac River, between mouth of Conecocheague and Antietam Creek, containing 100 acres. Signed before John Stull, Saml Beall Junr. Mary, wife of Thomas Cowan released dower rights.

BD2:436-439. Alexander Whitacre recorded deed 23 October 1776, from George Hoskinson for £32, part of tract called *Resurvey on Elizabeth's Delight,* metes and bound for 16 acres.

BD2:439 Jonathan Tucker recorded lease assignment 23 October 1776 from George Grafft and Christopher Massincope, assigns all rights to a certain field and smith shop.

BD2:440-442. George Grafft, from Chistopher Massincope, blacksmith. Whereas George did on 15 October 1775, warrant and agree in writing, to lease to him for term of 9 years, the first two years rent free, now agrees to let field adjoining barn. Signed by both before Robert Peter. I Christopher Massincope, assign all my rights to said lease.

BD2:442-443. Negro Peter, about 39 years old, recorded manumission 7 November 1776, from Israel Thompson. Signed before Jacob Young.

BD2:443 William Sabtiro recorded marks of cattle and hogs 13 November 1776.

BD2:443-446. Robert John Smith of Anne Arundel County, recorded deed 16 November 1776 from Silas Veatch, for £320, tract called *The Resurvey on the Pheasants Nest,* containing 32 acres, also part of *Poplar Spring,* containing 94 acres more or less, the graveyard excepted, with the improvements and appurtenances thereunto belonging. Signed before Jacob Young, George Scott. Jane Veatch, wife of Silas released dower rights.

BD2:446-448. John and Verlinda Chappel recorded deed of gift 20 November 1776, from Margaret Masters, in consideration of the natural love and affection which I have to my son in law John Chappel and my daughter, Verlinda, and 5 shillings, I grant the three following Negroes, Rachel, Bess and Doll, and their increase, as well as all my cattle, horses, mares, sheep and hogs, household furniture, plantation utensils, crop of every kind, with the intent that they shall furnish and provide for the said Margaret Masters, maintenance during her natural life. Signed by mark before Benj. Becraft, Robert Peter.

BD2:448-449. James Campbell recorded bill of sale 21 November 1776. Whereas Thomas Dyson, late of Frederick County, did on the 17th August 1775, sell unto Lawrence O'Neale, the following Negroes, to wit, one Negro named Dublin, one Negro wench named Cynthify, one named Nell, and their further increase, I, Lawrence O'Neal, for £144 paid by James Campbell, merchant, assign said Negroes and one Negro girl child of said Nell.

BD2:449-452. [Marginal note: Ex'd & delvd John Elder, per order] William Ramsey recorded deed 21 Nov. 1776, from Charles Beatty for £100 two tracts of land, *The Resurvey on Beaver Dam Level,* 64 acres, and part of *Dear Bought*, on west side of a draught of Captain's Branch which falls into Monocacy, containing 43 acres more or less. Martha, wife of Charles Beatty released dower rights.

BD2:452-455. [Marginal note: Examined and delivered to John Neill, 2 November 1785.] Thomas Neill recorded deed 21 November 1776, from Charles Beatty for £100, part of tract called *Tryall,* containing 115 acres of land, more or less. Signed C. Beatty before Wm Beatty, Abraham Haff. Martha, wife of Charles Beatty released dower rights.

BD2:455-457. John Ellis recorded deed 21 Nov 1776 from William Harvey Junr., for £77..10 all that tract called *Hazard,* beginning at north side of a branch that falls into Bennet's Creek, laid out for 50 acres. Signed by mark. Stacey, wife of William examined apart released dower rights.

BD2:458-460. James Crabtree recorded deed 21 November 1776, from Nathan Fraks, for £20 sells tract called *Hay Bottom,* containing 50 acres of land near Town Creek going into Potomac river. Signed by mark before F. Warring, Thos Cresap.

BD2:460-462. James Crabtree recorded deed 21 November 1776, from Nathan Fraks, [also spelled Freaks, Freakes, Fach, Feakes] late of Frederick County, in the province of Maryland, for £20, assigns parcel called *Crabtree's Folly,* containing 60 acres. Signed by mark.

BD2:462-463. Edward Boteler recorded bill of sale 21 November 1776, from John Demory for £22..10 sells one brown horse, one black mare, and one year old black colt, provided nevertheless that if sum paid, sale is of no effect. Signed by mark before Nathan Magruder Junr., Thomas Frizzle.

BD2:463-466. George Bright recorded deed 21 Nov 1776 from Thomas Morrow of Washington County, Maryland, for £120 sells tract of land called *Hard Fortune,* containing 50 acres. Darius, wife of the aforesaid Thomas Morrow released dower rights.

BD2:466-467. James Crouch recorded bill of sale 28 November 1776, from Conrad Merkle for £100, one Negro woman named Diane, her future increase, and one Negro boy named Tom. Signed before George Scott.

BD2:468 Wm Dickensheets recorded bill of sale 9 December 1776, from Wm Orput in consideration of a horse sold, the price of £12, have bargained and sold, Wm Dickensheets, 70 bushels of Wheat in Henry Landis, his mill, Signed before John Norris, Isaac Braselton.

BD2:469 Oliver Burch, planter of Prince George's County, recorded lease 11 December 1776, from Wm Offutt Magruder, in consideration of a yearly rent, lease for 99 years, 250 acre tract of land called *Rich Land,* witnessed by Robert Peter, William Wilson.

BD2:471-475. Charles Beatty, James Johnson, and John Manson, Supervisors of the Gunlock manufactury, to be erected in Frederick Town, recorded deed 13 November 1776, from Christian Steiner. Whereas it was resolved by the Convention of Maryland held at the City of Annapolis 7 December 1775, that a gunlock manufactury should be established in FrederickTown, for £16, assigns lot #1, on original plat of town, which lies south of the creek running through the lot, called Carroll's Creek, formerly conveyed by Daniel Dulaney to Jacob Baney in 1764, and by him to Christian Stoner 18 May 1774. Signed G.S. before Jacob Young, George Scott. Hannah Stoner released dower.

BD2:475-477. Davis Stanisfer recorded deed 13 December 1776, from Samuel Owings of Baltimore County for £53, part of tract called *Ohio,* on 6th line of *Frushes Folly,* containing 100 acres. Signed before John Moale, Bale Randall, J.P.s of Baltimore County. Deborah Owings released dower rights.

BD2:478-480. Adam Long recorded deed 13 December 1776, from Samuel Owings of Baltimore County, for £100, sells part of *Ohio,* on line of *Frushes Folly,* containing 180 acres. Signed before John Moale, Bale Randall, J.P.s of Baltimore County. Deborah Owings, wife of Samuel Owings, released dower rights.

BD2:481 Negroes Abraham, Hager and Joshua recorded manumission 16 December 1776, from William Morsell, for diverse good considerations, one Negro man, Abraham about 34 years old, one Negro woman, Hager, about 22, and Negro boy Joshua to be free at the age of 21 years, which will be the 21st of the 5th month, 1796. Signed before George Scott.

BD2:481-483. Jacob Harbaugh recorded deed 18 Dec. 1776 from Thomas Harris. Whereas the said Thomas Harris is son and heir at law of Thomas Harris, late of Frederick County, deceased, with a legal right, to all such lands unconveyed by Thomas Harris before his decease, this indenture, for the sum of 5 shillings paid by Jacob Harbough, assigns parcel called *Pleasant Level,* sold by William Biggerstaff to Thos Harris, recorded in Liber B. Signed before Robert Peter, Jacob Young. Ruth, wife to the said Thomas Harris released dower.

BD2:483-486. Joseph Flint recorded deed from John Ridout of the City of Annapolis, for £191..6 tract formerly called the third part of *Chatham,* but now on a resurvey called *Dalecarlia,* containing 549 acres. Signed before Dan'l of St. Thos Jenifer, Jas Anderson. Mary Rideout, wife of John released dower rights.

BD2:486-489. Uriah Shipley recorded deed 19 December 1776, from Philemon Barnes for £17, part of tract called *Horse Pasture,* containing 71 acres. Signed before Upton Sheridine, Joseph Wells. Rachel, wife of Philemon Barnes, released dower rights.

BD2:489-492. Casper Keller recorded deed December 1776, from Adam Keller for 5 shillings, two parts of tract granted Charles Beatty called *Trura.* Metes and bounds for 196 acres. Catherine Keller wife of Adam Keller released dower.

BD2:492-495. Sarah and Alexander Willson recorded agreement 3 January 1777. Articles of agreement, agreed to 14 December 1776 between Robert Briscoe of Frederick County, and Sarah Willson of the same county, widow, and Alexander Willson of the third part. Whereas a marriage is intended to be shortly had and solemnized between the said Robert Briscoe and Sarah Willson, and whereas the said Robert Briscoe, in consideration of the love and affection which he beareth toward the said Sarah Willson is desirous if the said marriage takes effect of making a provision for her in trust with payment of £100 to the said Alexander Willson, he is to insure that she shall have a house, outhouses and garden, to be improved to the value of £50, adjoining to her son the said Alexander Willson, in a distinct and separate lot of land now in possession of him the said Robert Briscoe, called *Robert's Delight,* for herself and family, and discharge of her dower or thirds which she may claim in his estate. Signed Robert Briscoe, Sarah Willson by mark, Alexander Wilson before Archibald Boyd, Elie Williams.

BD2:495-496. Gerard Briscoe recorded deed of gift, 4 Jan 1777 from Robert Briscoe of Montgomery County, in consideration of the natural love and affection which I bare unto my beloved son Gerard Briscoe of the county aforesaid, and in consideration have granted all my estate both real and personal, to have hold and enjoy, saving to myself, full free and ample possessions and enjoyment thereof during my natural live. Signed Robt Briscoe before Basil Brooke, John Baker, Anne Baker.

BD2:496-497. Jacob Michael recorded deed 13 January 1777, from Thomas Fletcher for £4..15, lots #116, 117 & 188 of land in Frederick Town, laid out for Thomas Price. Acknowledged.

BD2:497-501. Hugh Scott recorded deed 13 January 1777, from Peter Myer for £2000, parts of *Resurvey on Cool Spring,* 180 acres; part of *Resurvey on Shear Spring,* 60 acres; third, *Peter's Lott,* adjacent to *Friendship,* 172 1/4 acres; 4th *Resurvey on Lewis's Forrest*, 67 acres; 5th, *Resurvey on Hard Grubbing,* 50 acres. Sarah wife of Peter Myer, released dower rights.

BD2:501-504. [Ex'd & del'd Rezin Davis, 17 Oct. 1785.] David Mitchell of Hampshire County, Virginia, recorded deed 14 January 1777, from George Brent and Charity, his wife, for £100 tract *Round Bottom,* about two perches from a run into the Potomac on north side of the river, about a mile below the mouth of Little Cacapon Creek. Signed before Thos Cresap, F. Warring.

BD2:504-506. [Ex'd & del'd Rezin Davis, 17 Oct. 1785.] David Mitchell of Hampshire County, Virginia, recorded deed 14 January 1777, from William McGoughy for £45, tract *Harman's Disappointment*. Agnes McGoughey wife of William released dower.

BD2:506 Abraham Laken recorded marks of his cattle 15 January 1777.

BD2:506-507. Duckett Wells recorded his marks of creatures 15 January 1777.

BD2:507-508. Jacob Myers recorded bill of sale 15 January 1777 from Frederick Meddag for £12 Continental money, one red and white cow, and one heifer about 1 year old.

BD2:508 [Marginal note, delivered to Mathias Need, 19 March 1784]. David Harry recorded deed 17 January 1777, from Daniel Clapsaddle for £125, lot #109 in Elizabethtown. Catherine Clapsaddle released dower rights.

BD2:511-512. Jonathan Reid recorded power of attorney 23 January 1777, from James Ford in Craven County, South Carolina, empowered to sell tract called *Turnip Patch,* containing 60 acres, on branch of Dry Seneca. Witnesses James Reid, Alexander Reid. Came to Frederick County court.

BD2:512-514. Henry Dick recorded deed 30 Jan. 1777, from Joseph Chapline executor of Joseph Chapline, for £50, sells *Resurvey on Well Done,* containing 100 acres.

BD2:514-516. Arianna Scott of Prince George's County, recorded deed 24 Feb. 1777, made 28 Nov. 1776, from George French, for 2 shillings, assigns tract called *George's Adventure,* lying in Frederick County in that part lately called Washington County, by estimation 400 acres. Signed by George French.

BD2:516-519 George Scott recorded deed of trust 18 March 1777, from George French, made 27 February 1777, between George French, Ariana French, wife of the said George French, and George Scott of the third part, confirms deed above, to use and benefit of Ariana, formerly Ariana Scott, with George Scott, trustee, since date of marriage.

BD2:520-522. William Waters recorded deed 19 March 1777, from Thaddeus Beall for £35, tract called *Pleasant Ridge,* containing 50 acres. Signed before David Lynn, Edward Burgess. Acknowledged, no dower release.

BD2:522 Nathan Maynard recorded deed 22 March 1777, from John Hall of the City of Annapolis, Attorney at law, in consideration of £58 sells tract called *Middle Plantation,* near a place called Dog Wood Bottom, on a run of water called Linganore, containing 100 acres. Signed before R. Ridgely, G. Duvall.

BD2:524-529. Alexander Hamilton recorded deed 31 March 1777, from John Glassford, James Gordon, John Campbell Jr., Alexander Low and William Ingram, merchants of Glasgow, North Britain, by Henry Riddle, as attorney in fact for John Glassford and Sons, recorded in the Provincial Court, 7 January 1774, for 5 shillings, assigns two lots in Georgetown, #51, whereon a Joseph Belt did dwell, and lot #76, purchased by Archibald Henderson.

BD2:529-533. Henry Riddel recorded deed 31 March 1777, from Alexander Hamilton for 5 shillings, sells two lots #51 and #76, as above, beginning at SW corner of the wooden store house lately occupied by John Glassford & Co.

BD2:533-536. Leonard Marbury Deakins recorded deed 8 April 1777, from James Walker for £50 tract called *Resurvey on Subburbs,* 8 5/8 acres. Signed before Wm Beatty, and James Young. The wife of James Walker, came, examined apart, released dower. [No name inserted.]

BD2:536-538. John Twigg recorded deed 8 April 1777 from Lawrence O'Neale for £40, *Twigg's Adventure,* beginning at white oak near side of glade between Robert and John Twigg, containing 95 1/4 acres. Henrietta O'Neale released dower rights.

BD2:538-540. [Exam'd & del'd Abraham Plummer, 6 Nov. 1785.] Hezekiah Hyatt recorded deed 8 April 1775, from Lawrence O'Neale for £20, tract called *Hyatt's Luck,* on north side of Murly Run, for 51 acres; also 13 acres, part of *Resurvey on Conclusion.* Henrietta O'Neale released dower.

BD2:540-541. Francis Deakins recorded deed 8 April 1777, from Dan'l Veatch for £68..15, parcel called *Hopewell*, on Little Monocacy, for 50 acres.

BD2:541-543. Robert Smith recorded deed 8 April 1777, from Thomas Dorsey of Anne Arundel County, for £100, part of tract called *Dorsey's Risque,* for 72 acres. Signed before Humphrey R. Thompson, Cornelius Garrettson. Acknowledged before Dan'l of St. Thos Jennifer, a Justice of the Provincial Court.

BD2:543-545. Christian Ebersole recorded deed 8 April 1777, from Thomas Dorsey for £100, part of tract called *Dorsey's Risque,* adjacent to a tract that is a resurvey on part of *Sprigg's Delight.* Signed before Humphrey R. Thompson, Cornelius Garrettson. Acknowledged before Dan'l of St. Thos Jennifer, a Justice of the Provincial Court.

BD2:545-549. John Chapel and Verlinda, his wife recorded deed from William Masters, son of Margaret Masters, by some called William Windom, of Frederick, alias Montgomery County, for £100 assigns tract devised by Thomas Windom, deceased in his will of 14 March 1762, to Josiah Beall in trust for Margaret Masters during her life, and then to her son, William Masters, to receive his dwelling plantation, a part of *Fletchall's Chance,* containing 100 acres, which he has received from his mother and the heirs of Josiah Beall, all the personal estate, and he is now about to remove to Virginia, with his family. Signed and acknowledged before David Lynn, Robert Peter. Bathsheba, wife of William Masters released dower.

BD2:549-551. [Marginal note, deed delivered grantee 9 Oct. 1784] John Kipheart recorded deed 12 April 1777, from Joseph Wood Jr. for £87..10, one full moiety or share of lot #86 in Frederick Town. Ann Wood released dower rights.

BD2:551-553. [Ex'd & del'd Tisha (?) Allison, 27 June 1785] Richard Allison recorded deed 24 April 1777, from Ignatius Diggs of Prince George's County, for £5 sterling, *Resurvey on Easy Come By,* for 50 acres. Signed before John Read Magruder, David Crawfurd.

End of Volume BD2

Frederick County Deeds, Liber RP1

RP1:1-2. John Hollington recorded deed 20 May 1777 from George Gillespie for £1000, two tracts of land, *Struggle,* containing 176 acres, and *Resurvey on Three Friends,* part containing 5 acres. Martha Gillespie released dower.

RP1:2-4. George Gillespie recorded deed 20 May 1777 from John Hollington, for 5 shillings, *Struggle* containing 176 acres, and part of *Three Friends,* containing 5 acres.

RP1:4. Nathaniel Offutt recorded bill of sale 21 May 1777, from John Delozel, in consideration of the love and affection I have for my son-in-law, Nathaniel Offutt son of Ed, grants my Negro boys Tom, Feb., Will, Randzen and York. Signed John Delizel in presence of Nathan Offutt, Mary Offutt.

RP1:4-6. Samuel Snowden of Prince George's County, and John Snowden of Anne Arundel County, recorded deed 22 May 1777 from William Martinsen, formerly of Frederick County, but now of Augusta County, Colony of Virginia, for £40 paid by Richard Snowden, late of Patuxent Iron Works, for tract called *Bear Bacon,* for 100 acres. William Holmes, of Anne Arundel County appointed his attorney for sale.

RP1:6-9. William Holmes recorded trust deed 22 May 1777 from Edward Dorsey, and Elizabeth his wife, for £7..10, parcel called *Bear Bacon,* for 93 ½ acres. Signed before Basil Burgess, John Burgess.

RP1:9-10. Edward Doring recorded deed from Samuel Waters (son of John) for £143..4..4, the amount of a mortgage made 12 August 1769. Signed before John Burgess and Basil Burgess of Anne Arundel County. Signatures attested to by County Clerk of Anne Arundel.

RP1:11. William Holmes recorded affidavit 22 May 1777. On 7 Nov. 1776, Edward Penn, son of Benjamin, in the presence of Richard Estep, Edward Browning, John Holmes, Edward Browning 3d, James Conner, Josephus Burton, showed white oak on west side of East Paint Branch, which he says was shown to him by John Larkin, who informed him it was corner of Edward Doring's land, a part of *Bear Bacon.*

RP1:11-12. Nicholas Sybert recorded deed 22 May 1777 from Christian Lower of Berkely County, by deed of mortgage for £1100, land called *Pleasant Valley,* in Montgomery County, but lately in Frederick County, 300 acres; and part of *Pleasant Fields.*

RP1:13-15. Benjamin Spyker, May 1777 from Nicholas Sybert of Montgomery County, for £1531, three parts of tract, 113 acres, 56 acres, other, along with improvements, mills, waterways.

RP1:15-16. William Benson and Jas Simpson recorded deed 22 May 1777 from Benjamin Spyker, for £2120 tract called *Resurvey on Pleasant Valley,* and part of *Pleasant Fields,* in Montgomery County, 216 acres.

RP1:17-18. Jacob Rowland, miller, recorded deed made 9 May 1777, from Jacob Sharer of Washington County, for £40, part of *Resurvey on Kelly's Delight,* 28 acres. Signed before Sam'l Beall Junr., John Stull. Magdalena Sharer released dower.

RP1:18-19. John Fage recorded deed 22 May 1777, from Jacob Sharer of Washington County, for £160, two tracts, part of *Resurvey on Kelly's Delight,* 170 acres, and 2nd part starting on East side of Antietam Creek, called *Delight,* 100 acres. Signed before Sam'l Beall Junr., John Stull. Magdalena Sharer released dower.

RP1:20-21. George Leonard Backenbach recorded deed 26 May 1777 from John Wendel Storm and Michael Haverley, for £100, Pennsylvania, two tracts, *Resurvey on Turkey Range,* and part of *Fox Hole,* 45 and 58 acres. Wives (names left blank) released dower.

RP1:22. Charles Boley recorded deed, made 10 August 1777 from John Cump, shoemaker, for 5 shillings, sells lot #240 in Additional Lots to Frederick Town. Elizabeth wife of John Cump released dower.

RP1:23-25. Jacob Keplinger, blacksmith, recorded deed 26 May 1777 from George Leonard Beckenbaugh, for £100, Pennsylvania, three parcels, in whole 152 ½ acres, beginning at a black oak on south side of Half Mile Branch of Kittoctin, also the beginning of *Resurvey on Turkey Range,* and *Fox Hole,* 71 ½ acres, also 46 acres, and one other part of 30 acres. Anna Maria Beckenbaugh released dower.

RP1:25-26. William Magruder, son of Alexander, recorded deed 24 May 1777 from Alexander Magruder of Prince George's County, for natural love and affection, and for his better maintenance, assigns tract called *Lost Pen and Ink,* as patented. Elizabeth Magruder released dower rights.

RP1:26-28. Jacob Kendler recorded deed 24 May 1777 from William Beatty for £300, lot #65 in Frederick Town. Mary Beatty released dower.

RP1:28-29. Joshua Pigman recorded deed, made 2 May 1777, from William Murdoch of Prince George's County, for £578, tract called *Catch as Catch Can,* to line of Samuel Phillips part. 340 acres.

RP1:29-30. John Kellenger recorded deed 24 May 1777 from Ann Devilbiss, relict and executrix of Casper Devilbiss, for £150, *Resurvey on Poplar Bottom,* 85 acres, part of *Stouders Luck,* 65 acres and part of *Benjamin's Choice,* 14 acres. Signed by mark.

RP1:31-32. Isaac Hornace recorded deed 24 May 1777 from John Digges of Charles County, heir at law of Edward Diggs of Saint Mary's County, for £155, assigns tract north of Toms Creek, 115 acres.

RP1:32-34. William Benson and James Simpson recorded deed 22 May 1777, from Benjamin Spyker for £2120, tract called *Resurvey on Pleasant Valley and Pleasant Fields*, Catharine Spyker released dower rights.

RP1:34-35. Adam Hoover recorded deed 24 May 1774 from Henry Funk of Washington County, for £50 tract called *Locust Bottom.*

RP1:35-37. Henry Winemiller recorded deed 26 May 1777 from Joseph Doll of Fredericktown, joiner, lot #40 in Frederick Town. Charlotte wife of Joseph Doll released dower.

RP1:37-39. Valentine Adam recorded deed 25 May 1777 from John Middaugh, merchant. Whereas Susanna Beatty deceased was seized of *Dear Bought,* granted Daniel Dulaney, by estimation 100 acres, of which Johannes Middagh and Martha Middaght both of Prince George County, deceased, became possessed, and they died intestate, and John Middagh was son and heir at law, for £200 grants *Dulaney's Lot,* 154 acres. Mary wife of John Middagh released dower.

RP1:39-40. John Linganfelter recorded deed 25 May 1777 from William Chad, for £31..9, *Morley's Resort.* Ann wife of William Chad released dower.

RP1:41-43. Samuel Durbin recorded deed 1 June 1777 from Benedict Swope of Baltimore County, for £250, part of *Molly's Fancy,* on Pipe Creek, 193 acres. Susannah, wife of Benedict released dower.

RP1:43-44. Nicholas Lyster recorded deed 8 June 1777 from Samuel Durben for £450, part of *Molly's Fancy,* 167 acres. Signed by mark. Comfort, wife of Samuel Durban released dower.

RP1:45-46. John Renner recorded deed 31 May 1777 from Casper Shaaf, for £50, *Good Hill,* at beginning tree of *Bear's Den.* Alice wife of Casper Shaaf released dower.

RP1:46-48. Mathias Marten recorded deed 31 May 1777 from William Fout for £900, *Digge's Lot,* on north side of Toms Creek. 171 acres. Susannah wife of William Fout released dower.

RP1:49-50. Christian Louch recorded deed 3 Jane 1777 from Francis Deakins and William Deakins Junr. for £28..15, part of tract called *Good,* 14 3/8 acres. Eleanor, wife of Francis Deakins released dower.

RP1:50-52. Peter Wolf recorded deed 3 June 1777, from Jesse Wharton £212 part of *Diggs Lot,* at mouth of Toms Creek, conveyed to me in trust by the heirs of Edward Diggs deceased.

RP1:53-55. Peter Sholly recorded deed 3 June 1777 from Jacob Kreps for £190, tract called *Polton's Seal,* 97 3/4 acres. Magreth released dower rights.

RP1:55-57. Adam Troup recorded deed 3 June 1777, from Christian Shively and Jacob Shively for £1000 tract *Three Friends,* 208 acres. Susanna and Elizabeth wives of Christian and Jacob and Elizabeth, their mother, released dower rights.

RP1:57-60. John Nicholls recorded deed 3 June 1777,from Christian Kemp, part of *Resurvey on Dispatch,* 60 acres. Gertraud, wife of Christian Kemp released dower rights.

RP1:60-62. Isaac Honacre recorded deed 3 June 1777 from George Dickson, for £37..17, part of *Diggs Lot,* 6 ½ acres, 15 perches. Signed before Jacob Young, George Scott.

RP1:62-64. Frederick Hyser recorded deed 3 Jun3 1777, made 9 April from Francis Deakins and William Deakins Junr. for £179, part of tract *Resurvey on What You Please,* 150 acres. Eleanor, wife of Francis Deakins released dower.

RP1:64-67. Thomas Ricketts recorded deed 3 June 1777, made 1 March from Thomas Bayne for £80, assigns parcel called *Nonesuch,* containing 75 acres. Catharine Baynes released dower.

RP1:67-69. Isaac Hornacre recorded deed 3 June 1777, from Rudolph Neat for £10 *Resurvey on Benjamin's Good Luck,* 2 acres.

RP1:69-71. Michael Smith recorded deed 3 June 1777, from Adam Bower for £209, part of *Resurvey on Mend All,* and part of tract *I Hope it Well Done,* adjacent to *Last Shift,* and line between Michael Smith and Jacob Smith, 97 1/4 acres. Mary Dorothea Bower released dower rights.

RP1:72-75. William Harris, merchant of Chester County, Pennsylvania, recorded deed 5 June 1777 from Robert Beatty, for £1300 part of *Resurvey on the Pines,* and *Addition to the Pines,* containing 500 acres. Esther Beatty released dower rights.

RP1:75-77. John Simpkins recorded deed 3 June 1777, from Thomas Gilbert for £125, tract *Resurvey on Pilgrim's Harbor,* 66 acres. Elizabeth wife of Thomas Gilbert released dower.

RP1:78-79. Valentine Smelser recorded deed 5 June 1777, from Jacob Sharer of Washington County, Maryland, for £30, sells lot #123, to pay ground rents to Jacob Funk of 6 shillings on 29th September each year. Magdalena, wife of Jacob Sharer released dower.

RP1:80-82. Peter Toffler recorded deed 6 June 1777 from Woolrich Henninger for £10 part of tract on east side of Fishing Creek, containing 25 acres. Susannah, wife of Woolrich released dower.

RP1:82-84. Conrad Crown recorded deed 7 June 1777, from Peter Stock for £101..2..6, one house and lot #1, in Middletown, to pay annual rents of 7 shillings to owner of the town. Esther Stock released dower rights.

RP1:85-87. Martin Burntrager recorded deed 9 June 1777 from Jacob Kagga of Monham Twp., York County, Pennsylvania, for £130, 197 acres of *Chestnut Ridge*, signed before Jacob Young, Christ. Edelen.

RP1:87-89. John Meek recorded deed 21 June 1777, from John Spoon for £25, part of *Clem's Chance,* adjacent to *Petersham,* belonging to Charles Sholl, to tract called *Vulversham,* surveyed for Michael Havener. Two acres. Susannah, wife of John Spoon released dower rights.

RP1:89. Michael Troutman recorded deed 14 June 1777, from Adam Pancoast of Montgomery County, for £150 sell a certain Negro man named Anthony Waiter. Signed in presence of J. Troup.

RP1:89-92. John Troxell, late of Philadelphia County, but now of Frederick County, recorded deed 14 June 1777 from Michael Waggoner of Frederick County, for £2000 sells part of tract called *Resurvey on Harris's Delight,* metes & bounds given containing 273 acres. Signed in the presence of Jacob Young, John Haas. Elizabeth Waggoner released dower rights.

RP1:92-96. Peter Troxall recorded deed 16 June 1777, from Christian Keefer for £2450, five tracts hereafter mentioned. (1) *Resurvey on Digg's Lot,* conveyed to him by William Digges, recorded in Liber W:164, 100 acres. (2) tract on west side of Monocacy, near Tom's Creek patented to Unkle Unkles, by name of *Chance Medley,* 92 acres. (3) *Resurvey on Benjamin's Good Luck,* 50 acres. The last two tracts being made over by Conrad Hockersmith, in November 1774, recorded in Liber W:273-274, parts of *Resurvey on Digge's Lot,* conveyed by William Diggs to Nicholas O'Bryan for 50 acres and (5) part of *Diggs Lot,* 108 acres, conveyed to Christian Keefer by Lawrence Creager, recorded in Liber U:270. Containing in all 400 acres. Sarah, wife of Christian Keefer released dower.

RP1:96-99. Abraham Kise of Tawneytown, brewer, recorded deed 18 June 1777 from Nicholas Lazear, of Pennsylvania, lately of Tawneytown, lots whereon he lately lived in Tawney Town; part of *Resurvey on Brother's Agreement,* 10 acres, lot #4 on town plan, and another lot on the main road from Frederick to York Town, lot #16. Sophia, wife of Nicholas Lazear released dower rights.

RP1:99-101. John Hinds recorded deed 10 June 1777 from Thomas Beatty, for £20, tract called *Leave None,* on first line of *Discovery,* granted to Richard Stephenson, for 21 acres. Signed before Ally Morrow, and Joshua Ivory (by mark). Catharine, wife of Thomas Beatty released dower.

RP1:101-104. Elizabeth Hinds recorded deed 20 June 1777, from Thomas Beatty for £100, part of *Resurvey on Discovery,* for 175 acres. Catharine Beatty released dower.

RP1:104-105. Nicholas Kline recorded deed 20 June 1777, from Michael Weaver for £18, lot #237 in Addition to Frederick Town, covenants to build dwelling house. Catharine, wife of Michael Weaver released dower.

RP1:105-107. Thomas Maginnis recorded deed 22 June 1777, from Francis Deakins for £22, *Addition to the Rich Lands,* 30 ½ acres. Eleanor, wife of Francis Deakins released dower.

RP1:107-109. Valentine Linganfelter recorded deed 21 June 1777 from George Darr and Henry Leatherman. Whereas Andrew Livingston for £200 conveyed to parties above, on 28 March 1774, tracts, for £400, Darr and Leatherman, now assign to Linganfelter, tract called *Miller's Delight,* containing 100 acres, plus improvements. Amelia Darr and Margaret Leatherman released dower.

RP1:110-112. James Sergeant recorded deed 28 June 1777, from Thomas Frazier for £73..2..6, part of *Hawkins Merry Peep a Day*, adjacent to *Merryland,* signed before Wm Luckett Junr., Carlton Tanneyhill. Anne wife of Thomas Frazier released dower.

RP1:112-113. Frederick Whitacre, carpenter, recorded deed 28 June 1777 sold to John Hummell for £50, lot #108 in Frederick town. Catherine, wife of Frederick Whitacre released dower.

RP1:114-116. John Kemp recorded deed 28 June 1777 from Christian Kemp, for money amount not recorded, assigns tract *Small Gain,* 217 acres. Gertraud, wife of Christian Kemp released dower.

RP1:116-118. Legh Master recorded deed 30 June 1777, from Prudence England executrix and wife to Samuel England, deceased of Frederick County, for £76 grants to James Smith on behalf of Legh Master, tract *Arnold's Chance.*

RP1:118-119. George Main Junr recorded deed 30 June 1777, from George Main Senr for £20, part of tract called *Full Bottle,* containing 75 acres.

RP1:120-121. Conrad Kline recorded deed 1 July 1777 from John Logsdon, for £102 part of tract called *Bedford,* on Great Pipe Creek, adjacent to part conveyed to Morris Ellis. Margaret Logsdon, wife of John, released dower.

RP1:121-123. Isaac Runion and Mary Higgeman, widow, recorded deed 1 July 1777, from John Logsdon for 15 shillings, tractr on Great Pipe Creek containing 15 acres, part of *Logsdons Amendment.* Margaret Logsdon released dower right.

RP1:123-124. Elijah Beatty recorded deed 2 July 1777 from Ezekiel Beatty for £350 part of *Resurvey on part of Middle Plantation,* 1330 acres. Christian, wife to Ezekiel, released dower. Signed by mark.

RP1:125-126. Benjamin Cornal recorded deed 3 July 1777, from Gilbert Watson for £400 part of *Resurvey on Brother's Agreement,* containing 175 acres. Ann wife of Gilbert Watson released dower.

RP1:127-129. Thomas Fletcher recorded deed 2 July 1777, from Christian Lower of Bucks County, Pennsylvania, for £350, sells part of *Magruder and Bealls Honesty,* lying in Montgomery County. Acknowledged before Jacob Young, Wm Beatty.

RP1:129-130. Christopher Erb recorded deed 3 July 1777 from Michael Traut for £250, parts of *Spark's Delight, William and Ann,* and *Brookes Discovery on the Rich Lands,* beginning at part of a tract sold by Christoph Neiswanger to Leonard Painter, to part sold by Neiswanger to Frederick Black, metes and bounds for 200 acres. If £250 plus interest paid within two years, land goes back to Michael Traut.

RP1:130-131. Casper Mantz recorded deed 4 July 1777, from Charles Beatty for £160, lots #83 & 84 in Frederick Town. Martha Beatty released dower rights.

RP1:132-133. Simon Snook recorded deed 5 July 1777, from Charles Beatty for £111, part of tract called *Loss Gained,* beginning at John Silver's part, adjacent to *Lisbon.* Martha, wife of Charles, released dower right.

RP1:133-134. Frederick Goldie recorded deed 5 July 1777 from Daniel Lays for £26 part of lots #127 & 128 in Addition to Frederick Town, adjoining Jacob Michael's part of said lots. Signed before Christopher Edelen, John Haas.

RP1:134-137. James Somervell of Baltimore Town, recorded deed 5 July 1777, from Abraham Hayter for £2500 part of *Addition to Brooke's Discovery on the Rich Lands,* beginning at a tract called *Joseph's Chance,* to Samuel Ferguson's land. 501 acres. Excepting 2 acres where the meeting house stands for use as a Presbyterian Congregation and school, and two acres land to the nearest spring of water. Also a part of tract patented to Isaac Brook conveyed to Abraham Hayter by Andrew Pack, to a parcel laid off for Dann Baldwin. Susannah, wife to Abraham Hayter released dower.

RP1:137-138. John Nighcomer recorded deed 7 July 1777, from Mathew Maughens for £100 art of *Dry Meadow,* near a spring opposite the widow Shaffers, for 50 acres. Signed before Christopher Edelen, Jacob Young.

RP1:138-139. Balser Hawk recorded deed 8 July 1777, from Christian Pringle for £250 lot #20 in Frederick Town, to pay ground rents to Daniel Dulaney or his heirs. Elizabeth, wife to Christian Pringle released dower.

RP1:139-141. Barbara Gryder recorded deed 9 July 1777, from Peter Gryder, son of John Gryder, deceased, late of Frederick County, for £250, sells tract, part of *Molly's Industry,* formerly patented to Thomas Logsdon, and conveyed to John Gryder, now deceased, 18 July 1747, recorded in the records of Baltimore in Liber TB no E, folio 462-464, part of a tract called *Beaver's Delight,* conveyed by George Barnett to the said John Gryder, recorded in Frederick County Deeds, Liber B, folio 548-549, containing 100 acres, and deed from October 1765, recorded in Baltimore County, *Resurvey on Molley's Industry,* recorded in September 1768, in Baltimore County liber B no. O, folio 547-549, containing 50 acres. Margaret, wife to Peter Gryder released dower.

RP1:141-144. Robert Talbot recorded deed 10 July 1777, from John Logsdon and Anthony Arnold Junr., By a bond of obligation dated 19 March 1774, John Logsdon bound himself in sum of £90 to Anthony Arnold Jr., lot in town of New London, #6, part of tract called *Timber Ridge,* the lot formerly inhabited by a certain James White, and whereas the said Robert Talbot hath agreed for the absolute purchase of said lot, for consideration aforesaid and the sum of £22..10 paid by Anthony Arnold to John Logsdon, assigns lot above unto Robert Talbott. Deed signed by John Logsdon, Anthony Arnold. Receipt to Robert Talbott for £110. Mary wife of John Logsdon, and Hannah, the wife of Anthony Arnold Junr. examined apart and released dower rights.

RP1:144-145. Charles Sewell of York County, Pennsylvania, recorded deed 14 July 1777, from John Logsdon, for 5 shillings sterling and other services rendered to him, assigns part of tract, *Resurvey on Bedford,* containing 10 acres more or less. Signed before Rezin Hamond, and John Moale, of Baltimore County, Justices. A. Lawson, clerk of Baltimore attested.

RP1:145-146. Valentine Black recorded deed 19 July 1777, from Charles Beatty for £207 lots #83 & #84 in Frederick Town. Signed before Jacob Young, Chris. Edelen. Martha, wife to Charles Beatty released dower.

RP1:146-147. Jacob Goller recorded deed 20 July 1777 from Philip Grantler for £40 all that half lot #136 lying in Frederick Town, Signed before Jacob Young, Chris Edelen.

RP1:147-148. Abraham Haff recorded bill of sale 20 July 1777 from Elijah Hall, for £25 sells one yearling colt, one harrow plow and iron tooth harrow, two feather beds with their furniture, 7 pewter plates, two large pewter dishes, two large basins, several other items, but sale to be void if sum paid with legal interest by 1 October next. Signed Elijah Hall before Wm Beatty.

RP1:148-150. George Woolsey of Baltimore, recorded deed 23 July 1777, from Edward Lamb, sells all residue of tracts *Resurvey on Lamb's Choice,* and *Resurvey on Locust Neck,* for £1142. Metes and bounds given. Signed before Wm Winchester, John Chamberlain. Eleanor Lamb released dower.

RP1:150-151. Jacob Getzendanner recorded deed 24 July 1777, from George Michael Rohr for £110, lot #24 in Middletown. Mary, wife of grantor, released dower.

RP1:151-153. James Martin recorded deed 27 July 1777, from Blaney Allison, son and heir at law of Robert Allison, formerly of Charles Town in Cecil County, late of Frederick County, deceased, for £200, part of *Brooke's Discovery on the Rich Lands,* that Andrew Pack and Abraham Hayter, sold to Benjamin Pedan, for 64 acres. Signed before Jacob Young, John Haas.

RP1:153-154. Winebergh Judy recorded deed 27 July 1777 from Frederick Goldie for £65, two lots #127 & 128 in Frederick Town. Margaret, wife of Frederick, released dower.

RP1:154-155. George Rosensteel recorded deed 31 July 1777 from Thomas Bowles, for £267, lot #31 in Fredericktown.

RP1:155-157. Lewis Kemp recorded deed 2 August 1777, from Christian Kemp for £250, *Resurvey on Dispatch*, and *Kemps Delight.*

RP1:157-158. Joseph and Absolom Hedges recorded deed 2 August 1777 from Thomas Gilbert for £5, *Resurvey on Pilgrim's Harbour.* Elizabeth Gilbert released dower rights.

RP1:158-160. David Stottlemeyer, miller, recorded deed 4 August 1777, from Thomas Welsh of Harford County, for £64, tract called *Schley's Discovery,* and tract called *Goose Cap,* Hannah Welsh released dower rights.

RP1:160-161. Adam Main recorded deed 6 August 1777, from George Main for £20, tract called *Empty Bottle* containing 80 acres.

RP1:161-162. Philip Keller recorded deed 6 August 1777 from Christian Kemp for 5 shillings, part of tract called *Philadelphia,* 17 acres. Gertraut, wife of Christian Kemp released dower.

RP1:163-164. James and William Marshall recorded deed 6 August 1777, from John Marshall of Lancaster County, Pennsylvania. Whereas James Marshall, late of Lancaster County, deceased, in his lifetime, obtained a deed of sale from Alexander McKlean of Frederick, 400 acres of land, recorded in Liber O:1-2, assigns for 5 shillings, as executor of will of James Marshall, tract.

RP1:164-165. Nicholas Boone recorded deed 7 August 1777, made 12 July 1777, from Jacob Boon for £30, land called *Black Oak Hill,* 7 1/4 acres. Catherin wife of Jacob Boon released dower.

RP1:165-167. Nicholas Hows recorded deed 7 August 1777, from George Dickson, for £35, assigns lot #176, 175 & 174, in Frederick Town.

RP1:167-168. Leonard Storm recorded deed 8 August 1777, from Wendel Storm, made 21 June, for £210, his right to 1 ½ lots in Middletown, #3. To pay yearly ground rents to Conrad Crown of 7 shillings, 6 pence. Magdalena wife of Wendall released dower.

RP1:168-169. Michael Walker recorded deed 9 August 1777, from Thomas Jones of Frederick County, tract *Lamar's Generosity,* adjacent to *Virgin's Delight,* 25 acres. Kezia Jones, wife of Thomas Jones released dower.

RP1:169-171. Jacob Good recorded deed 9 August 1777 from Francis Deakins and William Deakins Junr., for £30, tract called *Good Beginning,* adjacent to *Resurvey on Skipton.*

RP1:171-172. Mary Smith, widow, recorded deed 11 August 1777, from Edward Stevenson, son of Richard Stevenson, for £10 tract called *Small Tennant Beginning,* laid out for 5 acres more or less. Signed before Daniel Stevenson, Chris. Edelen. Phoebe Stevenson, wife of Edward released dower.

RP1:172-173. John Jacob Young recorded deed 12 August 1777, from Thomas Welch of Harford County, for £50 Pennsylvania, one tract called *I Would Not,* containing 25 acres; and also part of another tract called *Resurvey on Trembling,* containing 25 acres. Signed before James McComas, Wm Smither. Receipt. Acknowledgment and Hannah Welch released dower. John Lee Gibson, Clerk Harford County attested to J.P.s

RP1:173-174. Malachi Boyer recorded deed 12 August 1777, from Michael Reader, for £400, sells 108 3/4 acres, *Resurvey on Lamb's Choice,* Signed before Upton Sheredine, John Corker. Barbara, wife of Michael Reader, released dower.

RP1:175-176. John Shellman recorded deed 14 August 1777, from Eleanor Charlton of Frederick Town, executrix of the will of Arthur Charlton, late of Frederick County, deceased, sells lot #159, in Frederick Town for £46..10 at public vendue, adjacent to Mr. George Murdoch.

RP1:176-177. Christopher Gough recorded deed 18 Aug. 1777 from Jacob Keller for £62, two parts of *Resurvey on Den of Wolves,* adjacent to *Sassafrass Bottom,* and *Resurvey on Ken's Choice,* containing 16 ½ and 19 1/4 acres. Signed by mark. Magdalena Keller released dower.

RP1:177-179. Frederick William Shiver of York County, Pennsylvania, recorded deed 18 August 1777 from Jacob Keller. Whereas Jacob Keller obtained a patent 29 Sept. 1762 for *Den of Wolves,* containing 727 acres by patent, recorded in BC&GS #161 folio 595, of which he has sold 100 acres to John Smith, 200 acres to Nicholas Knezott, 100 acres to Michael Keller, 35 acres to Christopher Gough and 17 acres to Robert Wood. Now for £925 he sells remaining parts not sold, be estimation containing 200 acres. Wife of Jacob Keller, not named, released dower rights.

RP1:179-180. Rudolph Crabster recorded deed 20 August 1777 from Thomas Fisher of York County, Pennsylvania, for £300, tract *Addition to Brooks Discovery on the Rich Lands,* beginning at the 5th course of a parcel made over by Andrew Parke and Abraham Hayter to Potter Coonce, metes and bounds given for 100 acres. Eve, wife of Thomas Fisher released dower.

RP1:180-181. Casper Keller recorded deed 20 Aug 1777 from Peter Troutman, carpenter, for 5 shillings, part of tract. Mary, wife of Peter, released dower rights.

RP1:181-182. Peter Trautman recorded deed 20 Aug 1777 from Casper Keller for 10 shillings, part of tract called *Less Ground.* Anna Margaret, wife of Casper, released dower rights.

RP1:183. Peter Trautman recorded deed 20 Aug 1777 from Casper Keller for 5 shillings, part of tract called *Less Ground,* containing 2 ½ acres. Anna Margaret, wife of Casper, released dower.

RP1:184-185. David Hoffman recorded deed 24 August 1777 from Jacob Klein for £150, tract called *Thomas Field,* for 70 acres. Magdalene, wife of Jacob Klein released dower rights.

RP1:185-186. Godfrey Leatherman recorded deed 20 August 1777, from George Coster, fuller, for £4..16, sells part of tract called *Fuller's Delight,* containing 58 1/4 acres, signed before Jacob Young, Christ. Edelin. Susanna Coster, wife of George, released dower rights.

RP1:187-188. Henry Leatherman recorded deed 20 August 1777, from George Coster, fuller, for £2 sells part of tract called *Fuller's Delight,* containing one acre more or less. Susanna Coster released dower rights.

RP1:188-190. James Yeast recorded deed 20 August 1777, from George Peter Koopenrider for £300, sells tract *Below the Nipple and Bubbly,* metes and bounds for 121 acres. Signed by mark before Jacob Young, Wm M. Beall. Caty, wife of the aforesaid George Peter released dower rights.

RP1:190-191. John Ekes recorded deed 21 August 1777, from Joseph Rhea [or Neal]for £540, sells part of tract called *Brooks Resurvey on the Rich Lands,* laid out for 201 acres of land. Signed before Wm Blair, Joseph Wood Junr. Margaret, wife of Joseph Neal released dower rights.

RP1:191-192. James Allison recorded deed 21 August 1777 from Samuel Beall Junr of Frederick County, for £60 sells part of tract called *Frenchman's Purchase,* containing 160 acres.

RP1:192-193. Conrad Maugens recorded deed 21 August 1777, from George Custer for £73..12, tract called *Stony Bottom.* Susannah Custer released dower rights.

RP1:194-195. Nicholas Fringer recorded deed 22 August 1777, from William Winchester for £13..10, signed before Jacob Shellman, John Hahn.

RP1:195-196. Thomas Johnson, governor, recorded deed 23 August 1777, from Thomas Beatty, Esq., for £63, part of tract called *Rocky Creek.* Signed before Christ. Edelen, Upton Sheridine. Catherine, wife of Thomas Beatty released dower.

RP1:197-198. John Beyman recorded deed 23 August 1777, from Nicholas Leatherman, for £20, tract on branch of Little Hunting Creek, for 40 acres.

RP1:198-199. Anthony Stoke recorded deed 23 August 1777, from Charles Beatty. Whereas Casper Myer, had parts of tract called *Lay* and *Tasker's Chance,* laid out into lots on the road leading from Frederick, and Beatty sold lots to Stokes, this is to correct deeds. Martha Beatty released dower.

RP1:200-201. John Bruner recorded deed 26 August 1777, from James Hook. Whereas John Bruner by his will devised to the said John Bruner, son of Jacob, tract which was due to him from James Hook, upon payment of £42..1..5, called *Hooks Neglect,* resurveyed by a *Hard Struggle,* beginning at tract called *Gleaning,* granted to Notley Thomas, containing 117 acres. Signed James Hook.

RP1:201-202. Benjamin Clary of Baltimore County, recorded deed 30 August 1777, from John Mobberly, for £120, part of *Moberly's Chance,* metes and bounds for 60 acres. Signed by mark. Chloe, wife of John released dower rights.

RP1:202-203. James Murrey of Frederick County, recorded deed 30 August 1777, from William DeCourse of Roan Co., near the fork of Attkin River, N.C. for £80, sells tract called Leonard's Frederick patent to Leonard DeCourse, father to William, standing near head draught to Sam's Creek, containing 50 acres. William DeCourse, signed before Joseph Murray and James Armstrong. Attested to before Upton Sheridine, Christopher Edelen.

RP1:204-205. Henry Lynn recorded deed 30 August 1777, from Henry Forney of York County, Pennsylvania for £100 Penn., tract called *Benjamin's Good Will.* Signed by mark. Magdalena Forney released dower rights.

RP1:205-206. John Adam Easter recorded deed 30 August 1777, from George Peter Cooperrider, for £60, part of tract called *Below the Nipple and Bubbly,* 100 acres of 220 acres at end of third line of tract laid out for William Griffith. Signed by mark, Catherine, wife of George Peter Cooperrider released dower rights.

RP1:207-208. Jacob Boone, blacksmith, recorded deed 1 September 1777 from Nicholas Boone, son and heir at law of Theobald Boone, for £50, part of *Resurvey on Share Spring,* 80 acres, and part of *Boon's Content,* 40 acres, and also the *Resurvey on Wagner's Fancy,* containing 1/4 acre, more or less. Barbara Boone, wife of Nicholas Boone, released dower.

RP1:209-210. John Marquart, stocking weaver, deed recorded 1 September 1777, for Catharine Boyer for £250 she paid to John Marquart for two lots #177 & #178 in Additional Lots of Frederick Town. Dorothea, wife of John Marquart released dower rights.

RP1:210-211 George Linganfelter recorded deed 3 September 1777, from Raphael Taney of Saint Mary's County, and William Diggs, Jr., for £106..16, assigns tract called *Resurvey on Brother's*

Agreement, containing 182 acres. Eleanor Taney, wife of Raphael Taney and Catherine Diggs wife of William Diggs released dower.

RP1:211-212. Nathaniel Burckhart recorded deed 3 September 1777, from Henry Eller for £136, assigns his interest in *Richard's Hunting Ground,* on west side of Linganore Creek, on the 12th line of *Duke's Woods.* Elizabeth wife of Henry released dower rights.

RP1:213. Joseph Burckhart recorded deed 3 September 1777, from Henry Eller for £74, part of *Richard's Hunting Ground,* 55 acres. Elizabeth Eller released dower rights.

RP1:214-215. Henry Aller recorded deed 3 Sept. 1777, from Jesse Wharton for £326, *Richard's Hunting Grounds,* containing 366 acres.

RP1:215-216. Ludwick Hannewell recorded deed 4 September 1777 from Richard Hill for £100, part of *Brook's Discovery on the Rich Lands,* 100 acres. Mary Hill released dower rights.

RP1:216-218. Samuel Summers recorded deed 6 Sep 1777 from Henry Griffith for £100, part of *Joseph's Friendship,* on Monocacy. Ruth Griffith released dower rights.

RP1:218-219. Jeremiah Browning recorded deed 6 Sep 1777 from Henry Griffith for £127, part of *Addition and Joseph's Friendship.* Ruth Griffith released dower rights.

RP1:219-220. William Albough recorded bill of sale 9 September 1771. I Nicholas Boone, in consideration of William Albough being security in my deceased father Handell Boone's estate, sell one bay horse by the name of Buck and one bay horse by the name of Guy, provided always that bond is met, then sale is void.

RP1:220-221. Thomas Reynolds recorded deed 13 September 1777, from Christian Stowder for £52, part of *Resurvey on PawPaw,* 50 acres. Barbara, wife of Christian Stouder released dower rights.

RP1:221-222. John Arnold recorded bill of sale 3 Sept 1777 from Hugh Kelly for £12..17, one bed and furniture, one table and four chairs.

RP1:222-224. William Murdoch Beall recorded deed 3 September 1777 from Asher Layton for £140, part of *Resurvey on Content,* granted William Eller Burton in 1751 on Little Bennett Creek, formerly belonging to Joshua Burton. Signed by mark. Charity, wife of Asher Layton released dower.

RP1:224. William Fought recorded deed 8 Sep 1777 from Henry Green, for £450, *Hammond's Strife,* on Little Pipe Creek, 100 acres. Signed Henry Green Senr before Upton Sheridine, Eleanor Sheridine. Elizabeth Green released dower rights.

RP1:225-226. Nathan Hammond recorded deed 6 September 1777, from Philemon Plummer for £154, tracts *Debutts Delight,* 50 acres; *Holleter Springs,* 54 acres and part of *Resurvey on Beatty's Range,* conveyed to him in 1769 for 8 acres. Sophia Plummer released dower rights.

RP1:226-227. [Ex'd & delivered Thomas Rand, 12 Sept. 1779] William Green recorded deed 6 Sept. 1777 from Henry Green for 5 shillings, *Hinter's Forest,* patented in Baltimore County, but now in Frederick County, 43 ½ acres. Also parcel called *This or None.* Signed by Henry Green Senr., Elizabeth Green released dower rights.

RP1:228-229. Henry McClary recorded deed 8 Sept 1777, from Henry Griffith of Montgomery County, for £115, assigns 115 acres of *Joseph's Friendship.* Signed before T. Sprigg Wootten, Joseph Wilson. Ruth Griffith released dower.

RP1:229-231. Frederick Mane recorded deed 11 Sept. 1777, from George Mane for £2 assigns tract, *All Bottle's Full,* metes and bounds given for 65 acres. Signed by mark before Christopher Edelen, John Haas.

RP1:231-232. Christian Keefer recorded deed 14 September 1777, from Michael Wagoner for £100, *Resurvey on Wagoner's Fancy,* as recorded in liber H:878-880, adjacent to *Stoney Meadows.* Mary, wife of Michael released dower.

RP1:232-233. Christian Keefer recorded deed 14 September 1777, from Michael Wagoner for £20, part of tract, *Resurvey on Share Spring,* containing 15 ½ acres. Mary wife of Michael released dower.

RP1:234-235. John Cronise recorded deed 16 Sept. 1777, from Thomas Schley for £51..9, lot #225 & 226, in Additional Lots of Fredericktown. Margareth Schley released dower rights.

RP1:235-236. Adam Scheffley, shoemaker, recorded deed 16 Sept. 1777, from Henry Lampbright for £59, lot #214 in Additional Lots in Frederick. Conditions of deed given by Daniel Dulaney, Esq., to John Cary, on part of John Keipher, recorded in Liber I, folio 338-340. Signed before Jacob Young, Christ Edelen. Margareth, wife of Henry released dower rights.

RP1:236-237. George Ramsberger recorded deed 17 Sept 1777 from Conrad Ricker, blacksmith. Whereas Leonard Smith, executor of Eleanor Medley, conveyed lot #30 in New Town, recorded in BD1:221-223. Elizabeth, wife of Conrad Ricker released dower.

RP1:238-239. Wm Murdoch Beall recorded deed 22 Sept. 1777, from Lawrence O'Neale, Sheriff of Frederick County. Whereas John and Thomas Hartley obtained a judgment in 1769 against William Parker, and his property, lots #1 & 2, on *Long Acre,* part of *Tasker's Chance,* on road through Frederick Town, were sold in 1774 to Beall, the highest bidder at the sale for £52..17..4, and Murdock paid sums due to the Hartleys, deed is made.

RP1:239-240. Lawrence O'Neale recorded deed 22 September 1777, from Wm Murdoch Beall for £50 sterling, deed made for the two lots above.

RP1:240-241. Michael Rohrer recorded deed 22 September 1777, from Lawrence O'Neale for £170, sells lots #1 and 2, lying on the left side of the road leading through Frederick Town, part of *Long Acre,* on *Tasker's Chance,* as above. Henrietta O'Neale released dower rights.

RP1:242-243. John Peltz Junr., brickmaker, recorded deed 24 September 1777 from Valentine Stickle for £153, lot #131 in Frederick Town. Signed before Chris Edelen, John Haas. Sevilla Stickle released dower rights.

RP1:243-244. Jacob Matery recorded deed 25 Sept. 1777, from Henry Shover, lot #82 in Frederick Town. Signed before Jacob Young, Chist Edelen. Ann, wife of Henry Shover released dower.

RP1:245-246. Lawrence O'Neale recorded deed 25 September 1777, from Doctor Charles Neale. Whereas by deed of mortgage made 2 March 1775, for £400, several Negroes (following) were mortgaged, and witness the condition of said mortgage not being complied with, I the said Doctor

Charles Neale have, in consideration thereof as well as the further sum of £80, convey unto Lawrence O'Neale the following Negroes: Ned, about 43 years, Charles about 40, boys named Ned 6 years and Ralph 4 years old, woman Sanga, about 30 years old and girls Nell about 9, Easter about 10 years old and Moll 12 years old, and a mulatto girl named Bett, aged 17 years, to serve by judgment of the court till age of 31 years.

RP1:246. Lewis Kemp recorded bill of sale 26 September 1777. Received of Capt. Lewis Kemp, £121, in full paid for Negro Anthony, sold by me, the said Negro being committed to the gaol in Frederick County as a runaway, and sold at public vendue to the highest bidder. Signed by Thos Beatty, sheriff before Jas Smith, A. Reintzel.

RP1:246-248. Yeat Plummer and Robert Plummer recorded deed 26 September 1777, from Jacob Harmon for £250. Tract bought from Jacob Thomas, called *Jacob's Cowpen,* on east side of branch of Bennetts Creek, containing 43 acres. Margreth Harmon released dower rights.

RP1:248-249. Peter Bainbridge recorded bill of sale 18 Dec. 1776 from Thomas Hagerty for £61, one horse valued at £16; one mare £12, two cows, £10; 2 sheep at 15 shillings, 2 beds and furniture, £8; 2 saddles, £5..10; two chests and sundries, 16 small pieces of pewter. Signed before Jacob Young.

RP1:250-252. Mary Triplett of Baltimore County, widow, recorded deed 30 September 1777, from Jacob Boone for £650, part of three tracts, *Resurvey on Share Spring,* 80 acres; another tract for 40 acres, and 1/4 acre of part of *Resurvey on Wagoner's Fancy,* Signed before John Haas, Christn Edelen. Catharine Boone, wife of Jacob released dower.

RP1:252-253. Michael Tressler recorded deed 1 October 1777, from Jacob Hoffman for £50, parts of lot #156 and #158, in Additional Lots of Frederick. Signed before Wm Beatty, Jacob Young.

RP1:254 -255. Thomas Ogle recorded deed 2 October 1777, from Thomas Schley for £100, all that messuage or dwelling house and other buildings and part of lot #54, containing 1/4 of the said lot in Frederick Town on southwest corner of lot #54, to part of lot belonging to George Hoffman, to lot of Jacob Steiner. Margaret Schley released dower rights.

RP1:255-257. Jacob Boyer Sr recorded deed 8 October 1777, from Anthony Stokes, well digger. Whereas Joseph Burneston sold lot #156 in Frederick Town. Barbara Stokes released dower rights.

RP1:257-258. John Bruner recorded deed 12 October 1777, from Jacob Matery for £100, part of lot #82 in Fredericktown.

RP1:258-260. John Summers, of Westminster, taylor, recorded deed 14 October 1777, from Valentine Wing, for £60, lot #31 in Westminster, beginning at line of Henry Springer, to the property of the heirs of Enoch Davis, deceased, part of *White's Level.* Signed by mark before Upton Sheridine, Christ'n Edelen.

RP1:260-262. Charles Smith of Baltimore County, recorded deed 15 October 1777, from John Spohn for £200, part of *Clem's Chance,* beginning at 2nd line of *Wertenberger,* metes and bounds for 82 acres. Susanna, wife of John Spohn, released dower rights.

RP1:262, Daniel Gaver recorded deed 16 Oct. 1777 from George Marker for £36, 20 acres *Marker's Delight.* On west side of Kittoctin Creek. Mary, wife of George Marker released dower rights.

RP1:263-264. Daniel Gaver recorded deed 16 Oct. 1777 from George Marker, for £91 sells tract called *Reaching.* 50 acres. Mary, wife of George Marker released dower rights.

RP1:264-265. Jacob Baggerly recorded deed 16 Oct. 1777, from Charles Carroll of Annapolis, for £50, tract *Smith's Lot,* or part of *First Dividend,* 50 acres.

RP1:265-267. John Wood recorded deed 26 October 1777 from Joseph Wood for affection he has for aforesaid son, John Wood, and for £10 assigns parcel called *Content*, being a part of *Resurvey on Welch Cabbin*,

RP1:267-268. Nicholas Fringer recorded deed 28 Oct. 1777 from Christian Gobble, for £60. 1 acre of *Friendship*, adjacent to part conveyed by Frederick Gobble to Enoch Davis. Christian Gobble signed by her mark before Joseph Wood Junr., Charles Clance.

RP1:268-270. Philip Marshall recorded deed 30 October 1777, from Peter Beaver of Hampshire County, Virginia, for £200, part of *Resurvey on Oxford,* on 5th line of *Resurvey on Learning.* Metes and bounds for 100 acres.

RP1:270-271. Basil Dorsey Jr., recorded bond, 31 Oct 1777, from George Burckhart, the condition is that said Burckhart will make over a deed for a tract of land called *Burckhart's Industry,* lying on Bush Creek, laid out for 25 ½ acres, also 63 acres and another tract of land, containing 50 acres, and one containing 268 ½ acres. Signed before Joseph Plummer, John Snyder.

RP1:271-272. Jacob Haff recorded deed 3 November 1777, from Charles Beatty for £8, beginning at tract called *Hughe's Potoma (?),* containing 2 acres. Martha, wife of Charles Beatty, released dower.

RP1:272-273. John Chrisman recorded deed 4 Nov. 1777, from William Winchester of Westminster Town, for £60 tract called *Resurvey on part of Bedford,* on lines conveyed by John Logsdon to William Winchester, containing 12 acres. Signed before Henry Lanebright, Abraham Bonham.

RP1:274-275. Seaport Bonder, blacksmith, recorded deed 8 Nov. 1777 from Dennis Bussard, for £150, part of tract called *Hard Quarters,* on draughts of Little Pipe Creek, laid off for 4 3/4 acres. Sophia, wife of Daniel Bussard released dower.

RP1:276-277. Seaport Border, blacksmith, recorded deed 8 Nov. 1777 from Henry Crowel, for £180, part of *Runnymeade,* a resurvey on the tracts *Williams Neglect,* and *Hard Quarters*, containing 100 acres. Also one other tract called *Hammond's Strife,* 10 acres. Signed before John Lawrence, Conrad Dudderar. Margaret, wife of Henry Crowel released dower.

RP1:278-279. Elisha Beall recorded deed 8 Nov 1777 from Edward Willson for £25 *Resurvey on Willson's Lot,* 16 1/4 acres. Signed by mark. Sarah, wife of Edward Willson released dower.

RP1:279-281. Henry Rife recorded deed 8 Nov. 1777, from Matthew Nouts, and Frederick Ridgelough, executors of George Nouts, deceased, for £270..10, sells tract *William's Neglect Resurveyed*, on Little Pipe Creek, 97 acres.

RP1:281-283. Christian Goiner recorded deed 13 Nov. 1777 from Thomas Gilbert for £350, lot #5, outlot in Frederick Town. Elizabeth Gilbert released dower.

RP1:283-284. George Delzhaven recorded deed 18 Nov. 1777 from John Stone for £100, part of *Smith's Mistake Rectified.* 75 acres. Signed by mark before Joseph Wood, Jr., John Haas. Elizabeth, wife of John Stone, released dower.

RP1:285-286. Marcus Harman recorded deed 14 Nov. 1775 from John Bachman for £30, *Jacobs Luck.* Christiana wife of John Barkman, released dower rights.

RP1:286-287. John McWilliams, weaver, recorded deed 19 Nov. 1777, from Frederick Sollars, son and heir at law of Frederick Sollers late of Frederick County, deceased, for £30 sells and assigns tract beginning at 11th line of *Arnold's Delight,* laid out for a certain Arnold Livers, containing 30 acres,

RP1:287-288. Henry Myers recorded deed 19 Nov. 1777, from Frederick Chrisman for £86, sells part of a tract of land called *The Resurvey on Gillis Range,* containing 43 acres. Elizabeth, wife of Frederick Chrisman released dower rights.

RP1:289-290. Henry Eller recorded deed 19 Nov. 1777, from Robert Wood for £32, assigns 9 3/4 acres of tract called *Long Slipe,* Catharine Wood, wife of Robert released dower rights.

RP1:290-291. Philip Evert recorded deed 19 Nov. 1777 from Robert Wood, for £28 assigns 9 1/4 acres of *Long Slipe,* Catherine Wood released dower rights.

RP1:292-293. Jacob Oster recorded deed 20 November 1777, from Jacob Massebough for £128 parcel called *The Nipple* on branch of Kittoctin Creek, 53 acres. Signed before John Wood Junr., John Haas.

RP1:293-294. Thomas Ogle recorded deed 21 November 1777, from Richard Butler, son and heir of Peter Butler, deceased, lot #95 in Frederick town, for which Thomas Ogle was high bidder at public sale.

RP1:294-295. Thomas Balding of Montgomery County recorded deed 28 Nov. 1777 from John Baynes Signed before Christ'n Edelen, Jacob Young.

RP1:296-297. Christian Rodes recorded deed 22 November 1777, from Thomas Gilbert for £300, lot #6 in Frederick town. Elizabeth Gilbert released dower rights.

RP1:297-298. John Shellman recorded deed 22 November 1777 from David Rayon, joiner, for £153, lot #23 in Frederick Town. Signed before Wm Blair, Wm Beall. Martha, wife of David released dower rights.

RP1:298-300. Michael Fisher of Baltimore County, recorded deed 25 Nov. 1777, from Valentine Rinehart for £78, part of *Phillipsburg,* 100 acres. Barbara, wife of Valentine Rinehart released dower.

RP1:300-301. Nicholas Lewis recorded deed 26 Nov. 1777, from George Rengar for £300, part of *Brooks Discovery on the Rich Lands,* 100 acres. Signed by mark.

RP1:301-303. Jonathan Agay recorded deed 26 Nov. 1777, from Valentine Larsh of Baltimore County for £231..15, part of *Addition to Brooks Discovery on the Rich Lands,* beginning at *Joseph's Chance,* to the 9th line of *Carrollton,* containing 206 acres. Signed Valentine Larsh before James Kerr, William Aisquith. Mary, wife of Valentine released dower rights.

RP1:303-304. James Kerr recorded deed 26 Nov. 1777 from Valentine Larsh of Baltimore County, for £228..7..6 part of *Addition to Brookes Discovery on the Rich Lands,* 203 acres. Mary, wife of Valentine, released dower rights.

RP1:305-306, Michael Traut and George Lutz recorded deed 1 Dec 1777 from James Brooke of Montgomery County, for £200 part of *Addition to Brook's Discovery on the Rich Lands,* 83 acres. Signed before Edw Burgess, Jos Wilson.

RP1:306-307. George Rosensteel recorded deed 26 Nov. 1777, from Christian Rodes for £300..10 assigns half lot in Frederick Town, adjacent to lot belonging to George Whitaker. Signed by mark.

RP1:308-310. Alexander Hamilton and Henry Riddell recorded deed 26 November 1777, from James Marshall and William Marshall for £2030 assigns several tracts, beginning at a small creek called Halls Run, tracts called *Alexander's Prospect,* 73 acres, and adjacent tract *Douthert's Chance,* 255 acres, also the *Resurvey on Almoney's Mistake,* 68 acres. Signed before Wm Blair, Joseph Wood, Jr.

RP1:310-311. John Hanson recorded deed 29 Nov. 1777 from Doctor James Beard of Washington County, for £590, two lots laid out for a certain Sykes Engbart on west side of Frederick Town, fronting the main road that leads from town. Anne, wife of James Beard released dower.

RP1:312-313. Frederick Hefner recorded deed 3 Dec. 1777, from Felix Souder of Washington County, Maryland, for £130, tract called *Cronise's Chance,* 65 acres, clear of elder surveys. Susannah, wife of Felix Souder released dower rights.

RP1:313-315. Peter Dysher recorded deed 20 November 1777, from Henry Zealer for £280, tract *Tuscarorah Gap,* adjacent to *Resurvey on Chestnut Hill,* 50 acres. Signed Henry Zealer before John Adlum, Wm Beatty. Mary Zealer released dower rights.

RP1:315-317. Richard Potts recorded deed 3 December1777, from Henry Hawke for £350 part of tract *Batchelor's Hall Resurveyed,* lying near Catoctin Creek, which Henry Hawkes purchased of Peter Creager, 132 acres. Catherine, wife of Henry Hawke released dower.

RP1:317-319. Richard Davis recorded deed 4 Dec. 1777 from Charles Beatty for £80, 29 acres of *Luckett's Neglect,* likewise the beginning of tract *Whiskey Grogg,* containing 29 acres. Signed. Martha Beatty released dower.

RP1:319-320. John Martin recorded deed 6 December 1777, from John Kepler of Frederick Town, for £127..20, assigns two lots in Frederick Town. Catherine, wife of John Kepler released dower.

RP1:320-321. Peter Kemp recorded deed 15 Dec. 1777 from George Bennet Kepler, cordwainer, for £45, lot in Frederick Town. Catherine, wife of George Bennet Kepler released dower.

RP1:322-323. John Fisher recorded deed 15 December 1777 from Peter Kemp for £100, *The Rich Bottom,* adjacent to *Fraley's Last Choice,* 60 acres and *Fraley's Last Choice,* 43 acres. Catherine, wife of Peter Kemp released dower.

RP1:323-324. John Comp recorded release of mortgage 15 December 1777, from Frederick Shaver, mortgage recorded in Liber S folio 110, dated 23 August 1773. Signed before Christ'n Edelen, Jacob Young.

RP1:324-325. Henry Goyer recorded deed 20 Dec. 1777 from George Zimmerman for £24, lots #177 and 178 in Frederick Town. Signed before John Haas, Wm Blair. Margaret, wife of George Zimmerman released dower.

RP1:326-327. Catharine Boyer recorded deed 21 Dec 1777 from Henry Goyer for £10, lots #177 & 178 in Frederick Town. Signed before John Haas, Wm M. Beall.

RP1:327-328. Otho Holland recorded deed 25 Dec. 1777, from Joshua Pigman for £100..6 tract *Catch as Catch Can,* beginning at 10th line of tract, running to middle of a spring on south side of Joshua Pigman's dwelling house, to 2nd line of Samuel Phillip's part, laid out for 59 acres. Jemimah, wife of Joshua Pigman released dower.

RP1:329-330. Jonathan Holland recorded deed 25 December 1777, from Joshua Pigman for £222.14, part of *Catch as Catch Can,* adjacent to Samuel Phillip's part, laid out for 131 acres. Jemimah Pigman released dower.

RP1:330-332. Thomas Schley junr recorded deed 5 January 1778, from Ann Burneston, widow of Joseph Burneston and William Burneston, eldest son and acting executor of the last will and testament of Joseph Burneston, deceased, late of Frederick County, for £39..15 part of lots 156, 157 & 158 in Frederick Town, purchased 15 May 1765 recorded in Liber J:586-588.

RP1:332-334. Thomas Schley junr recorded deed 5 January 1778, from Ann Burneston, widow of Joseph Burneston and William Burneston, eldest son and acting executor of the last will and testament of Joseph Burneston, deceased, late of Frederick County, for £30 part of the 3 lots #156, 157 & 158 in Frederick Town, adjacent to Jacob Boyer's part. Signed before Wm Beatty, Wm M. Beall.

RP1:334-335. Jacob Frushour recorded 10 January 1778 from John Frushour, for £200, *Resurvey on Fearnot,* 200 acres. Elizabeth, wife of John Frushour released dower, before Christ'n Edelen, James Johnson.

RP1:336-337. Anthony Stoke recorded deed 10 January 1778, from Ann Burneston, widow of Joseph Burneston and William Burneston, eldest son and acting executor of the last will and testament of Joseph Burneston, deceased, late of Frederick County, part of additional lots 156, 157 & 158, to Frederick Town, sold at auction to highest bidder for £6

RP1:337-338. Jacob Sinn recorded bill of sale 12 January 1778, from John Vertrees for £18, one white and brown cow, one iron stove, three iron pots, one clock. Signed before Richard Butler, Bigger Head.

RP1:338-339. Thomas Harwood Junr. recorded deed 13 Jan. 1778 from Thomas Ellcott for £450, tract *Solomon's Contrivance,* laid out for 9 acres and tract *Partnership,* adjacent to *Solomon's Contrivance,* 209 acres as in deed from Thomas Watkins, Elizabeth Hall, John Hall, Thomas Henry Hall and Henry Hall dated 5 November 1762 recorded in the Secretary's Office in Liber DD #5, folio 415-416, one of the Provincial Court Land Records. Signed before Richard Harwood Junr., Thos Harwood. Catharine wife of Thomas Ellcott released dower.

RP1:340-341. George Devilbiss recorded 17 January 1778, from Ann Devilbiss, widow. Whereas Casper Devilbiss, late of Frederick County, deceased, died seized of lot #3 in Tawney Town, in his will appointed Ann, his executrix and William Ballenger, executor, and when he refused to act, Ann has taken on executorship, and sold the aforesaid lot to George Devilbiss son of the aforesaid Casper Davilbiss for £300. Signed by mark, before Christ'n Edelen, Wm Blair.

RP1:342. Henry Smith recorded deed 2 January 1779, from James Marshall, made 13 December 1778, for £1300 currency in bills of credit, part of tract *Wet Work,* 200 acres. [Marginal note: Ex'd & del'd Henry Smith, 8 May 1779].

RP1:343-344. Christian Hufford Jr. Recorded deed 7 Sept. 1778, from Joseph Wood Jr. for £275 part of tract *Wood's Choice,* beginning at 46th line of *Resurvey on Spring Garden.* Ann Wood, wife of Joseph Wood Jr., released dower rights.

RP1:344-345. Daniel Hufford recorded deed 7 Sept. 1778, from Joseph Wood Jr. for £175 tract *Better than None,* containing by patent 110 acres. Ann Wood, released dower rights.

RP1:345-346. [Ex'd & del'd Peter, son and heir at law, 6 June 1792] Nicholas VanSalter recorded deed 2 May 1782, from Eleanor Wright, executrix of John Wright, for £100, tract called *Baker's Discovery,* beginning at a large white oak marked BC FC, being on the line between Baltimore County and Frederick County, metes and bounds for 50 acres. Signed by mark before Upton Sheridine, Eleanor Sheridine.

RP1:346-347. Captain George Cook recorded deed 4 May 1778 from Samuel Duvall for £1653 assigns tract *Addition to Grimets Prospect,* 551 acres clear of elder surveys. Signed before B. Johnson, Roger Johnson. Priscilla Ann, wife of Samuel Duvall, released dower rights, signed before Wm Beatty, Christ'n Edelen.

RP1:348-349. Conrad Duttero of York Co, Pennsylvania, recorded deed 11 May 1788, from Valentine Rape. Whereas Nicholas Bugher, late of Frederick County, deceased, by his will appointed Valentine Rape and his wife to be executors, and his wife renounced the executorship and refused the will, and Valentine proved the will, and sold to Conrad for £1938 sells part of parcel *Trura*, adjacent to Nicholas Warner's part, containing 270 acres. Signed before Wm Beatty, Christ'n Edelen.

RP1:350-351. John Staler recorded deed 17 April 1778, from Adam Wolfe for £250, part of *Hammonds Strife*, metes and bounds given for 71 acres. Signed in German script before Wm Beatty, Joseph Wood. Catharine Wolfe released dower rights.

RP1:351-352. George Battle recorded deed 18 April 1778 from Charles Carroll for £90..8, tract called *Mount Pleasant,* containing 120 acres.

RP1:352-353. Casper Mantz recorded deed 21 April 1778, from Jacob Bentz, for lots #14 & 15 in Addition to Frederick town lots on *Long Acre,* a part of *Tasker's Chance.* Margaret, wife of Jacob Bentz released dower.

RP1:354-355. Jacob Goller recorded deed 21 April 1778, from Jacob Bentz for £80 assigns lot #13 laid out in Addition to Frederick Town, by a certain Casper Myer, late deceased, part of tract called *Long Acre,* on tract *Tasker's Chance,* Signed by Jacob Bentz in German script, and by mark of Jacob Goller. Margaret, wife of Jacob Bentz released dower.

RP1:355-356. Henry Shover recorded deed 21 April 1778, from Jacob Bentz, for £44, lot #16 laid out in Addition to Frederick Town, by a certain Casper Myer, late deceased, part of tract called *Long Acre,* on tract *Tasker's Chance,* Signed by Jacob Bentz and Henry Shover in German script. Margaret, wife of Jacob Bentz released dower.

RP1:357-358. John Chisholm recorded deed 4th April 1778, from Thomas Dorsey of Ann Arundel County, for £30 sterling, near the mouth of Monocacy Creek, known as *Welch Tract,* metes and bounds given for 100 acres. Signed before Carleton Tannehill, Richard Waters.

RP1:358-359. [Marginal note, ex'd & del'd Col. Joseph Wood, 26 Jan. 1785.] Joseph Wood Junr., recorded deed 24 April 1778, from John Hammond for £24, part of *Resurvey on Good Neighborhood,* containing 16 1/4 acres. Signed before Wm Beatty, Wm Luckett Junr. Eve, wife of John Hammond released dower.

RP1:359-360. Thomas Gilbert recorded deed 24 April 1778, from John Simpkins, cordwainer, for £174, all his title, right to tract, *Resurvey on Pilgrim's Harbour,* beginning at 4th line, laid out for 66 acres. Signed before Jacob Young, Carleton Tannehill. Eunice, wife of John Simpkins released dower.

RP1:360-361. Richard Lilly recorded deed 27 April 1778 from Charles Carroll of the City of Annapolis, for £39..4, sterling, tract known by the name of *Bailey's Purchase,* on a small branch below the ford that leads from Nathaniel Wickham's to Joseph Ogle's, now laid out for 26 acres of land. Signed before Francis Fairbrother and Joseph Wood Junr.

RP1:361-362. Gilbert Falconer recorded deed 30 April 1778, from Thomas Null, now of Frederick Town, merchant, for £2000 part of *Resurvey on Wildcat Hill,* containing 319 acres. Elizabeth wife of Thomas Null released dower rights.

RP1:363-364. Solomon Lydert recorded deed 29 April 1778 from Jacob Bentz of Frederick, for £54, sells lot #11, in Addition to Frederick Town, laid out by Casper Myer, on *Long Acre,* a part of *Tasker's Chance.* Signed by both parties in German script. Margaret Bentz released dower.

RP1:364-365. Jacob Michael recorded deed 30 April 1778, from Jacob Bentz of Frederick, for £81, sells lot #3, in Addition to Frederick Town, laid out by Casper Myer, deceased, on *Long Acre,* a part of *Tasker's Chance.* Signed by both parties. Margaret Bentz released dower.

RP1:365-366. Richard Potts recorded deed 5 May 1778 from William House for £100 tract of land called *Resurvey on Long Bottom,* containing 124 1/4 acres. Sarah House released dower rights.

RP1:367. Christian Yeasterday recorded bill of sale 5 May 1778, from Townley Bruce for £750 assign one Negro girl slave named Cate, and three Negro boy slaves named Tom, Gerard and Dave, signed Townley Bruce, before Henry Slagle and Joseph Guinn.

RP1:367-368. Frederick Black recorded deed 7 May 1778 from Adam Hope and Margaret Patterson, executors of William Patterson, late of Frederick county deceased, for £418..10 assigns tract called *Brother's Agreement,* containing 112 acres.

RP1:368-369. Frederick Black recorded bond 7 May 1778 from William Patterson, bond for £800 to make a good deed to Frederick Black for 124 acres of land, according to deed of conveyance from

Peter Heillander late of said county, adjoining the land. Signed by William Patterson before Adam Hope, Carl Sutton. (German script).

RP1:369-370. Peter Weterall, blacksmith, recorded deed 9 May 1778, from George Schnertzell, watch and clock maker, for £300 part of tract called *Resurvey on Good Neighborhood,* adjacent to tract belonging to Henry Crosby, containing 142 acres. Barbara Schnertzell released dower rights.

RP1:370-371. John Rinner recorded deed 13 May 1778 from John Cookerly, for £20 part of *Resurvey on Bear Den,* containing 4 acres more or less. Signed in German script. Margaret, wife of John Cookerly released dower rights.

RP1:371-373. Jacob Myers recorded deed 16 May 1778, from Cornelius Carmack, for £850 all his interest to tract, being part of *Lewis's Forest,* beginning at tract called *Level Spring,* containing 150 acres more or less. Signed before Joseph Wood Junr., Aquilla Carmack. Mary, wife of Cornelius released dower rights.

RP1:373-374. Peter Weterall recorded deed 19 May 1778, from Henry Crowl and Joseph Bailer for £600 tract, part of *Resurvey on Good Neighborhood,* containing 290 acres. Signed before Upton Sheridine, Wm Albough, by Henry Crowell, and in German script, Joseph Bailer. Margaret, wife of Henry and Elizabeth wife of Joseph released dower rights.

RP1:374-376. John Dern recorded deed 21 May 1778 from George Turnbull of Taneytown, for £50, assigns lot #43 in Taney Town, signed and acknowledged before John Ross Key, Jno McAlister.

RP1:376-377. Peter Weterall, blacksmith, recorded deed 28 May 1778, from John Beckleheimer for £19, part of tract called *Good Neighborhood,* containing 4 ½ acres. Signed in German script.

RP1:377-378. John Shenkmeyer recorded deed 21 May 1778, from Valentine Shroiner of Frederick Town, sadler, for £25, lot #40 in Frederick Town. Elizabeth Shroiner released dower rights.

RP1:378-379. Josiah Russell, attorney at law, recorded deed 22 May 1778, from Lodwick Weltner for £1330 lot with brick dwelling house and improvements. Mary, wife of Ludwick Weltner released dower rights.

RP1:380-381. Jacob Sharer recorded deed 22 May 1778, from Andrew Flickinger part of tract called *The Forest,* granted Osborn Sprigg, for 300 acres, metes and bounds now laid out for 100 acres. Signed German script before Jacob Young, Chris'n Edelen. Catherine Flinger released dower.

RP1:381-383. Michael Nuss, recorded 23 May 1778, from Jacob Bentz, for £88, to the said premises, lots #9 and 10, in Addition to Frederick Town, Michael Nuss, yielding and paying yearly, on 1st Monday in May, the sum of 7 shillings 6 pence unto the said Jacob Bentz, his heirs and assigns, and he covenants and agrees to work with the said Richard Nuss, his heirs and assigns. Signed in German script by Jacob Bentz, Johan Michael Nuss, before Wm Beatty, Carleton Tannehill

RP1:383-384. Henry Brothers recorded deed 22 May 1778 from John Potts, brick maker, for £820 all that new built, brick messuage, tenement or dwelling house, and that part of lot of ground in Frederick Town, lot #131, containing 102 feet in front and 60 ft. in depth, part of lot was purchased by John Potts. Signed before Christ'n Edelen, Carleton Tannehill. Catherine, wife of John Potts released dower.

RP1:384-385. [Marginal note, ex'd & deld Michael Null 13 Nov. 1793. Peter Little recorded deed 26 May 1778, from John Ross of Frederick Town, taylor, for £100 assigns part of tract called *Brother's Agreement,* containing 100 acres. Signed John Ross, Anna Ross, before John McAlister, Jno Ross Key.

RP1:386. Lawrence Sheler recorded deed 26 May 1778, made 16 April 1778, from Charles Carroll of Annapolis, for £50, part of tract called *Earnest Choice,* beginning near the mouth of a valley, on north easterly side of Little Pipe Creek, near the main road, containing 50 acres. Signed before Francis Fairbrother, Joseph Wood Junr.

387. Anthony Stoke recorded deed 17 May 1778 from Michael Rhorer, of Frederick Town for £301 lot # [blacked out], on the left side of main road through town, tract called *Long Acre,* a part of *Tasker's Chance,* adjacent to lot where said Anthony now lives. Signed before Christopher Edelen, Jacob Young. Mary Rhorer released dower.

388-389. Philip Rodenpillar recorded mortgage 27 May 1778 from Philip Smith for £150, two tracts, *Stony Level,* originally granted John Smith, late of Frederick County, deceased, for 45 acres on 12 Nov. 1773, and *Weaver's Lot,* granted him in 17750 for 50 acres; provided nevertheless that if sums paid with lawful interest in current money of Maryland, rating dollars at 7 shillings and 6 pence each.

389-390. Henry Lands recorded deed 27 May 1778 from Nicholas Cope for £75, *Friendship Completed,* adjacent to parts conveyed to Christian Goble, Simon Baum, Frederick Baum and Elizabeth Conrad. Signed before Jacob Young, John Edelen. Catherine wife of Nicholas Cope released dower rights.

RP1:390-391. William Paxton recorded deed 28 May 1778 from Samuel Farquhar for £100, part of *Brooke's Discovery on the Rich Lands,* 100 acres. Signed Samuel Farquhar by mark and Elizabeth Farquhar by mark.

RP1:391-392. [Marginal note, exam'd & deld Wm Paxton, 22 April 1780]. William Paxton recorded deed 28 May 1778 from James Brooke of Montgomery County, for £100, part of *Brook's Discovery on the Rich Lands,* beginning at part James Brooke made over to Abraham Hayter and Andrew Park, to a line of *Epping Forrest.* 10 acres by estimation.

RP1:392-393. Mathias Kepelen recorded deed 29 May 1778 from Abraham Gill for £123, part of *Frenchman's Purchase,* 150 acres. Mary wife of Abraham Gill released dower.

393-394. Benjamin Norris recorded deed 28 May 1778, made 25 Feb 1778 from Aquilla Carmack, for £624, part of *Resurvey on Spring Garden,* and part of *Lubberland,* 62 ½ acres. Signed before Upton Sheridine, Joseph Wood Junr.

394-395. Philip Kuhn recorded deed 6 June 1778 from Henry Forer and Jacob Krombach. Refers to mortgage recorded 16 August 1772 in Liber P, folio 450-451, on tract *Pleasant Valley.* Both signed in German script before Joseph Wood Junr., James Johnson.

395-396. Andrew Colvill of Philadelphia, Penn., merchant, recorded deed 4 June 1778 from Adam Hope for £2500, part of *Owing's Chance,* adjacent to *Norris ___?,* 300 acres. Signed before Wm Blair, Mary Blair, John McAllister. Agness, wife of Adam Hope released dower.

396-397. John Goff recorded deed 9 June 1778 from Christian Sholl and John Gaskins of Frederick Town. Whereas John Gaskins purchased of Clement Sholl, lot #284 in Frederick Town. Agreement signed by all three parties.

397-398. Christopher Meisenkop of Lancaster County, Pennsylvania, blacksmith, recorded deed 10 June 1778 from Thos Schley, Senr., schoolmaster, lot #228 in Frederick Town. Margaret Schley released dower.

RP1:398-400. Balser Fox recorded deed 10 June 1778 from Handel Barrick for £150, part of *Benson's Folly,* between Taylor's Branch and Muddy Run, 50 acres, being part of *Resurvey on Cooper's Alley,* 43 acres and also part of *Resurvey on Neighborhood,* by Richard Reynolds, 7 acres.

RP1:400-401. Mathais Fickle recorded deed 11 June 1778 from James Pettit for £56..5, part of *Brooks Discovery on the Rich Lands,* beginning at 3d line of *Epping Forest,* containing 25 acres. Signed before Jno Ross Key, Jno McAllister. Martha Pettit released dower. [Del'd Christopher Smith per court order, 23 August 1792].

RP1: 401-402. Conrad Myers recorded deed 11 June 1778 from James Davison for £52..10, *The Exchange,* signed by mark. Jane Davison released dower.

RP1:402-403. Daniel Root recorded deed 12 June 1778 from Daniel Bussard for £475, part of *Hammond's Shift,* 90 acres. Sophia Bussard released dower.

RP1:403-404. [Del'd 13 March 1780 to Martin Koontz]. Martin Coonce recorded deed 12 June 1778 from Martin Reisinger for £100, 50 acres. Signed in German Script.

RP1:404-405. Peter Vion (or Dion) of Westminster town, recorded lease 28 June 1778, from John Criseman for £30, assigns two lots in Westminster, formerly laid out by name of *New London*, #45 & 46, adjacent to property of John and Henry Alspaugh, and originally part of tract *Timber Ridge.*

RP1:405-406. Mary Dornock recorded deed 28 June 1778 from John Criseman of Westminster town for £50, lot #18 on northeast of Main Street bounded by Christopher Myers and Peter Cryder. Signed before Wm Winchester, Frederick Chrisman.

RP1:407-408. Christian Remsberger recorded deed 16 June 1778 from George Hoetzel of Shenandore County, Virginia; George Gertzel Senr. Late of Frederick County, deceased, for £900 two tracts of land, *George and Margaret,* and 39 acres adjacent to Mathias Ringer. Margaret Kertzel released dower.

RP1:408-409. Melchor Boyer recorded deed 26 June 1778 from Edward Lamb of Westmisnter Town, for £93, tract called *Chance.* Eleanor Lamb released dower.

RP1:409-410. Jacob Shellman recorded deed 1 July 1778 from George Snider for £540, part of two lots conveyed by Casper Myer to Charles Sholl, a lot on Carroll Creek. The wife of George Snider (not named) released dower.

RP1:410-411. Jacob Shellman recorded deed 1 July 1778 from Jacob Bentz, lot in Frederick Town for 5 shillings, land lying at the bottom of four lots in Frederick, across the creek from the lots, and Jacob Shellman to have use of water. Signed by both men.

RP1:411-413. Martin Reisinger recorded deed 8 July 1778 from Martin Koontz for £100 part of *Christian's Folly,* laid out for 3 ½ acres more or less with buildings and improvements. Signed German script. Receipt. Christena, wife of Martin Coones released dower.

RP1:413-414. [Ex'd & del'd Ephraim Carmack, 17 Feb. 1801]. Levi Carmack recorded deed 7 July 1778, from Simon Meredith for £150 tract called *Chance,* beginning at a hill on north side of Israel's Creek, containing 26 acres more or less. Catharine wife of Simon Meredith released dower.

RP1:414-415. John Shellman recorded deed 10 July 1778, from Ezekiel Beatty for £400 assigns one fourth part of a lot #65 in Frederick Town, adjoining part in tenure of Jacob Kendle with buildings and improvements belonging thereto. Christena, wife of Ezekial Beatty released dower rights.

RP1:415-416. Wm Miller recorded deed 13 July 1778, from Thomas Pollhouse for £760 all those several parts of lots in Frederick Town, #3, adjoins a part of lots formerly belonged to Joseph Hardman, half of the length and 47 ft of the breadth of lot #224, parts of lot #202, and #203 and #204, and #205 and #206. Signed before John Wood Junr., John Eads. Elizabeth Pollhouse released dower.

RP1-417-418. Martin Lowderslagle recorded deed 17 July 1778, from John Chrisman, for £15 lot #8 in Westminster, adjacent to Peter Crowl on the southwest, and part of tract called *Timber Ridge,* signed before Jno Lawrence, Wm Winchester Junr.

RP1:418-419. Ludwick Renald recorded deed 19 July 1778, made 4 June 1778 from John Renard Replogle for £500, *Resurvey on Owings Chance,* 2 parts, 30 acres, the second part beginning at a tract called *Landstul,* containing 44 acres. Signed German Script. Barbary, wife of Jno Rhinehart Reppleogle released dower.

RP1:419-420. Abednego Hyatt recorded deed 24 July 1778, from Abraham Miller for £400 sells part of *Miller's Chance,* containing 216 acres. Mary Miller, wife of Abraham released dower.

RP1:420-421. Daniel Sheler recorded deed 31 July 1778, made 3 June 1778, from Lawrence Shelor of Frederick County for £50, part of *Earnest Choice*, containing 23 acres. Signed in German script, Lorentz Sheiler, before Joseph Wood Junr., Jno Carmack, Jno Ross Key. Mary Sheiler, wife of Lawrence Sheiler released dower right.

RP1:421-422. Peter Steven recorded deed 30 Sept. 1778, from Jacob Stoner for £100, part of *Resurvey on Spring Garden,* which said Jacob Stoner purchased of Azel Warfield, containing 50 acres of land.

RP1:423. Baltis Kinkle recorded a stray horse about 15 years old, complained he trespassed on his enclosure. Taken before John Haas.

RP1:423. Michael Allix with sureties Adam Brent and Charles Sholl, bond for £100 to state of Maryland, bond as Clerk of Market, to regulate same. Signed before Richard Potts.

RP1:423. Isaac Barr recorded his mark of hogs, 28 April 1778.

RP1:423-424. Thomas Yates recorded deed 30 September 1778, from Leonard Smith for £5 part of tract called *The Mistaken Rival,* containing 17 acres and 100 perches of land. Elizabeth Smith released her rights of dower.

RP1:424-425. John Jacob Schley recorded deed 24 September 1778, from Barbara Myers, widow of John Jeremiah Myers, lately deceased, and Peter Hoffman, executors. He died seized of lot adjoining John Linganfelter, lots #38 & #39, and John Jacob Schley was high bidder for £1800. Signed and acknowledged before Jacob Young, Christ'n Edelen.

RP1:426-427. Michael Barnsdoller of Philadelphia, Pennsylvania, recorded deed 22 September 1778, from John Wimmer for £900 assigns part of tract *Resurvey on Brother's Agreement,* metes and bounds for 150 acres. Signed by William Cornell and George Lambert by mark. Winche, wife of John Wimmer released dower rights.

RP1:427-428. Dewalt Martz recorded deed 21 September 1778 from Christopher Edlen, seized in fee simple of 4 acres part of a tract called *Stumbling Block,* assigns same for £30. Mrs. Rebecca Edlen released dower rights.

RP1:428. Thomas Burgee recorded release of dower 19 September 1778, from Priscilla Duvall wife of William Duvall, on tract *Duvall's Forest,* conveyed to said Burgee.

RP1:428-429. Isaac Keeper recorded deed 19 September 1778 from Thomas Burgee for £400, tract called *Bealls Good Will.* Signed by mark before Christ'n Edelen, John Ross Key. Eleanor wife of Thomas Burgee released dower rights.

RP1:430-431. Joseph Willson recorded deed 19 September 1778, from Jacob Miller in consideration of his love and affection for his daughter Catherine Willson, wife of Joseph Willson, and for £5, assigns tract called *Hamilton's Resurvey,* patented by John Hamilton, as described in deed recorded in Liber K:54-55, containing 100 acres. Catherine Miller, wife of Jacob released dower rights.

RP1:431-432. Robert Wood recorded deed 16 September 1778, from Thomas Bowles. Whereas Thomas Bowles on 26 Nov. 1764 executed a deed of trust by William Beall, for sundry goods and tracts to pay debts, recorded in Liber I:852, and subsequently all debts were paid and secured and William Beall deeded tract called *Bethlehem,* resurvey as *Wood's Design,* to Robert Wood, this clears deed by Thomas Bowles to Robert Wood for tract called *Bethlehem,* for 5 shillings.

RP1:432-434. Margaret Tressler recorded deed 15 Sep 1778 from Thomas Schley Junr for £100, part of several lots parts of lots #157, 158 and 159, in Additional Lots of Frederick Town, being lots purchased by Joseph Burneston, deceased, on 29 August 1777 cross lines with Jacob Michael's parts of lots. Signed by both parties before Jacob Young, Christ'n Edelen. Catherine, wife of Thomas Schley released dower.

RP1:434. Samuel Cowens recorded supersedeas 21 Sept. 1778 against Philip Koop and Jacob Miller for £65, before Christian Edelen.

RP1:434-435. Daniel Jacobs recorded deed 12 Sept. 1778 from Edward Willson for £500, several tracts, 150 acres, part of *Abner's Choice,* 96 3/4 ac. Part of *The Two Brothers;* 24 3/4 acres on *Resurvey on Willson's Lot,* and 28 ½ acres. Sarah Willson, released dower.

RP1:435-436. Thomas Mathers recorded indenture 12 Sept 1778 from Thomas Johnson, Esq., Governor of Maryland, for and in consideration of the yearly rent hereafter stated, and considerations, covenants and agreements, he leases all that parcel of land, part of *The Three Springs,* containing 103 acres from the 1st March last past, for and during the term of 18 years, to pay rent of £6. Tenant to plant within 5 years, and to leave at least an orchard of 100 bearing apple trees. Signed by Thos Johnson before Jno Ross Key, Roger Johnson.

RP1:437. William Murdoch Beall recorded qualification as Justice, 11 September 1778 before Chris'n Edelen

RP1:437. Michael McGuire qualified as Deputy Sheriff, 9 September 1778, before same witness.

RP1:437-439. Wm Bell, merchant, of the City of Philadelphia recorded deed 29 July 1779, from Capt. Hugh Scott. Whereas a certain Peter Myers, late of Frederick County, was seized in the following tracts of land, called *Resurvey on Cool Spring,* containing 180 acres, and part of *Shear Spring,* conveyed in April 1759, to said Peter Myers for 60 acres, found to contain 58 ½ acres; and land called *Peter's Lot,* containing 172 acres clear of elder surveys, part of a tract called *Resurvey on Lewis Forest,* sold to Peter Myers by William Lewis in 1762, for 67 acres, but containing only 65 acres; and part of *Resurvey on Hard Grubbing,* metes and bounds given for the sum of £2000 and whereas the said Hugh Scott is seized in his own right, of a tract called *The Orchard,* containing by estimation 272 acres. Signed by Hugh Scott before Mary Graham and Thomas Jones. Acknowledged before Wm Winchester Junr., John McAlister.

RP1:439-441. Herman Yost recorded deed 5 Sept. 1778, from Michael Storm for £550, tract *Turkey Range,* on Half Mile Branch, to 4th line of Jacob Keplinger's part, containing 100 acres. Magdalena Storm released dower.

RP1:441-442. John Kaufman recorded deed 5 Sept. 1778, from Thomas Polhouse, for £23, lot #235 in Addition to Frederick Town. Signed before Joseph Wood Jr., John Haas. Elizabeth, the wife of Thomas Polhous, released dower rights.

RP1:442-443. Thomas Wallace recorded deed 4 September 1778, from Christian Rhode, for £61, lot #194 in Additional Lots of Frederick Town. Signed by mark. Barbara, wife of Christian Rhodes released dower rights.

RP1:443-444. John Raitt recorded deed 2 Sept. 1778 from Ruth Hammond for £230, part of parcel called *Friendship,* left to her by last will and testament of her father, Major Nathan Hammond, and devised to her by deed of partition between the said Ruth Hammond, Ann Hammond and Hannah Raitt, in May 1776, and recorded in Frederick County land records. Signed before Elizabeth Duckett, George Raitt.

RP1:444-445. Clement Wheeler recorded deed 2 September 1778, from Thomas Awberry of Loudoun county, Virginia, for £18, part of island above the mouth of the Monocacy. Signed before Wm Luckett and Carleton Tannehill.

RP1:445-446 Baker Johnson recorded deed 31 August 1778 from Thomas Beatty, sheriff of Frederick County for £48, parcel, part of *Rocky Creek,* adjacent to piece of land sold the public to erect a magazine on main road, leading to Frederick Town, and on the other side adjacent to George Bear's land.

RP1:446-447. William Bentley recorded deed 27 August 1778, from Christopher Steel, for £50, part of tract called *Choice,* and part of *Spring Plains,* containing 16 ½ acres. Signed in German Script. Before Joseph Wood Junr., John McAllister. Catharine Steel released dower.

RP1:448-449. Peter Fisher recorded deed 24 August 1778, from Peter Creager of Frederick County, and with lawful power of attorney from my brother, Michael Creager of the State of Virginia, for and in consideration of £12, sells part of tract called *Resurvey on Anchor and Hope,* signed before Jacob Young, Christ'n Edelen.

RP1:449-450. Ludwick Byerly recorded deed 25 August 1778, from Peter Smith for £225, lot #46 in Frederick Town, to pay yearly rents to Daniel Dulaney. Elizabeth, wife of Peter Smith released dower.

RP1:450-451. Andrew Lock, alias Andrew Sluss recorded deed 24 August 1778, from George Smith for £22, part of *Addition to Brook's Discovery on the Rich Lands,* laid out for 11 acres. Signed in German script by both parties before Wm Blair, John McAlister. Christiana Smith released dower.

RP1:451-453. [Presbyterian Church elders in index] George Bair, Conrad Rote (or Conrad Read), Valentine Black and Conrad Doll, elders and wardens of the Reformed Calvinest Church in Frederick Town, recorded deed 24 August 1778, from John Brunner and Michael Stokes, sons and heirs at law of John Bruner, late of Frederick County, deceased, for 5 shillings, a half part of lot #80 for use and benefit of the church. Signed before Chrisn Edelen, Jno Ross Key.

RP1:453-454. Frederick Stengle recorded deed, 10th [ ] 1778, from Casper Peckenpaugh, made 20 August 1778, for £60, all his interest in a lot of ground lying in Middletown, to have benefit of springs of water on lot. Signed by mark. Susanna Beckenback, released dower.

RP1:454-455. Mark Harmon recorded release of mortgage 20 August 1778 from Christian Koonce. Whereas by indenture of mortgage made in June 1772, for £40, parcel of land called *Not in Mountain,* metes and bounds given for 30 acres. For payments of sums with interest, in sum of £54..8 shillings, mortgage released before Jacob Young, Chrisn Edelen.

RP1:456-457. Jacob Thomas recorded deed 20 August 1778 from Benjamin Whitmore for £220, *Biggs Adventure,* a part of *Benjamin's Good Luck,* with the lines of John Peter Wetzell's part. Signed by mark. Mary Whitmore released dower.

RP1:457-459. James Cooper recorded deed 20 Aug. 1778 from James McMahon, son and heir at law of John McMahon, who in his life time, sold by bond to James Cooper a certain tract, and now upon payment, deed is made for part of *Brook's Reserve,* online of *Resurvey on Buck's Forest,* between the plantation of the said James Cooper and the late David White, deceased, laid out for 183 acres. Signed by both parties before Wm Blair, Jno Lawrence.

RP1:459-460. Thomas Karr recorded deed 19 Aug. 1778, made 19 April, from Robert Love, for £600 sells part of *Brook's Grove,* next to Adam Kerr's, containing 80 acres. Signed before Joseph Wood Jr., John McAlister. Phoebe Love, wife of Robert, released dower rights.

RP1:460-461. Martin Harry of Washington County, recorded release of mortgage 19 August 1778, from Wm Wister and Saml Miles of the City of Philadelphia, Martin Harry by deed of mortgage made in 1774, assigned lot in Elizabeth Town, number one, together with buildings for £148..4 released mortgage.

RP1:462. Martin Harry recorded power of attorney from Wm Wister and Saml Miles of Philadelphia, Pennsylvania, to Valentine Adams, to release mortgage to Martin Harry.

RP1:462-464. Martin Harry of Washington County, Maryland, recorded release of mortgage 19 August 1778, from Wm Wister and Saml Miles, for £148..4 shillings, lot number one, in Elizabeth Town, formerly in Frederick County, but now in Washington County, lot #1. Signed by all parties before R. Ridgely, Chas Beatty. [Duplicate of 460-461 above, with different witnesses. Acknowledged in open court before Wm Ritchie, Clerk of Frederick County.

RP1:464-465. Adam Lechliter recorded deed 19 Aug. 1778 from John Smith for £300 Continental currency, part of *Resurvey,* containing 100 acres. Signed in German script. Barbara Smith released dower rights.

RP1:465-467. John Cornell recorded deed 18 Aug. 1778 from Henry Kensor for £400 common money, assigns part of tract called *Transylvania,* adjacent to *Frenchman's Purchase,* containing 120 acres. Eve Kensor released dower.

RP1:467-469. Frederick Stemple, blacksmith, recorded deed 18 Aug. 1778 from Solome Lyder for £60, lot #7 in Middletown. Signed in German script, Salome Leittert.

RP1:469-470. George Good recorded deed 18 Aug. 1778 from David Maxwell for £80, part of *Brother's Agreement,* containing 120 acres. Signed by mark before Joseph Wood Jr., Jacob Good, John Ross Key. Elizabeth Maxwell released dower rights.

RP1:471-472. George Good recorded deed 18 Aug. 1778 from David Maxwell for £400, part of *Brother's Agreement,* bought of Rudy Brubach, 28 acres, metes and bounds given containing 58 acres. Elizabeth Maxwell released dower rights.

RP1:472-473. Henry Wolf recorded deed 8 Aug 1778 from George Burkett for £52..18, assigns tract *Burkhart's Folly,* metes and bounds given for 170 acres. Mary, wife of George, released dower.

RP1:474-475. William Renner recorded deed 3 August 1778 from Azel Waters of Montgomery County, Maryland, for the sum of £1000 current money, assigns 119 acres of tract, part of a *Resurvey on Joseph's Friendship,* signed and acknowledged. At same time, came Lucretia Waters, wife of Azel and released dower rights, before Jos Wilson, Ger'd Briscoe. Justices of the Peace, attested to by Brooke Beall, Clerk Montgomery County seal.

RP1:476-477. Henry Ramsburger recorded deed 3 August 1778, from Anthony Stokes, for £300 assigns lot #6 on the main road leading from Frederick Town to Conococheague, signed in German script before Wm Beatty, Carleton Tannehill. His wife, not named, released dower rights.

RP1:477-479. [Marginal note, ex'd & delivered to Henry Bitesell on 4th Dec. 1784] Henry Bitesell recorded deed 3 Aug 1778 from Andrew Barringer, for £500 parcel of land called *Andrew's Rosenburgh,* being a resurvey on a tract of land called *Punch Spoon,* containing 77 acres of land. Signed in German script, before Jno Blair, Sam'l Blair, Jno McAlister. Eve Rosanna Baringer, wife of Andrew, released dower rights.

RP1:479. John McGarry recorded bill of sale 3 Aug. 1778 from William Dealy of Toms Creek, weaver, for £30, one cow, one English loom and gears.

RP1:480-481. Andrew Hechinger recorded deed 1 August 1778 from Peter Creeger for £800, *Resurvey on part of Anchor and Hope.* 1 3/4 acres. Signed by mark. Mary wife of Peter Creager released dower.

RP1:482-483. Anthony Kinder, of Pennsylvania, stocking weaver, recorded deed 1 Oct. 1778 from William Winchester of Westminster Town in Frederick County, for £3, assigns lot #68 in Westminster, on the Main street, adjoining a lot belonging to Samuel Crowe. Signed before John Yingling, John Chrisman, Jno Ross Key.

RP1:483-485. John Yingling recorded deed 1 October 1778, from John Chrisman of Westminster Town, for the sum of £1500 assigns two tracts of land, *Resurvey on Timber Ridge,* containing 60 ½ acres, and the second is *Resurvey on part of Bedford,* for 72 acres. Signed before W Winchester, David Fisher, John Ross Key. Mary, wife of John Chrisman released dower rights.

RP1:486-487. David Fisher of Westminster Town, Frederick County, recorded deed 1 October 1778, from William Winchester, for six pounds, two lots in Westminster Town, #s 85 & 36. Signed before John Yingling, Jno Chrisman, Jno Ross Key.

RP1:487-489. David Fisher recorded deed 1 October 1778, from Peter Franks of Baltimore County, for £12, lot #37 in Westminster. Signed in German script before W Winchester, John Chrisman, Jn Ross Key.

RP1:489-491. Charles Wood recorded deed 2 October 1778, from Charles Beatty for £73 tract granted Charles Beatty under the name of *Bruce's loss,* on south side of a large spring flowing into Linganore Creek, containing 61 acres. Signed before Wm Beatty, W Winchester. Martha, wife of Charles Beatty released dower.

RP1:491-493. [Ex'd & delivered Heugh Reynolds, 25 Sept. 1780.] William Reynolds recorded deed 14 October 1778, from Thomas Neale, merchant, for £1400 tract known by the name of *Stone Choice,* on a branch of Monocacy Creek, containing 150 acres. Signed before Wm M Beall, Jno Ross Key. Elizabeth, wife of the aforesaid Thomas Neil released dower.

RP1:493-494. [Ex'd & del'd to James Bonham, August 8, 1782] Mary Bonham recorded deed 15 October 1778, from Thomas Schley, for £245, two lots #225 and #226 in Frederick Town, on Market Street. Signed before John Haas and Chris'n Edelen. Margareth Schley released dower.

RP1:494-496. John Wederburn of Baltimore Town, merchant, recorded deed 19 October 1778, from Thomas Samuel Pole of Frederick County, for £450 and the payments of the rents and performance of covenants and agreements in these presents, hereafter mentioned, sells two lots being in Wesminster Town, #27 and #28, adjacent to lot of Christian Toms, southwest of the lands of William Winchester; part of tract called *White's Level,* Signed Thos Saml Pole before W Winchester Junr., W Winchester and John Ross Key.

RP1:496-498. George Ramsburgh recorded deed 10th August 1779, from Peter Stilley, made 30th July 1779. Whereas a certain Osborn Sprigg, deceased in his lifetime, was seized of a lot called *Abel's Spring,* formerly in Prince Georges County, but now in Frederick County, originally granted in May 1734 to Abel Person for 100 acres of land, which tract above mentioned Osborn Sprigg by his last will, devised his daughter Priscilla Sprigg, late wife of Barton Lucas, and whereas Rachel Sprigg, widow and executrix of the said Osborn Sprigg, on behalf of the above mentioned Priscilla, who has then an infant under the age of 21 years, obtained a special warrant to resurvey said tract, and by virtue thereof added the quantity of 39 acres, and obtained a patent under the name of *Father's Gift and Uncles Good Will*, on 28 April 1763, and the aforesaid Barton Lucas and Priscilla his wife, obtained a special warrant, concerning the last mentioned tract of land on 28th April 1763, added 41 acres of vacant land, and whereas Barton Lucas and Priscilla conveyed said tract in 1764, to Peter Stilly, late of Frederick County, deceased. Now, this indenture witnessed that Peter Stilley, son and heir of the aforesaid Peter Stilly, deceased for £1450 assigns all that tract of land, called *Forest Hall,* being a *Resurvey on Father's Gift and Uncles Good Will,* lying in Frederick County, metes and bounds given for 180 acres. Signed before Christ'n Edelen, Philip Thomas. Mary Stilly, widow of Peter Stilley, deceased, acknowledged release of dower.

RP1:499-500. Christiana Springer recorded deed 26 October 1778, from Richard Butler, for £500 Continental Currency, assigns tract called. *Resurvey on Trunstile,* on Monocacy Creek, containing 148 acres of land. Signed before Jacob Green, Carleton Tannehill.

RP1:501-502. [Exam'd & del'd Philip Boyer 21 Nov. 1780] Peter Kemp recorded deed 27 Oct. 1778, from Charles Wood for £200, tracts called *Charles Choice and Bruce's Loss,* beginning at tract called *Chittam's Castle,* adjacent to Peter Kemp's part of *Wood's Choice,* for 40 ½ acres. Sarah, wife of Charles Wood released dower.

RP1:502-204. John Shroyer recorded deed 28 October 1778, from John Diggs heir at law of Edward Diggs, for 5 shillings, his share of tract, a part of *The Meadows,* containing 172 acres.

RP1:504-505. John Shroyer recorded deed 28 October 1778, from Jesse Wharton of Saint Mary's County, for 5 shillings, all his title to tract where John Shroyer now lives, a part of *The Meadows,* containing 172 acres.

RP1:506-507. Richard Iams recorded deed 29 Oct. 1778 from John Beall of Montgomery County, for £201..10, assigns part of *Choice Enlarged,* 100 3/4 acres. Signed before Richard Thompson, William Baker. Mary Beall released dower rights. Brook Beall, clerk of the court, attested to signers as justices of Montgomery County.

RP1:508-509. [Examined & delivered to Mr. Geo Woolsey, 22nd August 1779] William Bell recorded deed 16 August 1779, from Pearce Lamb, for £2800, part of two tracts, called *The Addition,* and *Lamb's Choice,* metes and bounds given, adjacent to Thomas Durbin's tract, containing 155 acres. Signed Pearce Lamb before W Winchester, Jno Lawrence. Catherine Lamb, his wife, released dower.

RP1:510-511. Andrew Warman recorded deed 2 November 1778, from Charles Wood for £75, part of *Charles Choice,* containing 20 acres. Signed before Upton Sheridine, John Lawrence. Sarah, wife of Charles Wood, released dower.

RP1:511-512. Andrew Warman recorded deed 2 Nov. 1778, from Joseph Wood for £400, tract called *Policy,* surveyed for Joseph Wood 7 Nov. 1752, beginning at tract *Partnership,* taken up by John Campbell and Lawrence Robinson, containing 55 acres. Signed before Upton Sheridine, John Lawrence. Mary, wife of Joseph Wood released dower.

RP1:513-514. Henry Zealor recorded deed 3 November 1778, from Henry Shover for £400, part of northeast corner of lot #82, in Frederick Town. Signed German script before Wm Beatty, Christ'n Edelen. Ann Mary, wife of Henry Shover released dower.

RP1:514-516. Godlieb Miller recorded deed 4 Nov. 1778 from Henry Shover for £400, £400, part of northeast corner of lot #82, in Frederick Town. Signed German script before Wm Beatty, Christ'n Edelen. Ann Mary, wife of Henry Shover released dower.

RP1:516-518. Philip Boyer recorded deed 6 Nov. 1778 from Charles Wood for £12..4..4, part of *Wood's Grove,* bounded by tract, *Chittam Castle,* 4 acres. Sarah, wife of Charles Wood released dower.

RP1:518-519. Yost Cover recorded deed 9 Nov. 1778 from William Fout for £770, part of *Hammond's Strife,* 100 acres. Signed by mark. Susanna, wife of William Fout released dower.

RP1:519-520. Philip Shade, britches maker, recorded deed 9 Nov. 1778 from Michael Stoker for £1200 part of lot #82 in Frederick Town, beginning 124 ft. from southeast corner, adjoins Samuel Miller's part of said lot. Signed German script before Jacob Young, Christ'n Edelen. Mary, wife of Michael Stoker released dower.

RP1:521-522. [Ex'd & del'd Phil Creamer 27 April 1805.] Casper Creamer recorded deed 11 Nov. 1778, from Benjamin Cornell for £3, assigns part of *Brook's Discovery on the Rich Lands,* beginning at tract previously conveyed by Cornell to Creamer, metes and bounds for 1 ½ acres. Signed before John McAlister, William Blair. Sarah, wife of Benjamin Cornell released dower.

RP1:522-523. Daniel Long, recorded deed 11 November 1778, from Benjamin Cornell, mason, for£240, part of *Addition to Brooke's Discovery on the Rich Lands* adjacent to part conveyed to Cornell by John Scholfield, 78 ½ acres. Sarah Cornell released dower rights.

RP1:524-525. Sebastian Derr recorded deed 12 Nov. 1778. Whereas Thomas Schley for £110 paid by Margaret Trisler, 21 Sept. For two lots in Frederick Town, and she sold same to Sebastian Derr. Deed signed by Thomas Schley, witnessed by Jacob Young, Christ'n Edelen. Margaret Schley released dower.

RP1:525-527. Henry Sharrer recorded deed 12 Nov. 1778, from Christian Meissencope of Lancaster County, Pennsylvania, blacksmith, for 5 shillings, lot #225 in Frederick Town, adjacent to Peter Toffler's lot. Signed in German script before Michael Hubley, Charles Hall. Margaret Meissencope released dower.

RP1:527-528. Michael Smith recorded deed 19 nov. 1778 from Wm Digges Senr of Prince George's County, for £50, part of *Digge's Lot,* 100 ½ acres. Signed before Thomas Clagett, Wm Lyles Jr., Catherine Digges released dower. John Read Magruder, attested to Justices of the Peace of Prince George's County.

RP1:528-530. Frederick Missal, butcher, recorded deed 10 Nov. 1778, from Martin Waltz, house carpenter, in Frederick Town for £996, lot #48 in Frederick Town. Signed before John Haas, Christ'n Edelen. Barbara, wife of Martin Waltz released dower.

RP1:530-532. Joseph Gordon recorded land commission and deposition, issued to Wm Winchester Sr., Wm Roberts Sr., John McAlister and Patrick Wattson to perpetuate the bounds of tract *Bedford.* Deposition of James White, age 48 years, on 10 Nov. 1768, deposed that in 1762 as deputy surveyor he was called upon to make a survey for John Holland on Great Pipe Creek, beginning at *Head's Industry.* Deposition of William Head, aged about 45 years, was on of the chain carriers for tract *Bedford,* beginning at *Head's Industry.*

RP1: 532-533. Jacob Smith recorded deed 17 Nov. 1778 from Paul Beard, for £150, tract *Mansinger*, beginning at George Stump's land, containing 67 ½ acres. Signed by mark. Agnes, wife of Paul Beard released dower.

RP1:534-535. Heugh Kerr recorded deed 17 Nov. 1778 from Jacob Slagle of Bonwick Twp., Pennsylvania. For £192, tract called *Half Moon,* on Great Pipe Creek. Barbara Slagle released dower.

RP1:535-537. Jacob Miller recorded deed 18 Nov. 1778 from Philip Bier, cordwainer, for £2800, assigns all his moiety of lot #63 in Frederick town. Eve Catherine, wife of Philip released dower.

RP1:537-539. Henry Poole of Anne Arundel Co., recorded deed 18 Nov. 1778, from John Dorsey of John for £315, part of *Mount Pleasant.* Mary, wife of John. released dower.

RP1:539-541. Jacob Hoff recorded deed 18 Nov. 1778 from Jacob Clyne for £1500, a part of tract called *Anchor and Hope,* on east side of Catoctin Creek, containing 50 acres. Mary Clyne released dower rights.

RP1:542-543. Jacob Groff recorded deed 18 Nov. 1778 from Philip Thomas for £9, two lots #6 & #7, in Addition to Frederick Town, purposed by the said Philip Thomas of the Trustees for the Poor, they being part of the poor house. Jane C. Thomas released dower.

RP1:543-545. John Shroyer recorded deed 19 Nov. 1778, from John Protzman, for £860, part of resurvey on tract called *Middle Part,* at end of *Second Chance,* containing 100 acres more or less. Signed before Christn Edelen, Wm Luckett Jr. Acknowledgment.

RP1:545-546. Jacob Hummer recorded deed 28 Nov 1778 from Samuel Chase, Esq. Of Anne Arundel County, for £100, part of tract called *Choyce,* laid out for 140 acres. Signed before Jos Cowman, Jr. Acknowledged before one of the judges of the General Court, Nichs Thomas.

RP1:546. On the back of John Goff's deed, recorded in folio 396 of this liber was the following endorsement: Appeared Christian Sholl and John Gaskin and acknowledged deed, at same time Catherine wife of Christian Sholl and Jane, wife of John Gaskin released dower rights, signed before Jacob Young, John Haas.

END OF VOLUME RP1

INDEX:

Be aware that German surnames beginning with G, K and even H may have sounded similar to the land records clerk and the letters used interchangeable, e.g. see RP1:407-408, for George Hoetzel of Shenandore County, Virginia; George Gertzel Senr. Late of Frederick County, deceased, and Margaret Kertzel who released dower rights. Spelling was not in the least way consistent throughout this period, so be sure to browse the indexes - this is true of all surnames.

TRACT NAMES:

APPENDIX:

JUSTICES OF THE FREDERICK COURT
OTHER OFFICIALS ACTIVE IN THIS VOLUME as WITNESSES (1773-1778)

BEALL, Samuel aka, Sam'l Beall Jr. (1713-1778). Resided on *Kelly's Purchase*, now Washington Co.. He served as justice from 1763-1775, the son of John Beall of Alexander and Verlinda Magruder Beall. Samuel Beall Jr. Married Eleanor Brooke and was the father of Brooke Beall of Georgetown, and grandfather of Upton Beall, both clerks of the Montgomery County Court. He was younger than Samuel Beall, son of Ninian, grandson of Col. Ninian, who took the name Samuel Beall Sr. and married Jane Edmonston.[7] He was one of the "Twelve Immortal Justices of the Frederick County Court, who repudiated the Stamp Act - November 23, 1765" celebrated on a plaque in the Frederick County Courthouse.

BEALL, William Murdock (1742-1823), son of Nathaniel and Ann (Murdock) Beall. He resided in Frederick Town. From 1770 he served as Frederick County Clerk of Court receiving alienation fines on recording deeds. Justice in Frederick County, 1777 to at least 1794.

BEATTY, Charles (1736-1804). He lived in Georgetown, Montgomery County and was the son of Thomas Beatty, and brother of Justice Thomas Beatty Jr. He was married twice, first to Mary Middagh and second to Verlinda Offutt. He served in the Lower House of the Legislature from Frederick County in 1771.[8] He was a land speculator who sold lots in Georgetown in partnership with George Frazer Hawkins.

BEATTY, William (1739-1803). Chosen to serve on Committee of Observation in September 1775. Resident of Manor Hundred, Frederick County. Sheriff of Frederick County in 1776, Judge of the Orphans Court from 1777 to at least 1783.[9]

BLAIR, Willliam (1730-1778). Served as justice from at least 1767; on Committee of Correspondence, and as an associator from Tom's Creek Hundred.[10] His will filed in Frederick County named a wife and several children[11]. He was one of the twelve justices of the Frederick County Court, who repudiated the Stamp Act - November 23, 1765.

---

[7]Edward C. Papenfuse, Alan F. Day, David W. Jordan and Gregory A. Stiverson, *A Biographical Dictionary of the Maryland Legislature, 1635-1789. 2 vols.* (Baltimore: Johns Hopkins University Press, 1797, 1985) pg. 124; Eleanor M.V. Cook, *The Brooke Beall Family and the John's Family,* mss. dated July 1986, copies at the Maryland State Archives and Montgomery County Historical Society; also, Nettie Leith Major, "Ninian Beall, 1625-1717" in *MGSB,* Summer 1979, vol. 20, #3, pg. 214-225.

[8]Ibid., pg. 126-127.

[9]Henry C. Peden Jr., *Revolutionary Patriots of Frederick County, 1775-1783,* Westminster, Md., Family Line Publications, 1995, pg. 29.

[10]Peden, Jr., *Revolutionary Patriots of Frederick County, 1775-1783,* pg. 38.

[11]Abstracted in *Western Maryland Genealogy,* vol. 5:132.

BOOTH, Bartholomew . Served on the Committee of Observation in 1775. [12]

BOYD, Archibald. Clerk of the Committee of Observation in 1775.[13]

BURGESS, Edward. (1733-1809) . He was born in Anne Arundel County, and married Mary Davis, daughter of Thomas Davis and Elizabeth Gaither. Around 1773, he moved into the lower district of Frederick County and became involved in politics. He was an Anti-Federalist. He was a Justice of Frederick County, and held the same position in Montgomery County, at its formation. He was elected a representative to the Lower House of the Maryland Assembly ten times from 1777 to 1799. In 1776, he became a Captain in the Flying Camp of Revolutionary War soldiers. He settled near Logtown on the left side of the road from Georgetown to Frederick, somewhere near today's Gaithersburg High School. *Belt's Desire.* He also owned other real property, some with improvements. Between 1779 and 1790 he purchased about 1200 acres of land, much of this land was attached and sold by court order between 1792 and 1798 for debts. Therefore Edward Burgess was a prime example of the type of person who could take up the Anti-Federalist cause. He had debts which the issuance of paper money might help to alleviate.[14]

CHAPLINE, Joseph (1746-1821), with brothers James and William, sons of Justice Joseph Chapline (1707-1769) are active in this volume, selling lots in Sharpsburg, and other real estate they inherited in the Antietam Valley.[15] He lived at *Mt. Pleasant* near Sharpsburg, and pursued a legal career in Frederick Town.

CRESAP, Michael (1742-1775) son of Justice Thomas Cresap (1703-1788), served as witness in this volume, he lived in Western Maryland, in part of county which became Washington County.[16]

CRESAP, Thomas, Justice from March Court 1748/9.[17] b. 1703 Skipton, Yorkshire, d. 1788. He acted as Maryland's agent to the Cherokee and Iroquois Indians, and settled out at Old Town on the Potomac River, now Allegany Co. He was a Justice of Prince George's County from 1739-1748, and served Frederick County as a Justice from 1748 through 1775, as well as in other capacities, including as deputy surveyor. [Papenfuse, p.244]

DEAKINS, William Jr. (1742-1798). Served as Justice of the Peace in Frederick, and then Montgomery Counties.

DULANEY, Benjamin. Clerk and Record Keeper of Frederick County, bonded 2 May 1773. Libers BD1 and BD2, are from his initials.

DULANEY, Daniel, Esq. Chief Justice, Frederick County Court. from March 1748/9 through 1751[18] He died in 1753, and his sons Daniel Dulaney and Walter Dulaney, both of Anne Arundel County, are present in this volume, because of their extensive interests in Frederick Town lots and other Frederick County real estate.[19]

---

[12]Henry C. Peden Jr., *Revolutionary Patriots of Frederick County, 1775-1783,* Westminster, Md., Family Line Publications, 1995, pg. 41.

[13]Henry C. Peden Jr., *Revolutionary Patriots of Frederick County, 1775-1783,* Westminster, Md., Family Line Publications, 1995, pg. 44.

[14] *Montgomery County Story,* Vol. 30, no. 2, pg. 273.

[15]Papenfuse, op.cit., pg. 210-211.

[16]Henry C. Peden, *Revolutionary Patriots of Washington County, Maryland 1776-1783,* Westmisnter, Md., Family Line Publications, 1998, pg.83

[17] Millard Millburn Rice, *This Was the Life: Excerpts from the Judgment Records of Frederick County, Maryland, 1748-1765,* Redwood City, CA: Monocacy Book Co., 1979, Appendix C, pg. 285.

[18]Rice, op.cit..

[19]Papenfuse, et.al., op.cit., pgs 284-289.

EDELEN, Christopher. On the Committee of Observation in 1775. A member of the State Constitutional Convention in 1776. Sheriff In October 1779.[20]

HAWKINS, George Fraser. (1741-1785). Son of John Hawkins (1713-1757). Resided in Prince George's County on Potomac River, opposite of Alexandria. Married to Susannah Trueman Somerville.[21] With Charles Beatty, developer of Georgetown lots.

HEUGH, Andrew.(1727-1789) Served as a Justice from 1756[22] through at least 1775. Lived in Lower Potomac Hundred, Frederick County, which later became part of Montgomery County. Served in the Lower House of the Legislature, 1769-1770.[23]. Was one of the twelve justices who repudiated the Stamp Act, November 23, 1765.

JONES, Charles. (1712-1798). Served as a Justice from 1754.[24] He was one of the twelve justices of the Frederick County Court who repudiated the stamp act. He lived on *Clean Drinking Manor* on the west side of Rock Creek, jsut north of the present line with the District of Columbia. In 1777, he became the first judge of the Orphans Court of Montgomery County.[25]

JENIFER, Daniel of St. Thomas (1723-1790). Lived near Annapolis in Anne Arundel County, he was a Justice of the Provincial Court, 1766-1773 and appointed Rent Roll Keeper of the Western Shore in 1768. He also held other offices.[26]

LYNN, David (d. 1779) (first Grand Jury foreman 1748/9), served as Justice from 1754.[27] An immigrant from Dublin, Ireland, he was a Surveyor, and one of the Commissioners to lay out Georgetown in 1751, served as a Justice through 1775. David Lynn died before 16 December 1779, when Andrew Heugh and Roger Brooke prepared the inventory of his estate, filed 18 February 1780 in Montgomery County; David Lynn, was administrator, Sarah Lynn, Caty Lynn signed as next of kin[28]. He was also the father of John Lynn, who resided in Allegany (now Garrett County).[29]. On 10 May 1790, his widow Elizabeth made her will, which was probated in Montgomery County 9 Sept. 1803.[30]

LOWNDES, Christopher (1713-1785). A well to do merchant who lived at *Bostwick* in Bladensburg, Prince George's County. He was married to Elizabeth Tasker and therefore, brother-in-law of Daniel Dulaney.[31] .

---

[20]Henry C. Peden Jr., *Revolutionary Patriots of Frederick County, 1775-1783,* Westminster, Md., Family Line Publications, 1995, pg. 110.

[21]Papenfuse, et.al., op.cit., pgs. 423-424.

[22]Rice, *op.cit.*

[23]Papenfuse, *op.cit.,* pg. 439.

[24]Rice, *op.cit.*

[25]Jones Family File, Montgomery County Historical Society Library, Rockville, Md.

[26]Papenfuse, *op.cit.,* 485-486.

[27]Rice, *op.cit.*

[28]Eleanor M. V. Cook, *Abstract of Estate Record Book Liber A, 1777-1780, Montgomery County, Maryland,* non-published manuscript, dated March 1993, at of the Montgomery County Historical Society, pg. 35.

[29]Papenfuse, *op.cit., pg 558*

[30]Mary Gordon Malloy, Jane C. Sween, Janet D. Manuel, *Abstracts of Wills, Montgomery County, Maryland, 1776-1825,* Washington, D.C., Gray Printing Company, copyright by authors, 1977. Pg. 87.

[31]Peden, *Patriots of Prince Georges County*, pg. 194.

LUCKETT, William (1711-1783). He operated a ferry across the Potomac River to Virginia, which was later operated by his son-in-law, Thomas Noland. He was an Innholder in Frederick County by 1754 and served as a justice, intermittently from 1757 through 1775.[32]

PRATHER, Thomas, (1704-1785) Justice from March Court 1748/9 through 1762. He was Sheriff in 1762, and served intermittently as Justice through 1775. He was a brother of John Smith Prather[33]. Jannet Prather was one of estate administrators in Washington County.[34] She also appeared as witness occasionally with him.

PRICE, Thomas (1732-1795). Served as a Justice of the Peace from 1758.[35] He was one of the twelve justices who repudiated the Stamp Act, November 23, 1765. He lived in Sugarland Hundred; his daughter Matilda Bowen Price, married Upton Beall 29 December 1796.

STEUART, Adam. Served as justice from at least 1772 in Frederick County, and later in Montgomery County. Often witnessing Georgetown transactions.

STULL, John. (1733-1791). Served as justice from at least 1772 in Frederick County. His home plantation, *Whiskey,* was located near Elizabethtown which, after division of county, became Hagerstown, the county seat for Washington County. His second wife was Mercy Williams, daughter of Joseph Williams, a tavern keeper. He was elected to the State Legislature by 1775.[36]

WARRING, F. Served as justice of the peace. No other information found at this time.

WINCHESTER, William (1710-1790). Born in London, he emigrated to Annapolis in 1729 at age 19. Lived Pipe Creek Hundred. Acquired over 1000 acres of *White's Level,* and surveyed the town of Winchester in 1764, which today is Westminster, the Carroll County seat. An earlier town name was New London.

YOUNG, Jacob. Served as Justice of the Peace in 1777, and in the House of Delegates, 1777-1778.[37]

---

[32]Papenfuse, *op.cit., pg. 553;* Harry Wright Newman, *The Lucketts of Port Tobacco.,* Washington, D.C., author, 1938.

[33]Rice, op.cit.; Papenfuse, *op.cit.,* pg 659.

[34]Peden, *Revolutionary Patriots of Washington County,* pg 290.

[35]Rice, *op.cit.*

[36]Papenfuse, *op.cit.,* Vol. 2, pg 792.

[37]Peden, *Revolutionary Patriots of Frederick County, Maryland, 1775-1783,* pg. 407.